IMAGES
of Rail

RAILROADING IN ELLIS COUNTY

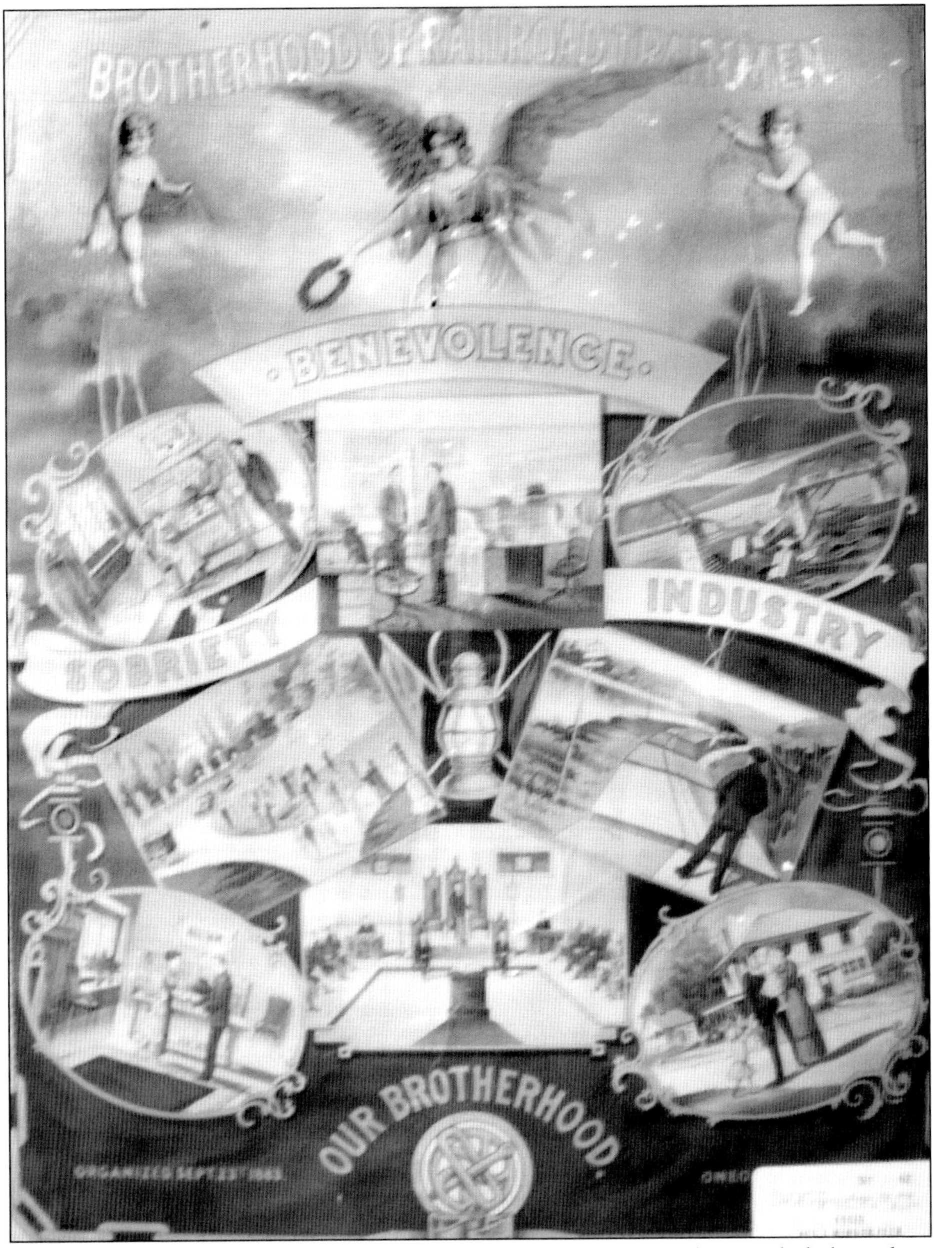

The Brotherhood of Railroad Trainmen was founded in 1883. Members included conductors, brakemen, baggagemen, flagmen, and dining-car stewards. The Ennis H. G. Wagner Lodge No. 416 formed around 1890. The members participated in an 1898 picnic with the Denison and Cleburne lodges. In 1904, Ennis officers included J. G. Evans, master; J. Beaty, vice master; J. T. Reinhardt, secretary; E. S. Overhiser, financier; M. M. Miller, journal agent; and P. A. Griffin, convention delegate. (Courtesy of Joe Pool.)

On the Cover: Railway agent W. A. Cardwell is pictured outside the Ennis depot and express office in the late 1940s. With his dog, Falla, they were part of the everyday life of many Ennis residents over the decades. (Courtesy of Dane Williams, part of the Ford Curry Collection.)

IMAGES
of Rail

RAILROADING IN ELLIS COUNTY

Laurie J. Wilson and Peggy Holland Rankin

ARCADIA
PUBLISHING

ISBN 978-0-7385-7915-3

Published by Arcadia Publishing
Charleston SC, Chicago IL, Portsmouth NH, San Francisco CA

Printed in the United States of America

Library of Congress Control Number: 2010921325

For all general information contact Arcadia Publishing at:
Telephone 843-853-2070
Fax 843-853-0044
E-mail sales@arcadiapublishing.com
For customer service and orders:
Toll-Free 1-888-313-2665

Visit us on the Internet at www.arcadiapublishing.com

This is dedicated to our parents, Ed and Jeanne Jeffrey,
and Thomas and Juanita Holland.
Each inspired us in ways that words can never adequately convey.

Contents

Acknowledgments 6

Introduction 7

1. The Early Years 11
2. Depots, Stops, and Places along the Way 21
3. Cotton and the Rail 33
4. Ennis Named Division Headquarters 43
5. The Interurban 65
6. Trains That Came Through 77
7. The People of the Rail 93
8. Preserving the Past 111

Acknowledgments

We have met many of the men of this railroad. We have walked the now barren land where they once built an engine from the ground up. We have visited depots that once thrived with activity and excitement. We have walked back in time and have come to understand what it is that drives them; their determination that the days of the rail are not forgotten. This book could not have been done without them.

We owe a debt of gratitude to Steve Howerton, Mary Ludwig, Shannon Simpson, and Dane Williams. They were unfaltering sources of information, guidance, and support.

The staff of the Ennis Railroad and Cultural Museum, Jerry Becker, Nita Bozek, and "conductor" Bill Martz, was always there. They answered questions, went through pictures, and answered more questions. We cannot thank them enough.

There are numerous individuals who helped in a multitude of ways. They shared their photographs and their memories, helped with fact checking, dug through historical documents, and so much more. Our heartfelt thanks go to Regina Adams, the late Carolyn Ballew, Bob Banner, Lloyd Bigham, Randy Bigham, Neil Blackstone, Kevin Bohanon, Jimmy and Ginger Boon, Larry Burns, Virginia Crilley, Darlene Denbow, Kathy Eriksen, Karen Kay Esberger, Ruby Essary, Forrest Fountain, Doris Gerron, Ervin Glaspy, Sugar Glaspy, George Graves, Dottie Henderson, Jerry Herring, David Hopkins, Alvin "Beano" Houdek, Jeanette Houdek, John and Barbra Kauffman, Eddie Luksa, Helen Sims, Ray Telfair, Jim and Helen Templin, Barry and Anita Thompson, Joe Pool, Buddy and Betty Wells, Dave Wilemon, and Anita Williamson. Along with their assistance every effort has been made to insure the accuracy of the spelling of all names in this book. And our thanks to the folks at Ennis Office Supply and our local Ennis Walgreens for always coming through for us.

Though no longer with us, the writings on the history of the rail by the late Ralph Essary and John Percival were used extensively. Also critical to the research of this book was the wealth of historical records in the Ennis Public Library, the City of Ennis, the Sims Library of Waxahachie, and the Ellis County Museum, as well as in historical issues of the *Ennis Daily News* and *Waxahachie Daily Light*, to all of which we extend our sincere gratitude.

We also want to express our gratitude to our editor with Arcadia Publishing, Luke Cunningham, who helped to make our vision of this book a reality. We especially thank our husbands and children; without their patience, support, and willingness to make this a huge part of their lives for the past year, we could not have done this.

INTRODUCTION

Few Texas cities have the railroad pedigree of Ennis, Texas. Born in the midst of the golden era of railroad expansion, sited at a location appropriate to best accommodate the line and named for a railroad magnate, Ennis is a bona fide Texas railroad town. Likewise, Ellis County is a county that has been uniquely shaped by the railroad.

In 1871, the northern terminus of the railroad arrived in Ellis County at the place that would become the City of Ennis one year later. The year 1871 was a landmark year of railroad expansion in America as the transcontinental railroad had been completed just three years earlier and the Houston and Texas Central Railroad Company (H&TC) lacked just 33 miles of track to connect the ports of Galveston and Houston to the emerging trade center that is known today as Dallas-Fort Worth. Optimism was high in 1871 as the promise of prosperity drove the railroad on to the north.

So great was the frenzy to build railroads following the Civil War (more than 35,000 miles of railroad track was built from 1866 to 1873) that the railroad industry quickly became a leading national employer, second only to agriculture. Unbridled competition and greed fueled the race to build a nationwide railroad system and eventually led to irrational investment speculation, overly generous government subsidies and unprecedented land grants that were inadequately collateralized. The inevitable happened in September 1873, when major railroad defaults rapidly undermined the national economy (of 364 American railroads, 89 failed) and the so-called Long Depression began. It would last until 1879.

In the midst of economic crisis, the railroad system in Ellis County flourished. During this period, investors in Waxahachie funded and constructed the Waxahachie Tap Railroad that connected Waxahachie to the H&TC line in the community of Garrett, just north of Ennis. The project began in 1875, was completed in 1879 and was purchased by the H&TC Railroad soon after completion. In 1881, the Chicago, Texas and Mexican Central Railroad (CT&MC) arrived in Midlothian and in 1885, the Fort Worth and New Orleans Railroad (FW&NO) became the second railroad to serve Waxahachie. Later the FW&NO was extended through Midlothian. In 1890, the Missouri, Kansas and Texas Railroad (MKT) was completed from Southern Ellis County through Waxahachie and into Dallas County. In 1894, the Texas Midland Railroad (Ennis to Paris, Texas) reached Ennis. This line was subsequently purchased by the H&TC in 1928 and ultimately abandoned in 1943.

On December 6, 1890, city fathers of Ennis were successful in securing one of the most important economic development deals in the history of Ellis County when they entered into agreement with the Houston and Texas Central Railroad Company (H&TC) to move the division headquarters from Corsicana to Ennis. Development incentives granted by the city included approximately 90 acres of land (the site for the division headquarters, machine shops, roundhouse and rail yard), perpetual free water rights (for the steam locomotives) from city water reservoirs, and a $25,000 bonus. The true economic impact of this agreement would be obvious over the coming years.

A "Twenty-fifth Anniversary" article about Ennis appeared in the *Dallas Morning News* on February 15, 1896. Excerpts from the article describe a prosperous and growing railroad town:

> This is the headquarters for the northern division of the Houston and Texas Central from Hearne to Denison and for the Fort Worth branch, comprising a total mileage of 256 miles. It is both a freight and passenger division and all of the men reside here. The shops are very complete and are prepared for rebuilding a locomotive from the track up. Three hundred men are employed and the pay roll amounts to $17,000 monthly. The town has twenty-two dry goods houses, nineteen grocery stores, five druggists, four jewelers, four hardware dealers, three lumber yards, four dentists, thirteen doctors, twelve lawyers and the usual number of other enterprises of a town of 6,000 people. To appreciate the importance of Ennis as a great trade mart and distributing point a person has but to appear in one of the principal streets on a busy day, especially during the cotton season. The streets present one connected mass of cotton bales. Ennis has a cotton oil mill that can crush 150 tons of seed a day. Two splendidly outfitted ginning plants are operated here, being electric lighted and having an aggregate capacity of 150 bales in ten hours. The Ennis Compress has been in operation fourteen years and has a capacity of 800 to 900 bales a day. Ennis ships annually an average of some 20,000 bales of cotton. Last season the local shipment [cotton] was 25,927 bales. Cotton is only one of the products of the farmer that find a market here. Grains, hay, fruits, vegetables and live stock are largely produced here. During the last year probably as many as 250 new residences were erected in Ennis, costing from $500 to $5,000 each. During the same time about a dozen one and two-story brick business houses were built.

As the county prospered, the International and Great Northern Railway (I&GN) was constructed across Southern Ellis County in 1902; and in 1906, the Trinity and Brazos Valley Railway Company (T&BV), later known as the Burlington–Rock Island Railroad (BRI), was completed through Bardwell, Waxahachie and Red Oak. By 1910, a well-developed network of more than 120 miles of railroad track crisscrossed Ellis County.

In 1913, the H&TC Division Headquarters agreement was tested as management of the H&TC Railroad attempted to relocate the Ennis division headquarters and all major facilities (offices, machine shops, roundhouse and rail yard) to Mexia, Texas. Following a protracted legal battle, the Court of Appeals of Texas ruled in favor of Ennis on March 2, 1918, and the appellate court decision was ultimately upheld by the U.S. Supreme Court on March 29, 1920. Ennis would be home to the H&TC Northern Division Headquarters for years to come.

The year 1913 also marked the inaugural service of the Interurban Electric Railway System (Southern Traction Company, later known as the Texas Electric Railway Company) in Ellis County. Two separate lines commenced scheduled service in October. The first between Waco and Dallas (serving Waxahachie and Western Ellis County) and the second between Corsicana and Dallas (serving Ennis and Eastern Ellis County). The Interurban service was extremely popular due to fares that were lower than steam passenger fares, schedules that offered more frequent motor car service, and stops that were more convenient for regional and local travelers. At its peak, the Interurban carried more than 800,000 passengers a year. The Interurban ceased operation in 1948 as a result of an expanding highway system and increased availability of the automobile.

As the railroads grew, so did the economy of Ellis County—both in size and diversity. The railroads of Ellis County provided reliable, relatively fast transportation that served as a catalyst for economic growth and development for decades—well into the 20th century. The railroads made it possible to access national and international markets. Approximately 50 percent of all cotton grown in Ellis County was exported to Europe (most via the ports of Galveston and Houston) and a substantial part of the remainder was destined for the American textile mills on the eastern seaboard. Because of ideal soil conditions and the railroads, Ellis County became the top cotton-producing county in the United States. The *New York Times* reported (headline: "1914 Record Cotton Year") "Ellis County, Texas, was the banner cotton county of the United States having grown 143,714 bales, approximately 75 per cent. [*sic*] more than the entire crop of Missouri or Florida, about three times that of California and nearly six times that of Virginia."

Truly cotton was king in Ellis County, and Ennis was justifiably known as the place "where railroads and cotton fields meet."

The railroads brought farm implements and the construction materials, equipment, and machinery for cotton gins and cottonseed oil mills. The railroads also delivered the consumer goods that stocked the shelves of the county's mercantile establishments. The railroads helped establish Ellis County as a leading center for the manufacture of bricks. In 1914, Ferris and Palmer were home to no less than eight brick manufacturing facilities that produced more than 500,000 bricks daily. The railroads even played a key role in health care as the H&TC Railroad operated a hospital in Ennis until 1916.

In 1934, the Southern Pacific Railroad acquired the H&TC and commenced operations in Texas and Louisiana under the name of its subsidiary company, the Texas and New Orleans Railroad (T&NO). By 1937, the Southern Pacific Railroad (SP) was the third largest industrial corporation in America, surpassed only by AT&T and the Pennsylvania Railroad. Southern Pacific operations in Ennis continued under the name of Texas and New Orleans Railroad (T&NO) until 1961, when the Southern Pacific Railroad name was applied to its Texas subsidiary.

The streamlined Sunbeam, a quintessential icon of Texas steam locomotive passenger service, was introduced on September 19, 1937. The T&NO's Sunbeam was designed for speeds up to 100 miles per hour and provided a new standard of elegance and passenger comfort. The train had a total seating capacity of 280 passengers in coach, observation, and dining cars. The Sunbeam (and Hustler) operated between Houston and Dallas with scheduled stops in Ennis and Bremond and other flagstops to discharge revenue passengers. The Sunbeam was authorized to operate at speeds up to 75 miles per hour between Ennis and Hearne and reduced the scheduled travel time by two hours from Dallas to Houston. The trip took four hours and 25 minutes (at an average speed of 62.5 miles per hour). The Dallas to Houston trip was successfully promoted as "265 miles in 265 minutes".

During the World War II years, the level of activity in the Ennis rail yard increased dramatically. Twenty-one tracks (several exceeding a mile in length) were operated in the rail yard to meet burgeoning war needs. Three shifts worked around the clock. Troop trains, munitions trains and oil trains were a common sight. Twenty to thirty trains typically transited Ennis daily during the period, but railroad workers of the era recalled one particular 24-hour period in which 100 trains were routed through Ennis. Proudly and sadly, America sent her sons and daughters to war from railroad stations like the Ennis station and they were met at the station as they returned home. Most reunions were joyous; others reflected the grievous loss of a loved one as flag-draped coffins were brought home to their final resting place. Southern Pacific (Texas and New Orleans) employees who gave their lives in service to their country during World War II are memorialized on a monument in Pierce Park, along the railroad tracks in Ennis.

Following the war (1947–1948), thirty-five freight train crews were based in Ennis, and three passenger trains operated each direction between Dallas and Houston. The first diesel locomotive visited Ennis in 1947, and by 1950, force reductions were occurring within the trades that worked on the steam locomotives. The Sunbeam's retirement began in 1949 as new diesel locomotives were brought into service. The last Sunbeam was removed from passenger service in 1956, and scheduled passenger service between Dallas and Houston ceased on June 7, 1958. The development of the National Defense Highway System (Interstate Highway System, approved by Congress in 1956), America's love affair with the automobile and the arrival of safe and cost effective air travel echoed the death knell for the passenger train.

In 1965, the Ennis division headquarters of the Southern Pacific Railroad (then called the Austin-Dallas Division) was officially closed. The Union Pacific Railroad acquired the Southern Pacific Railroad in 1996 and presently provides railroad freight service in Ellis County along with the Burlington, Northern and Santa Fe Railroad (BN&SF).

April 10, 1993, marked the opening of the Ennis Railroad and Cultural Heritage Museum. The museum building, which is owned by the City of Ennis, was acquired from the Southern Pacific Railroad and opened after extensive restoration and remodeling was lovingly and painstakingly completed by City of Ennis employees. Housed in the Ennis passenger depot (formerly a Van Noy railroad restaurant building, *c.* 1915), the museum contains the most complete collection of railroad artifacts and memorabilia that chronicles the history of the railroad in Ennis and Ellis County. The museum is widely regarded as one of the finest railroad museums in the Southwest.

Today we most frequently come into contact with the railroad at the railroad crossings that dot Ellis County. These railroad crossings are among the few remaining tangible reminders of our railroad heritage . . . a heritage that encompasses almost 140 years of technological, social, and economic change. These railroad crossings symbolize a confluence of people, places, and events that have shaped our history, made us the people that we are today, and built the county we call home. Like these railroad crossings, this pictorial history of the railroad in Ellis County is a "time crossing" that will transport you on a journey . . . a journey to fascinating bygone days . . . a journey we hope you will thoroughly enjoy.

—Steve Howerton
City Manager
Ennis, Texas

One

The Early Years

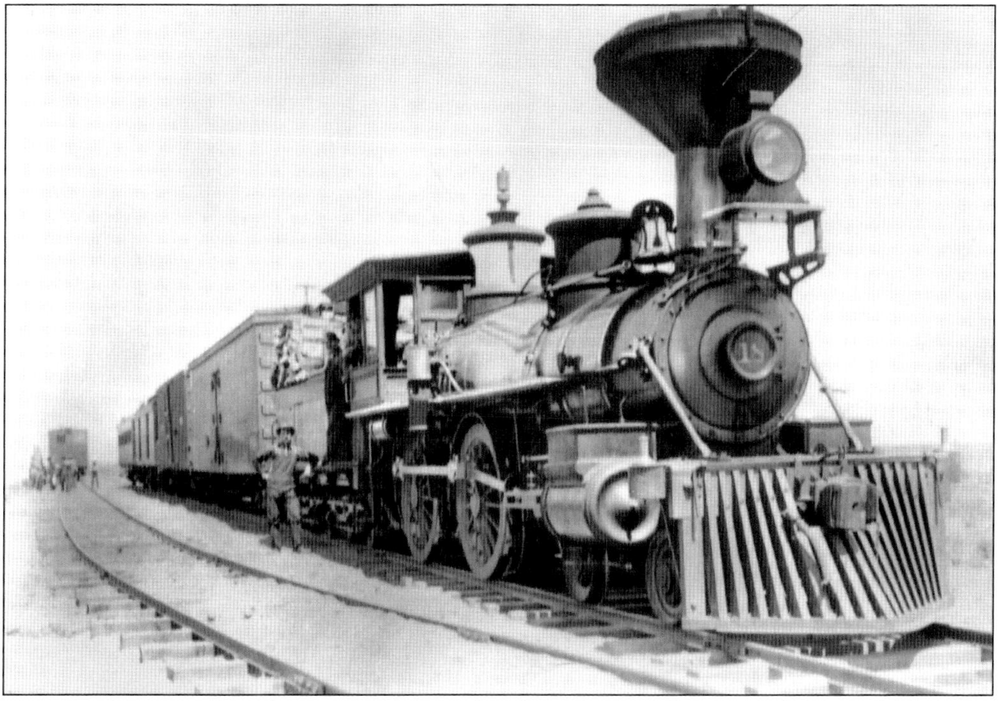

In 1872, the Houston and Texas Central Railroad (HT&C) made its way through Alma, Ennis, Garrett, Palmer, and Ferris, then on to Dallas. In 1872, the amount of water and wood a locomotive could carry dictated its range, from 10 to 20 miles at that time. It was also a decisive factor in the location of cities founded by the H&TC, including the newly founded town of Ennis. It would be one more decade before another rail was built. The Waxahachie Tap Railway was the vision of many of the founding pioneers of Waxahachie. Yet for all the prosperity the rail brought to these communities, it also dealt a blow to others. Burnham and Oak were casualties of the rail as the communities drifted out of existence with its arrival as residents relocated. Years before, the Great Northern Stage Route ran through Waxahachie as it connected communities from San Antonio, Texas, to Memphis, Georgia. And then came the rail. Pictured above is an engine and tender built that first year, 1872. (Courtesy of City of Ennis.)

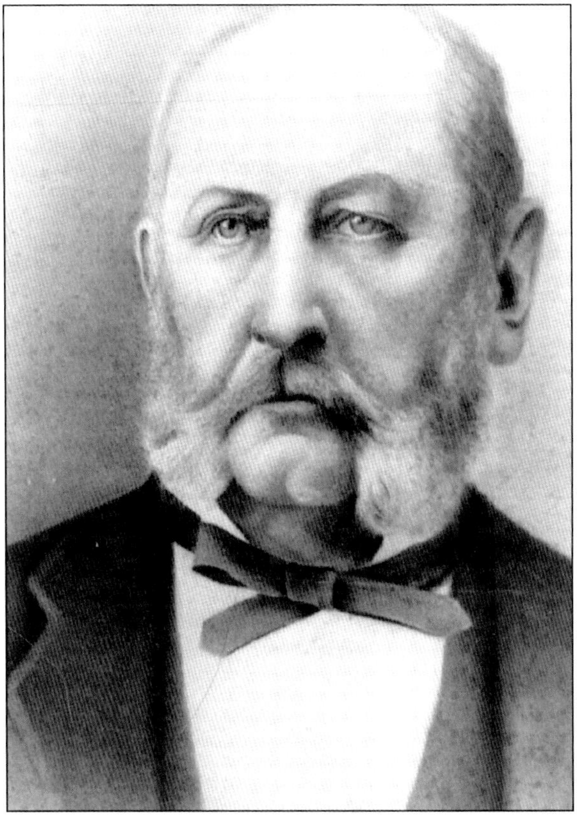

When the town of Ennis, Texas, was founded in 1872 by the Houston and Texas Central Railroad, it was named for one of the major officials of the company. Cornelius Ennis, pictured at left, was among the first investors of the Houston and Texas Central Railroad. He served on the company's board of directors for several years and held other roles, including comptroller and general superintendant. He served as mayor of Houston from 1856 to 1857, and during the Civil War, he was successful at running cotton and munitions through Union blockades. He also invested in newspapers. His oldest daughter, Nettie Ennis, was married to Alfred H. Belo, then president of the *Galveston News* and *Dallas News*. A younger daughter, Caroline Ennis, married Ceasar Lombardi, a later president of the *Dallas News*. An 1875 bird's-eye view of the town named for him is shown below. (Both, courtesy of City of Ennis.)

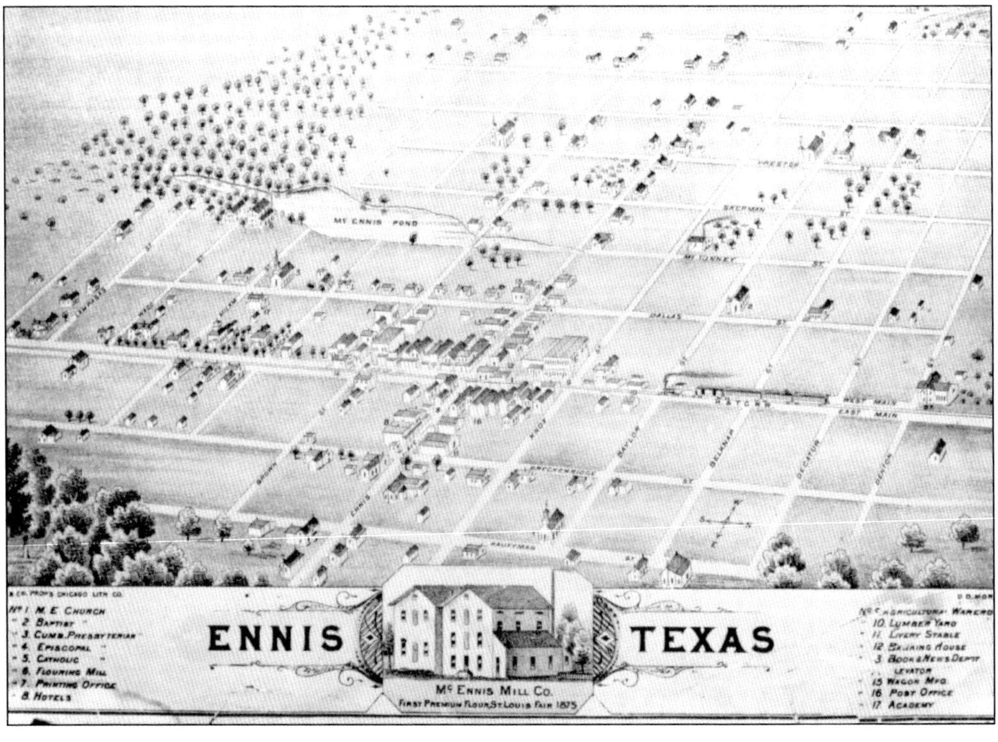

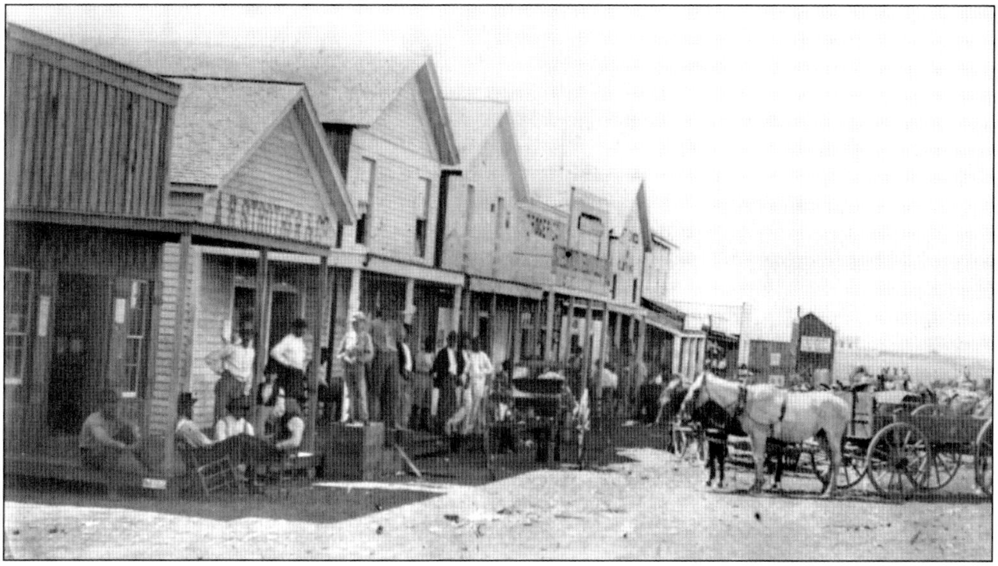

The Panic of 1873 was the beginning of a financial depression that took the country years to recover from. Over expansion of the railroads sent the financial markets into collapse beginning with Jay Cooke and Company in September 1873. The Houston and Texas Central made its way through Ellis County to Dallas by 1872. Dallas temporarily became the unexpected terminus of the Texas and Pacific Railway until financing was available to continue the line to Fort Worth. Formed and incorporated with the building of the rail, Ennis survived the harsh financial climate from its humble beginnings, pictured above in early 1875, to a prosperous city. West Knox Street is pictured below in 1907 with the depot prominently visible at the end of the block. (Above, courtesy of Mary Ann Novy Lamkin; below, courtesy of Joe Pool.)

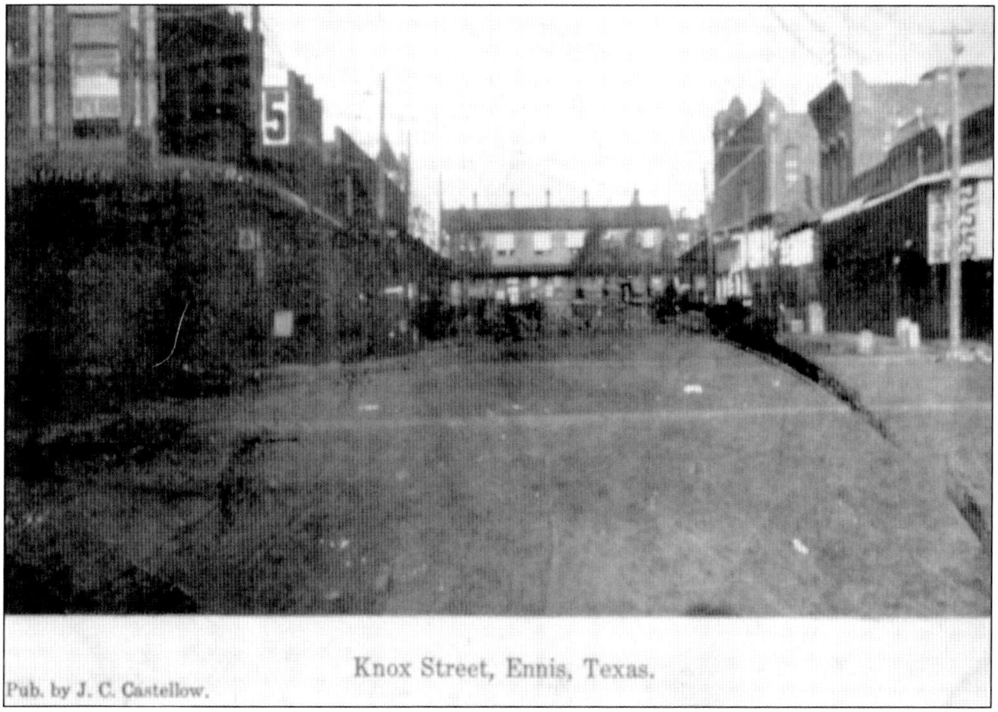

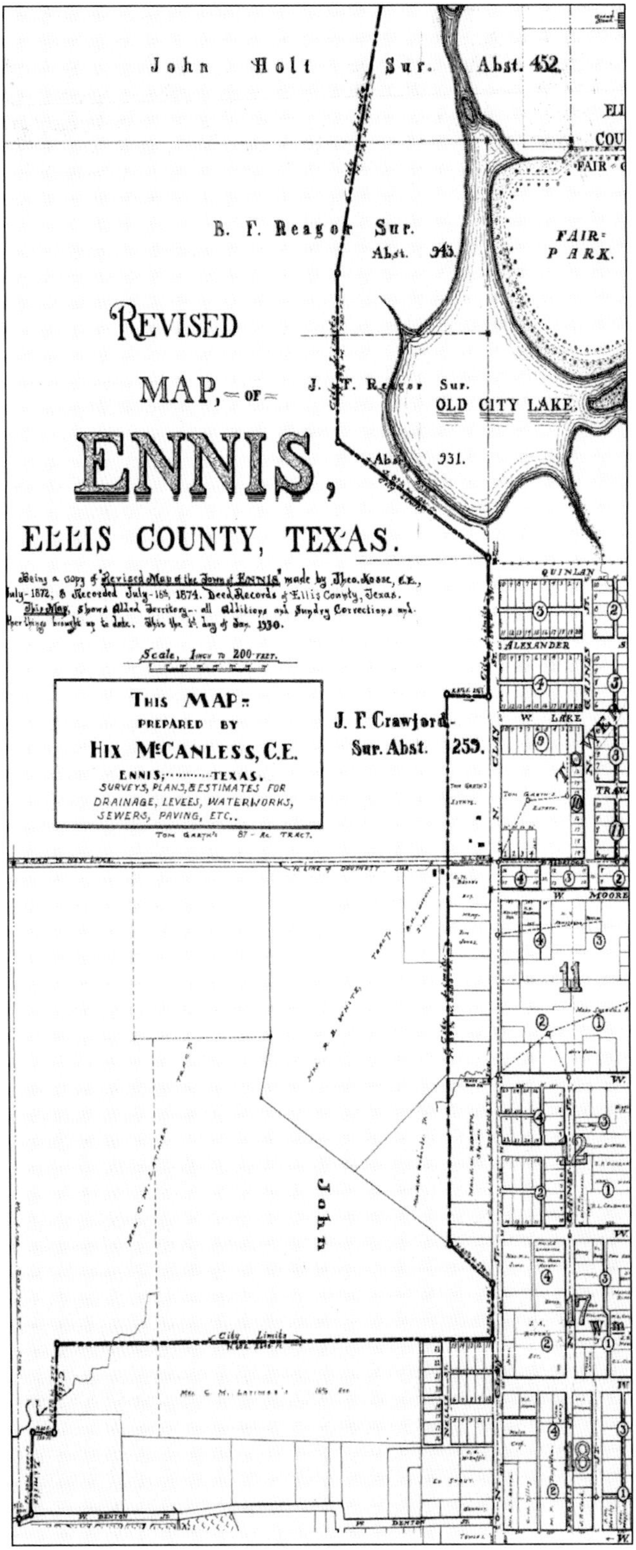

The effort for Ennis to become a division point for the Houston and Texas Central Railroad in 1891 was achieved in part through the efforts of Joseph Baldridge. In addition to raising the $25,000 bonus required by the railroad and providing 90 acres of land north of the city for the roundhouse, machine shops, and rail yard, the community also raised $13,000 to build Old City Lake, pictured in the upper portion of the photograph at left. The lake would provide the perpetual water source as required by the Houston and Texas Central Railroad for the steam locomotives. The city's commitment to building City Lake and another lake 3 miles to the west in 1895 to provide a supplemental water source was a major step in bringing the city of Ennis into serious consideration in the choice of a division point location. (Courtesy of Ellis County Abstract and Title Company.)

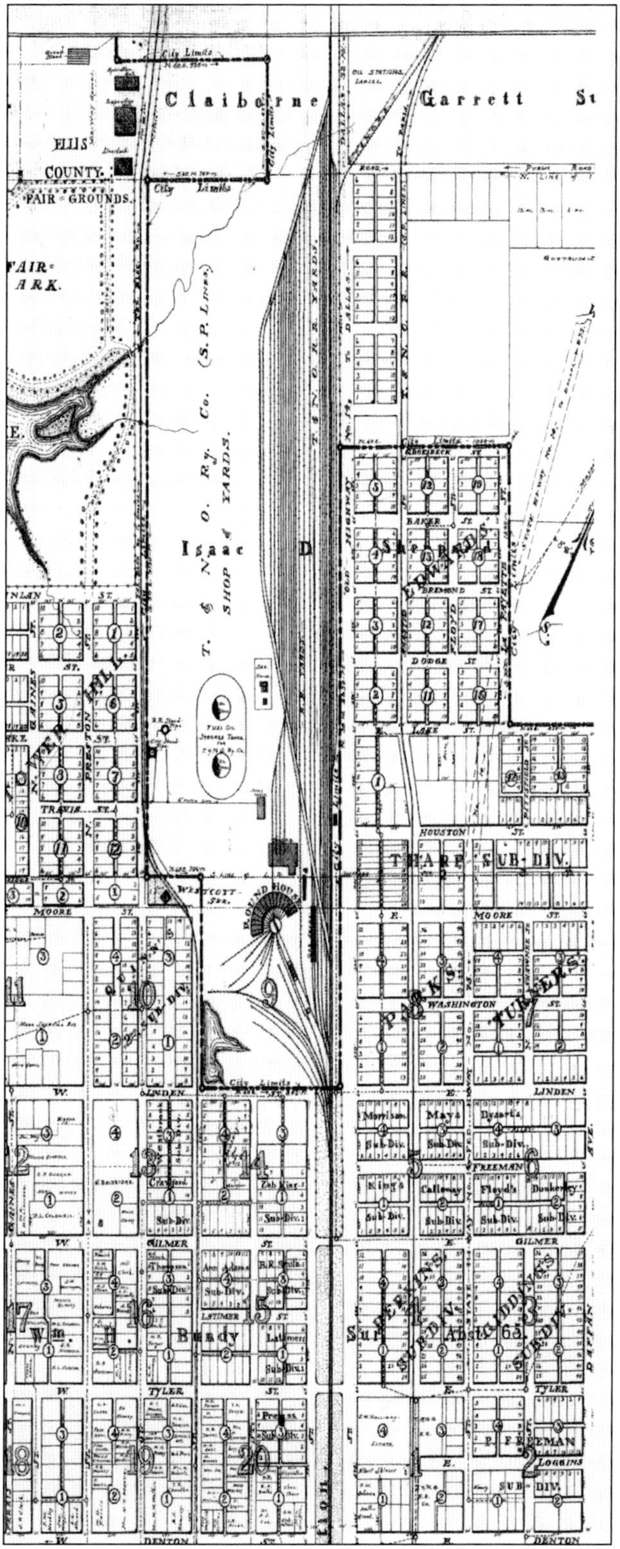

The location of the rail yards and machine shops was based on the location of the lake. Built just miles to the east of the lake, the yards were 1 mile north of the city's downtown area. Pictured at right, the shop yards expanded north of the roundhouse and the machine shop building north of it. The rail yards can be seen to the northeast of the roundhouse. Fuel oil storage tanks are designated above and to the left of the roundhouse. Several other buildings are also visible, including a section house and supply house located between the fuel oil storage tanks and the rail yards. (Courtesy of Ellis County Abstract and Title Company.)

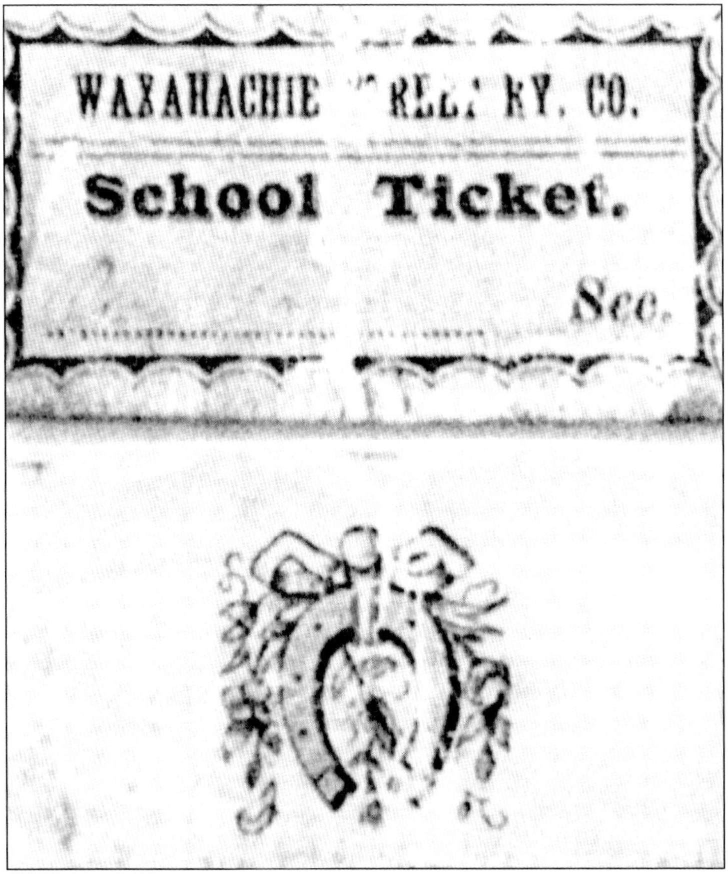

The Mule Car Street Railway system of Waxahachie operated from around 1890 to 1913. The Waxahachie Street Railway Company was established in 1889. Pictured at left is each side of one of its student tickets around 1900. The Lake Park Street Railway Company was founded in 1891. Both companies ceased operations with the arrival of the Texas Electric Railway in 1913–1914. Pictured below around 1899 a mule car can be seen making its way along Main Street between Rogers and College Streets in the courthouse square. (Both, courtesy of Ellis County Museum.)

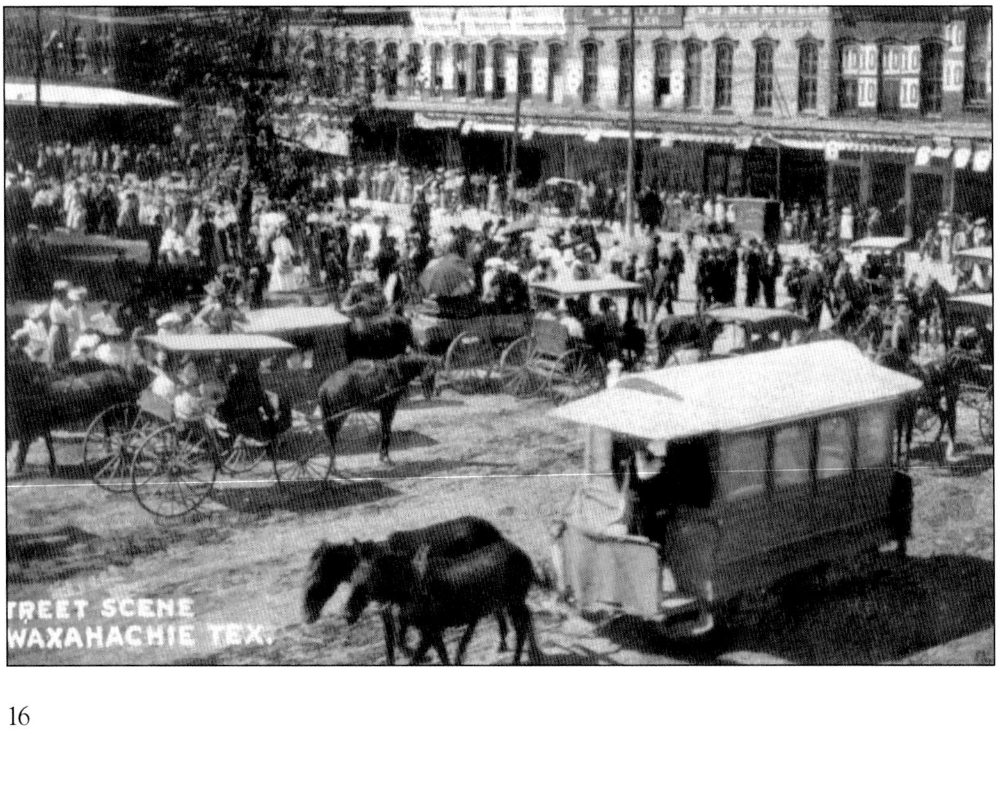

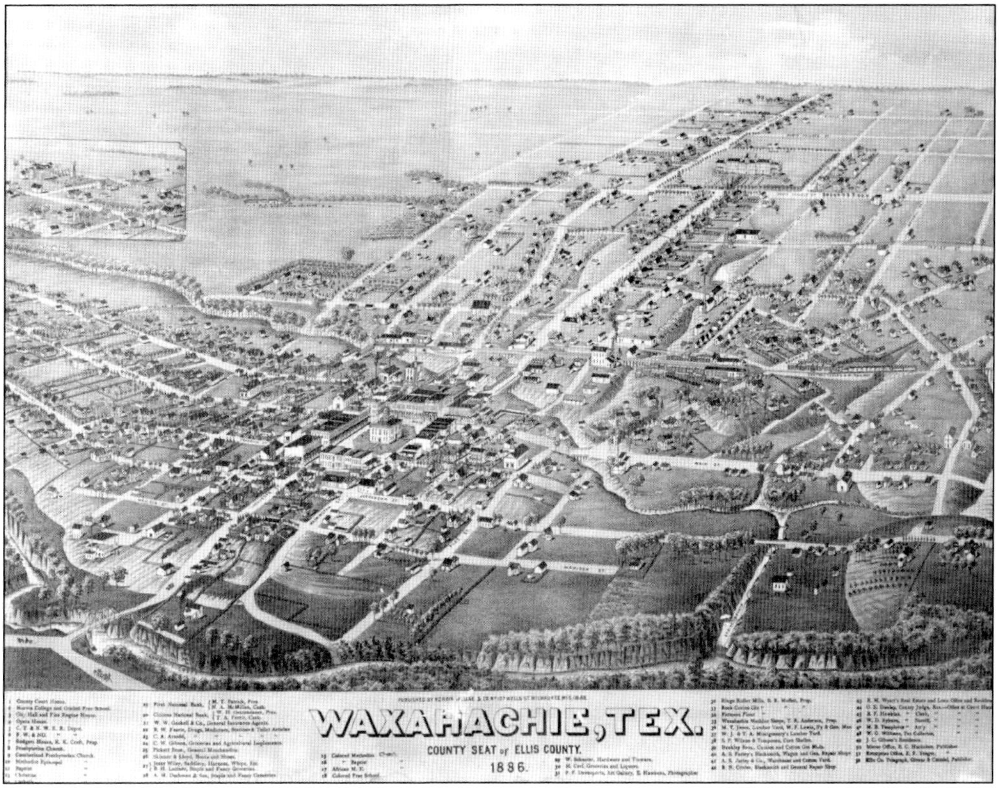

The Waxahachie Tap Railroad Company was granted a charter by the state legislature on January 25, 1875. Incorporators on the charter included G. L. Adkisson, J. F. Aldredge, W. L. Carrick, Stephen A. Clift, H. H. Dunn, Justus W. Ferris, H. W. Graber, Benjamin F. Hawkins, H. McLain, James B. Meredith, Marshall T. Patrick, Clark D. Pickett, David G. Ransom, John S. Siddons, Aaron Trippett, John G. Williams, and Nathaniel G. Wise. Six months later, thousands celebrated as the first ground was broken for the Waxahachie Tap in June 1875. Ground-breaking events included a barbecue, speeches, a band-led procession, and festivities at Waxahachie's Temperance Hall. The terrain was rugged, the necessary capital came slowly, and it was late 1879 before the line to Garrett was completed. Within months, however, thousands of bales of cotton and hundreds of railcars of lumber were transported by the Tap, demonstrating the growth and prosperity the rail could provide. The 1886 bird's-eye view (above) shows the Tap in the upper left of the photograph. (Courtesy of the Ellis County Museum.)

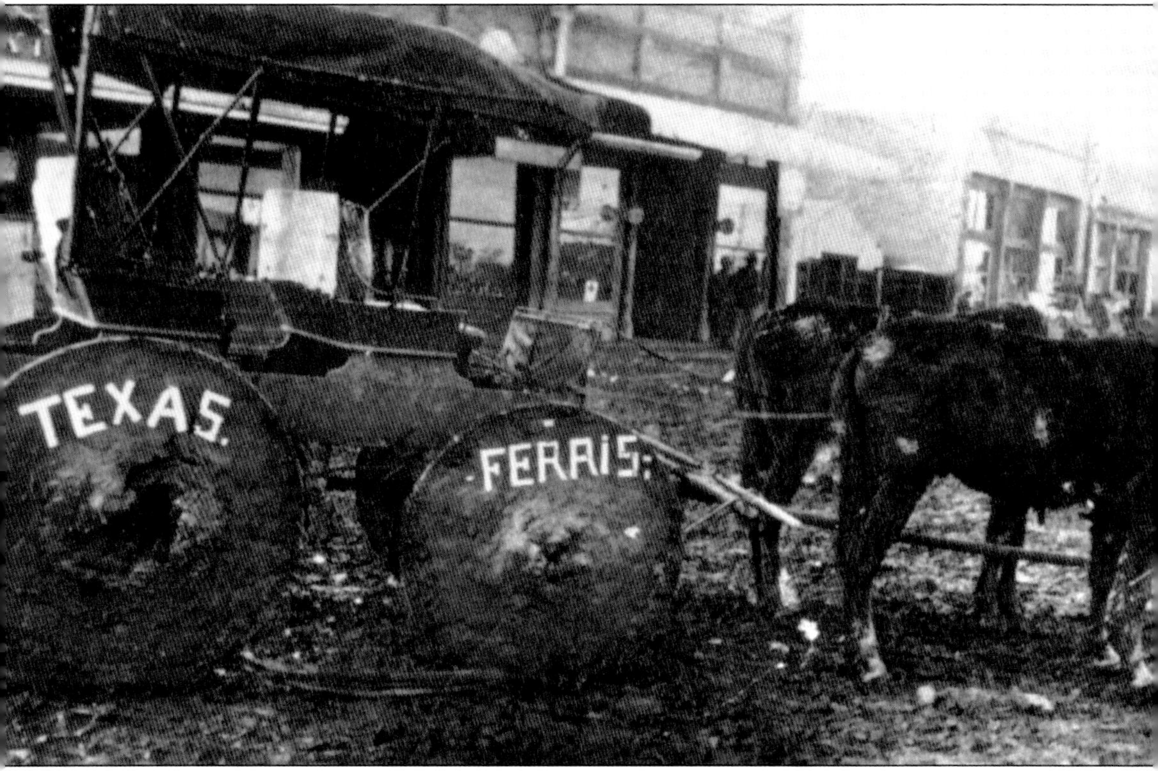

The McKnight colony was founded in the early 1850s by members of the McKnight, Andrews, Orr, McFarland, and Berry families, all of Tennessee. Twenty years later, Ferris was formed when 100 acres of land was granted to the Houston and Texas Central Railroad by members of this pioneer colony. Named for Judge Justus W. Ferris of Waxahachie, a founder of what would become Citizens National Bank, Ferris served as a chairman on the Committee on Railroads. Within a decade of the arrival of the rail, the town claimed cotton gins, gristmills, and numerous other businesses. In Ferris's early years, the Houston and Texas Central Railroad Depot agent would record the news of the community and, at week's end, pass it around, providing the growing town with its first news service. By World War I, brick manufacturing began and would prove to be a lasting industry for the community. The rail provided the means to transport this commodity. Pictured above is a mule-drawn wagon, an early form of transportation in Ferris, Texas. (Courtesy of Ellis County Museum.)

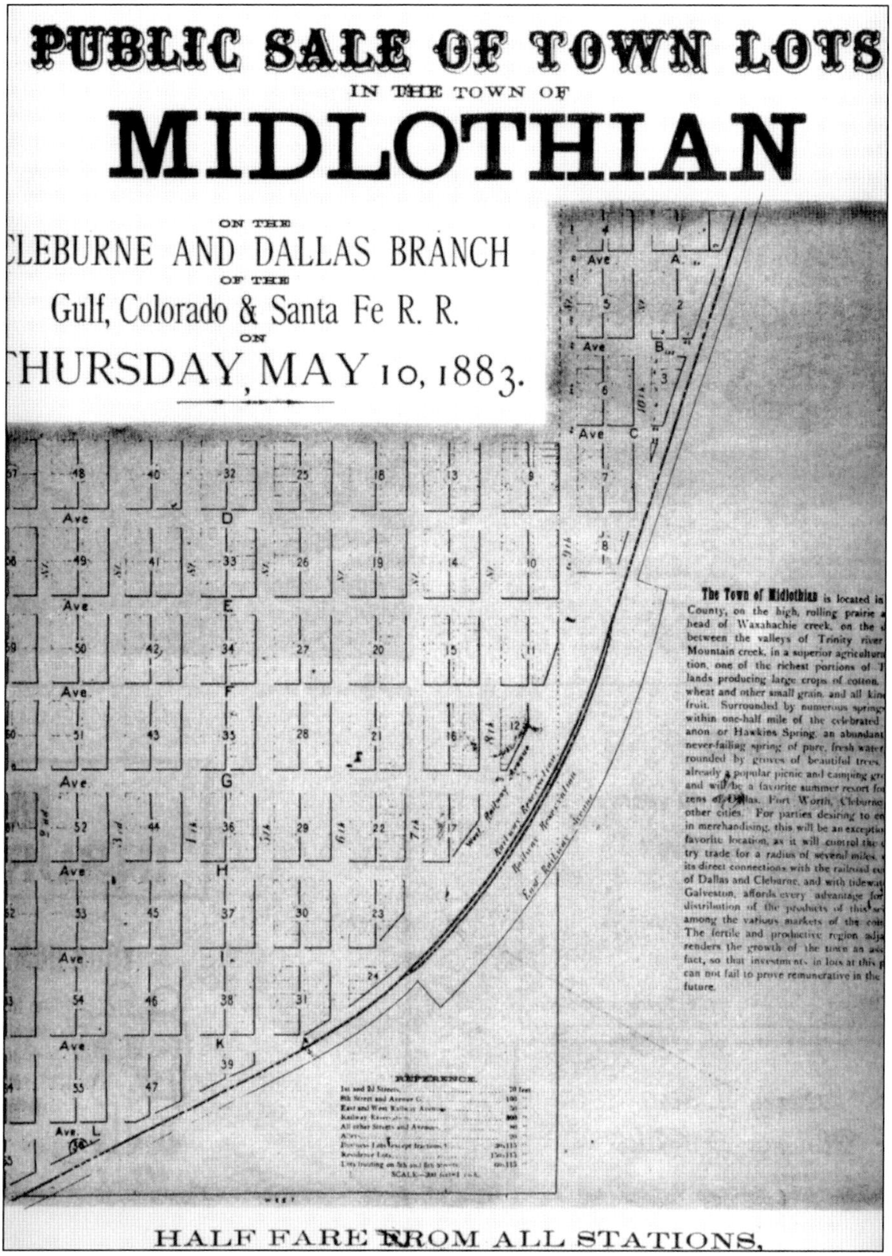

Midlothian was originally known as Lebanon after early settlers arrived in 1847. The Hawkins and Newton families were instrumental in the development of the community in its early years and beyond. By 1882, the Gulf-Colorado–Santa Fe Railroad had decided to make the area a stop on its route from Dallas to Cleburne, and the town's name was changed to Midlothian. In May 1883, two hundred acres were divided into lots for sale to the public, as pictured above in a Midlothian newspaper advertisement of the time. In July 1886, the Fort Worth and New Orleans Railroad reached Midlothian and, in that same month, connected with the Central Texas and Northwestern Railway in Waxahachie. The railroads provided the town with the means to transport trade items, and soon cotton gins were built, and a stockyard was located near the depot. (Courtesy of Karen Kay Esberger.)

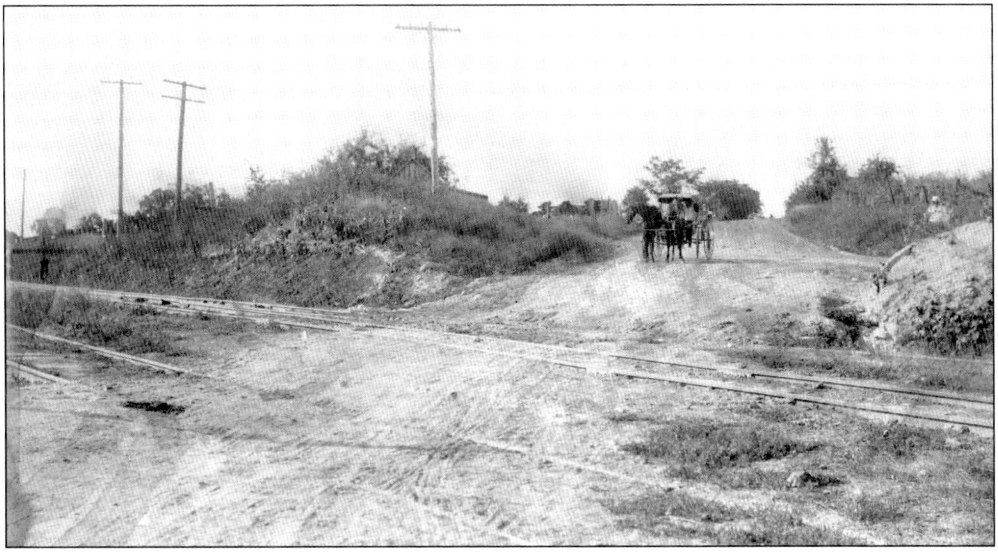

Horses and horse-pulled wagons were the means of transportation throughout Ellis County from its earliest years. Roads were formed by the repetitive use of the animals and the people that travelled them, as seen above. The rail brought changes to the way people travelled and how its commerce was transported to market. Pictured above, a horse-drawn carriage is seen approaching from the north toward the Missouri-Kansas-Texas Railroad crossing at Matthews Street (formerly Italy Road) in Waxahachie. Below several individuals can be seen at the same railroad crossing at Matthews Street in a northwest view toward Waxahachie. To the left side of the photograph is the Planters Cotton Oil Company facility. (Both, courtesy of Ellis County Museum.)

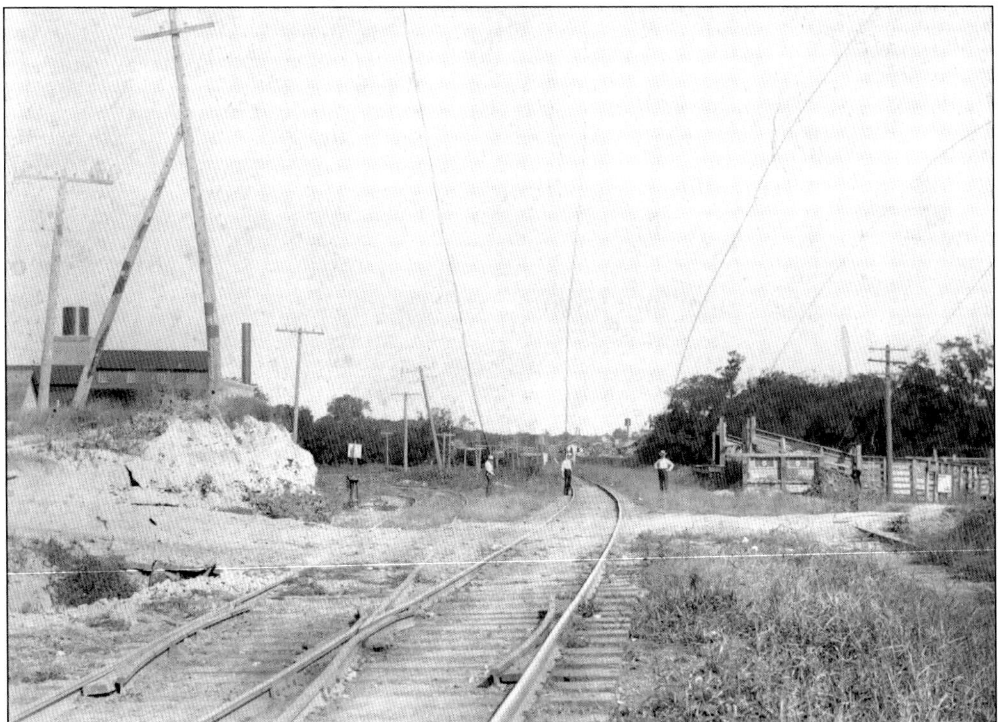

Two

Depots, Stops, and Places along the Way

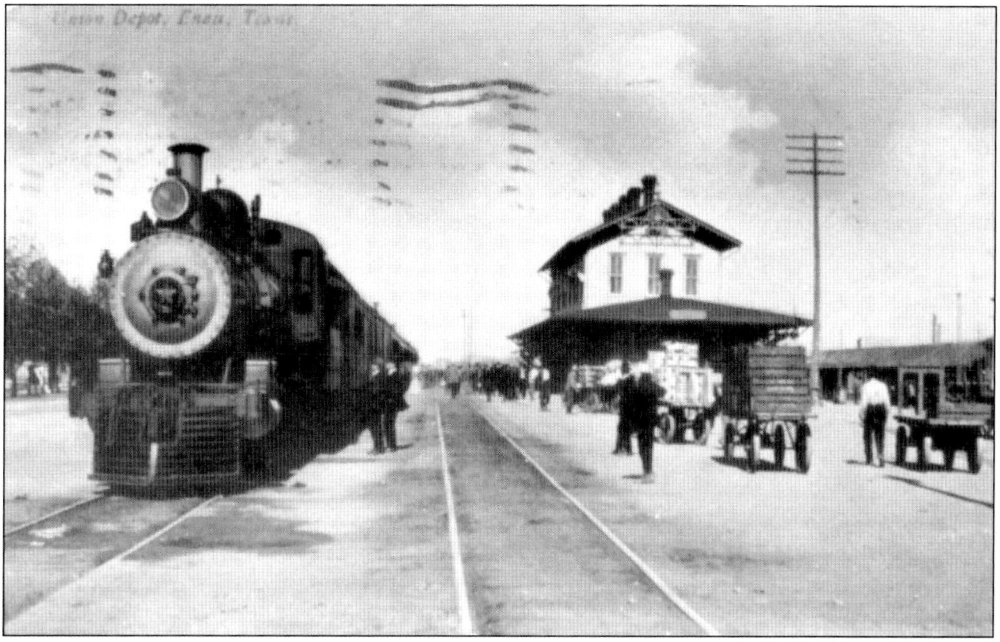

Ennis was established when the Houston and Texas Central Railroad reached this point on its way from Houston to Dennison in 1871. When the city was laid out, 300 feet were allocated for the railroad reservation, making the city's Main Street the widest in the United States. J. M. Dickson was the first railroad agent, and the first depot was built in 1872. Twenty years later, when the city became a division point for the railroad, a new depot was built (pictured above) at the same location in the 100 block of Northeast Main Street. The arrival of the rail in Ennis was not without difficulties. Initially the community of Burnham, south of Ennis, expected the rail to run through it. When this did not occur, reports from that time tell of gun fights that killed at least one and wounded others. As the arrival of the rail was the making of Ennis, it was also the beginning of the end of Burnham. The first train came through Ennis on September 1, 1872. (Courtesy of Steve Howerton.)

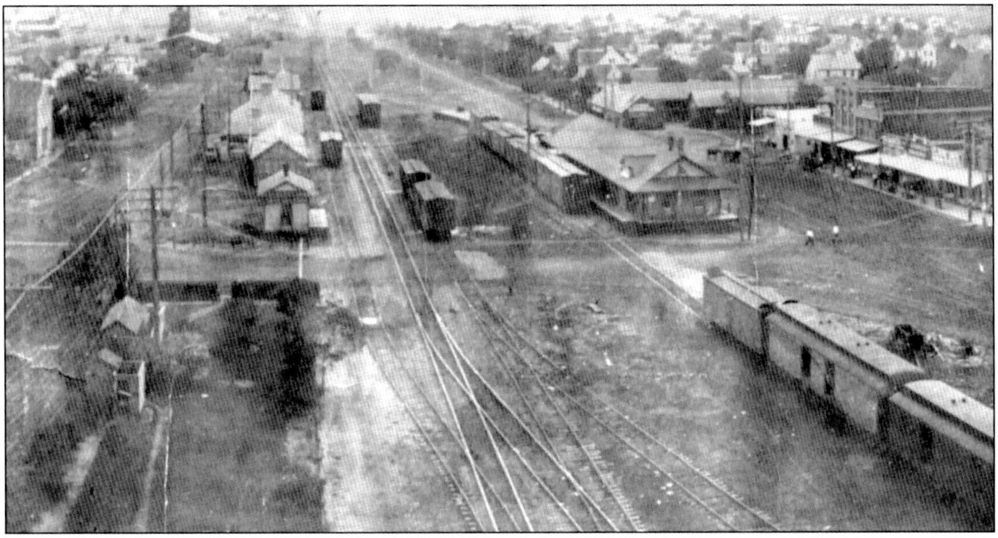

The freight depot of Ennis, pictured above in 1910, was built on Southwest Main Street. To its south, the Ennis Lumber Yard once ran along Main Street from Brown Street to Milam Street. The Houston and Texas Central Railroad Division Point Hospital (pictured below) was located at 909 North Kaufman in Ennis. It opened in mid-1904. The building was purchased from George Botzler. The hospital closed around 1916. In 1918, division doctors included C. P. Cook, W. P. McCall Sr., F. L. Story, and T. W. White of Ennis; J. T. Carter of Alma; E. House of Ferris; T. L. Barnett of Midlothian; and W. D. Boyd and W. C. Tenery of Waxahachie. Dr. Walter Price McCall Jr. was one of the last practicing division doctors of Ennis. (Above, courtesy of City of Ennis, below, courtesy of the A. L. Bohanon Jr. family.)

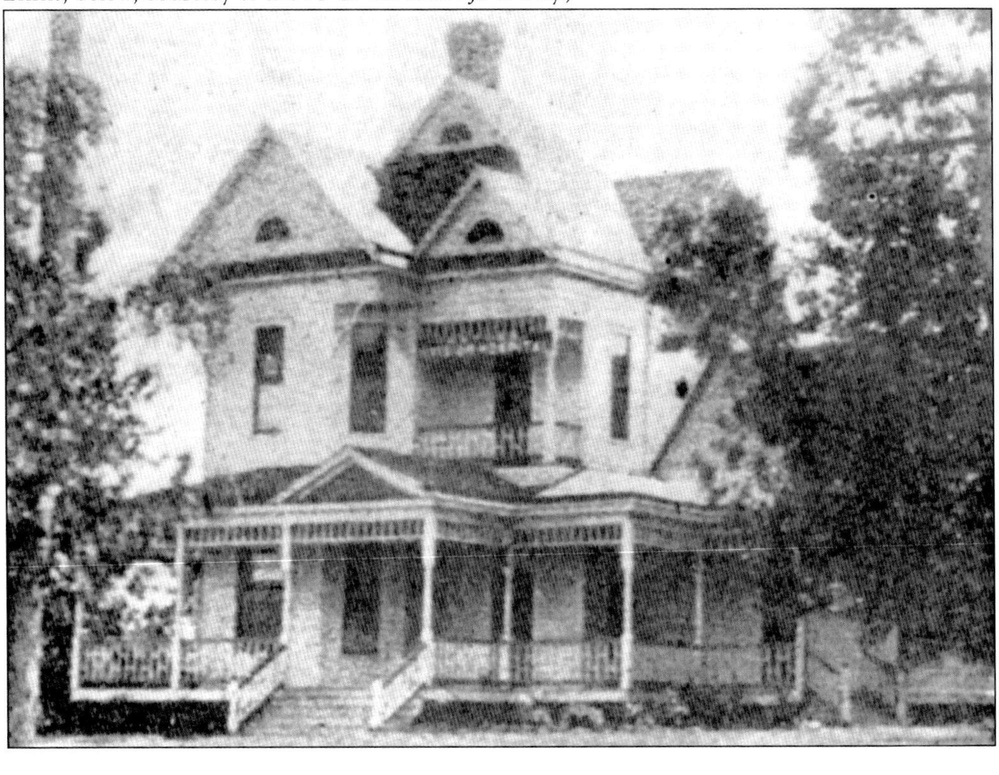

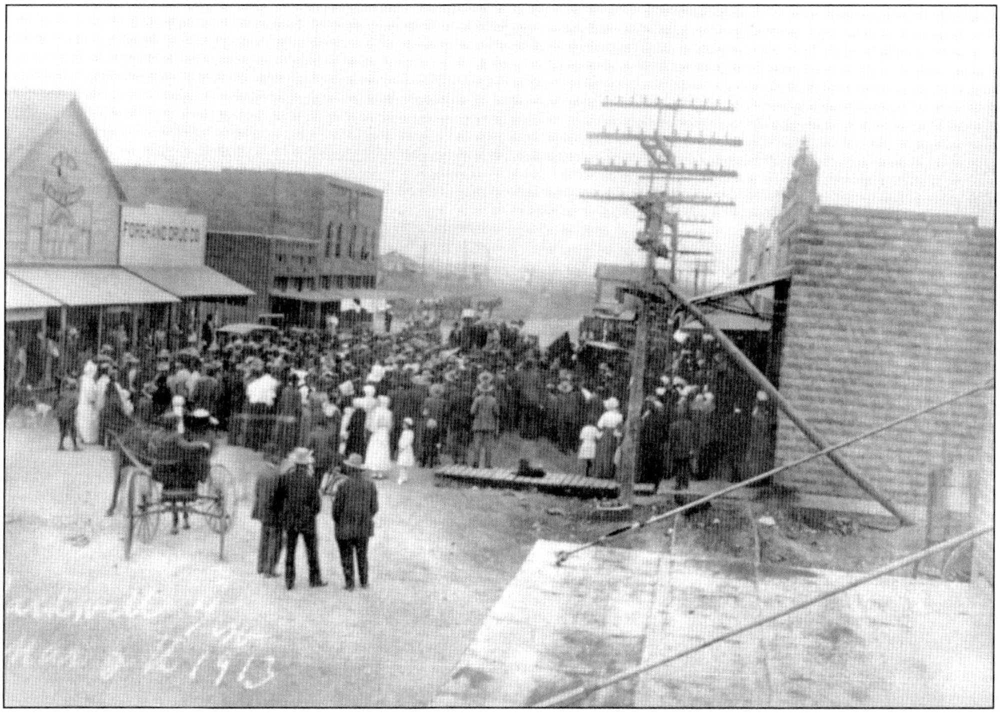

The City of Bardwell moved almost 1 mile east of its original location when the Trinity and Brazos Valley Railroad came through in 1906. Bardwell's Main Street is pictured above in 1913, where members of the community gather to wait for election results. Pictured along the left of the photograph, from left to right, are the Woodsmen of the World building (two stories), Forehand Drug Company, Bruce's Feed Store, and the Masonic Lodge at 301 Main Street. The depot, pictured at right in the mid-1940s, was moved south of the city around 1960. The street in the foreground is Commerce Street. The roofline of the Masonic Lodge can be seen to the left of the depot, and Chapman's Mercantile Store is to its left. (Both, courtesy of Joe V. Pool.)

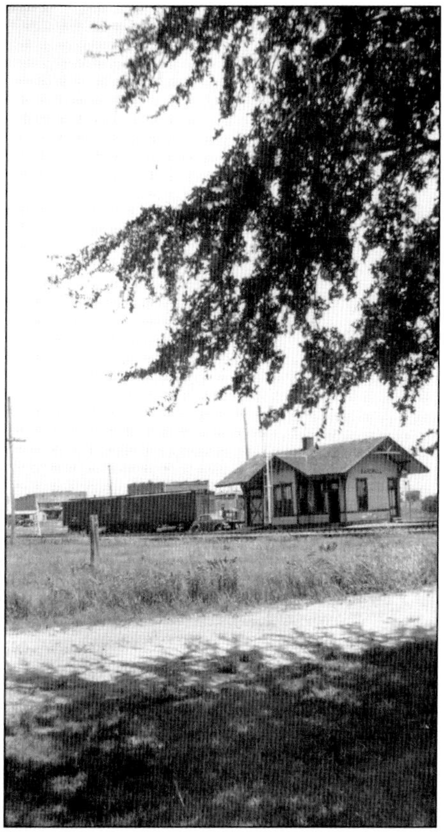

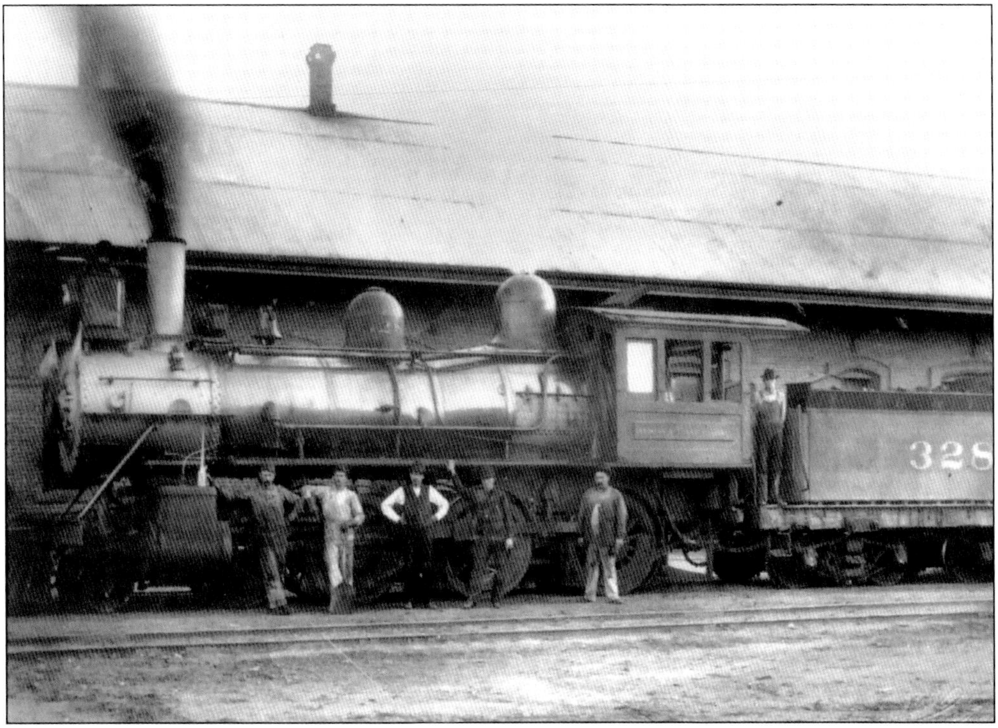

The Houston and Texas Central Railroad Depot in Waxahachie was located on the west side of North Rogers Street from the mid-1880s to 1904 and is pictured above, behind engine No. 328, around 1896. The engine was built by Cooke in 1892 and was scrapped in 1928. The depot can be seen below on the lower right-hand side of the photograph just below the Cumberland Presbyterian Church in this view taken from the Ellis County Courthouse in the early 1900s. The new depot that replaced it was built on the east side of North College Street, with the original depot becoming the freight depot. (Both, courtesy of Ellis County Museum.)

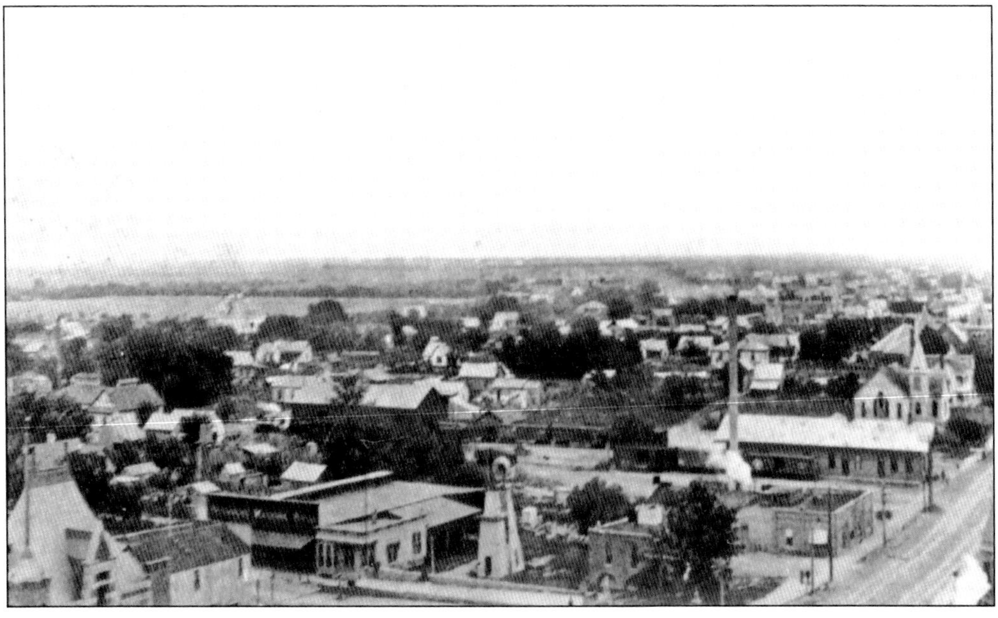

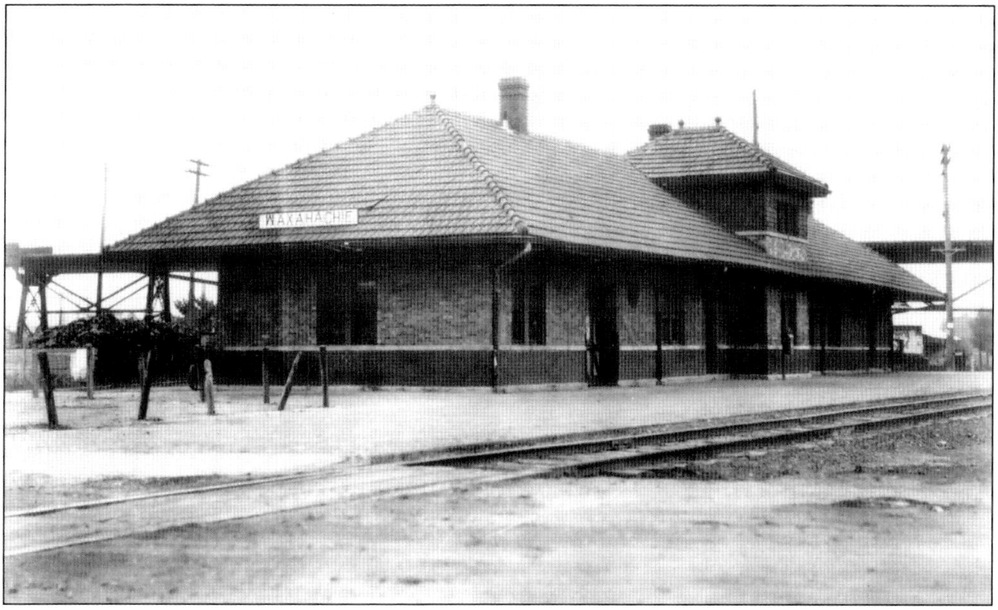

The Missouri-Kansas-Texas Railroad (M-K-T) arrived in Waxahachie in 1887. During the course of its construction, flash floods destroyed much of the graded roadbed near the Waxahachie Creek's low-lying areas. The M-K-T Railroad Passenger Depot, located along the rail between South Rogers and South College Streets, is pictured above around 1915. The M-K-T Railroad Freight Depot was located along the rail at the end of South Monroe Street to the west of the passenger depot. Passenger service on the M-K-T, also known as the Katy, continued until 1964. Pictured below is William Charles Clay, a baggage agent for the Houston and Texas Central Railroad. He is seen in the baggage depot in Waxahachie around 1916. (Both, courtesy of Ellis County Museum.)

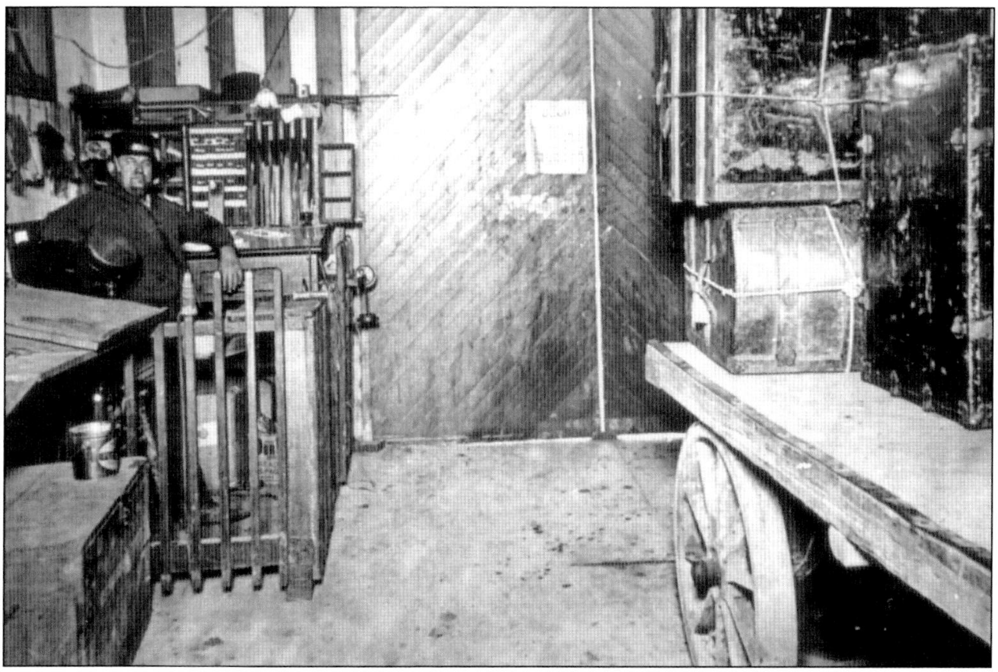

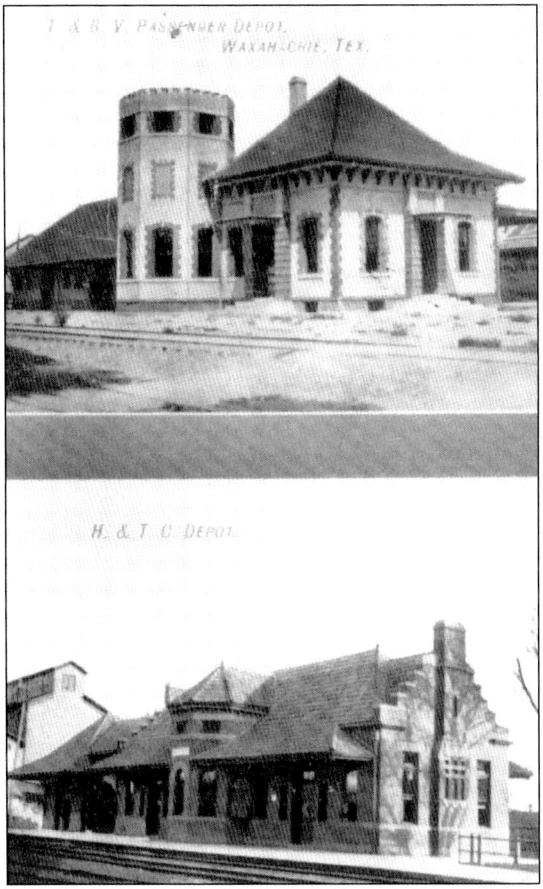

The Trinity and Brazos Valley Railroad Depot, in the upper portion of the photograph at left, was located between South Rogers and South College Streets. It later became the Burlington–Rock Island Railroad Depot. In the lower portion of the photograph is the Houston and Texas Central Railroad Depot, located between North Jackson and North College Streets, which was built to replace the earlier depot located on North Rogers Street. It was constructed around 1900, and both are pictured around 1908. (Courtesy of Ellis County Museum.)

This rear view of the Trinity and Brazos Valley Railroad (T&BV) is pictured below around 1915. The T&BV Railroad was the third rail line to reach Waxahachie and was completed in 1907. To the right of the photograph, engine No. 51 can be seen pulled alongside the depot. (Courtesy of Ellis County Museum.)

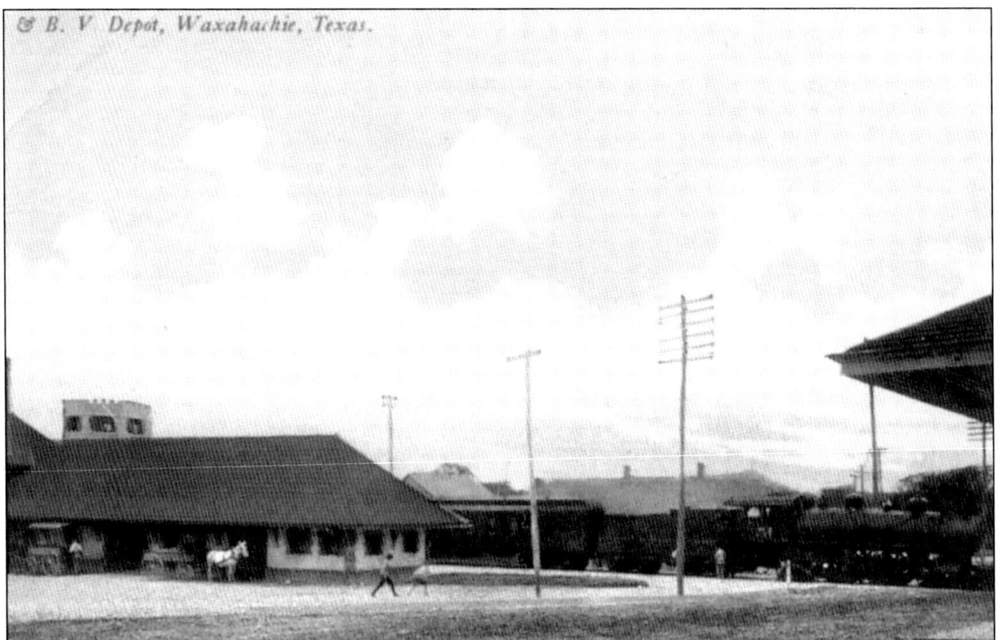

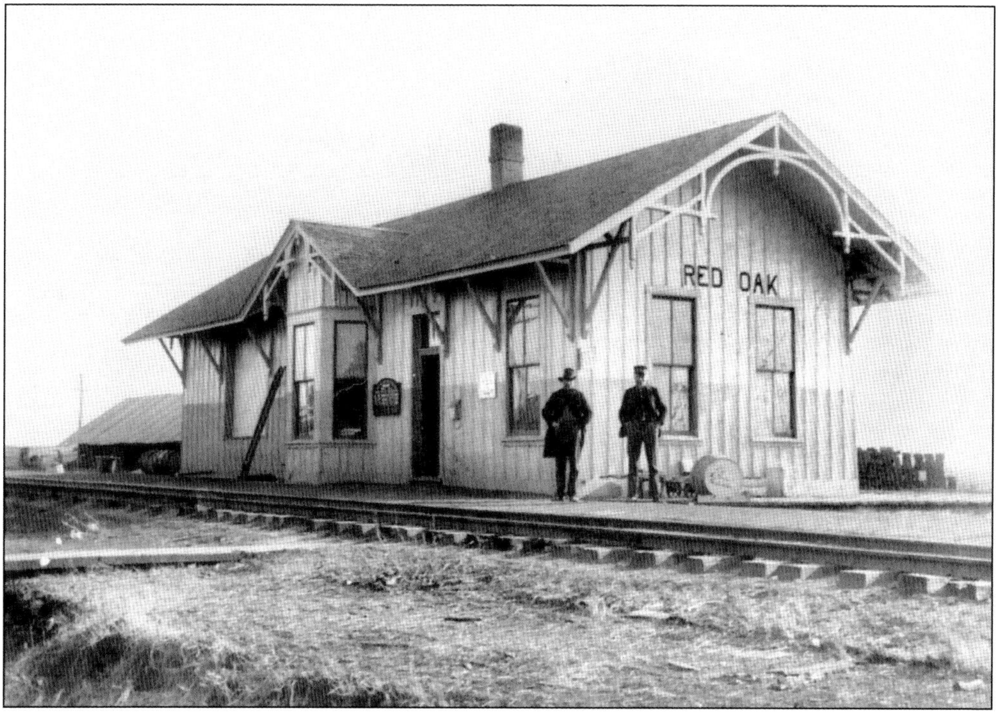

Red Oak's downtown area grew within blocks of the railroad. Pictured above is the Missouri-Kansas-Texas Railroad Depot around 1905. In front of the depot are James Andrews (left), agent for the railroad from 1896 to 1908, and ? Holder, a section foreman. Red Oak's downtown area, looking down Waller Street to Ligon and Beddo General Merchandise Store, is seen below, also around 1905. Main Street is the cross street in the foreground, with Ligon and Beddo Dry Goods and Grocery Store to the left. (Both, courtesy of Ellis County Museum.)

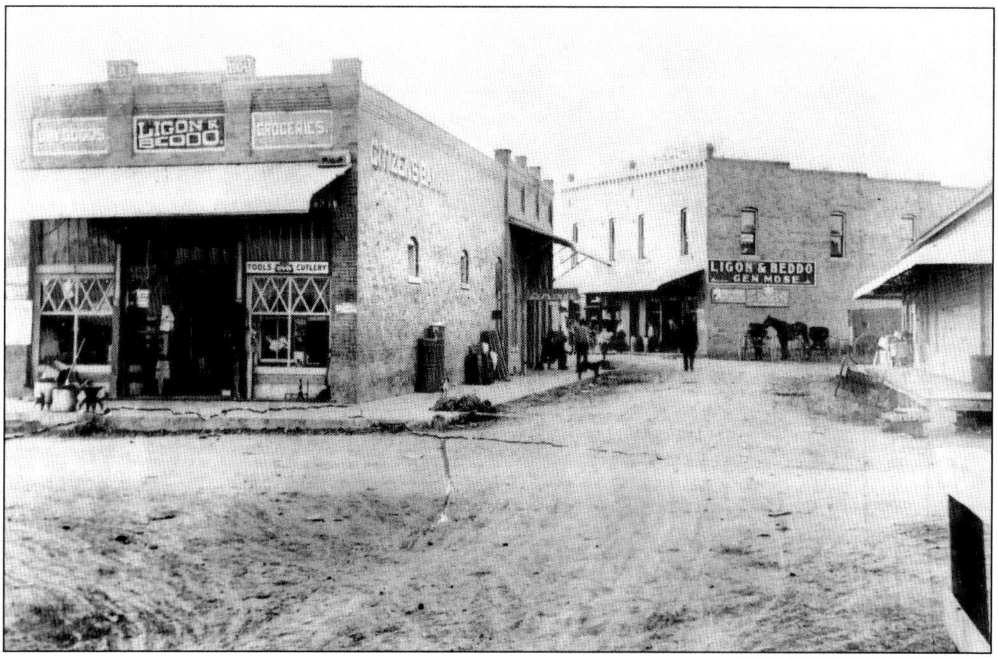

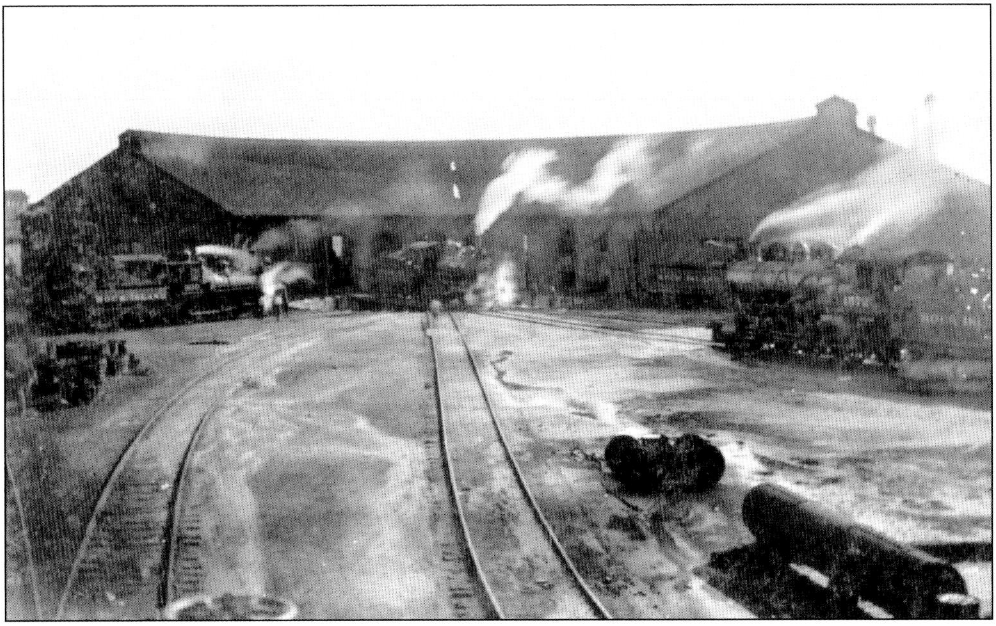

The Ferris Roundhouse was located a few miles outside of the city. Built in the late 1890s, it was closed by the end of the 1920s. At the left of the photograph is Rock Island Engine No. 300, and to the right is engine No. 1572. Inbound and outbound tracks leading to the turntable are visible in the foreground. (Courtesy of Ellis County Museum.)

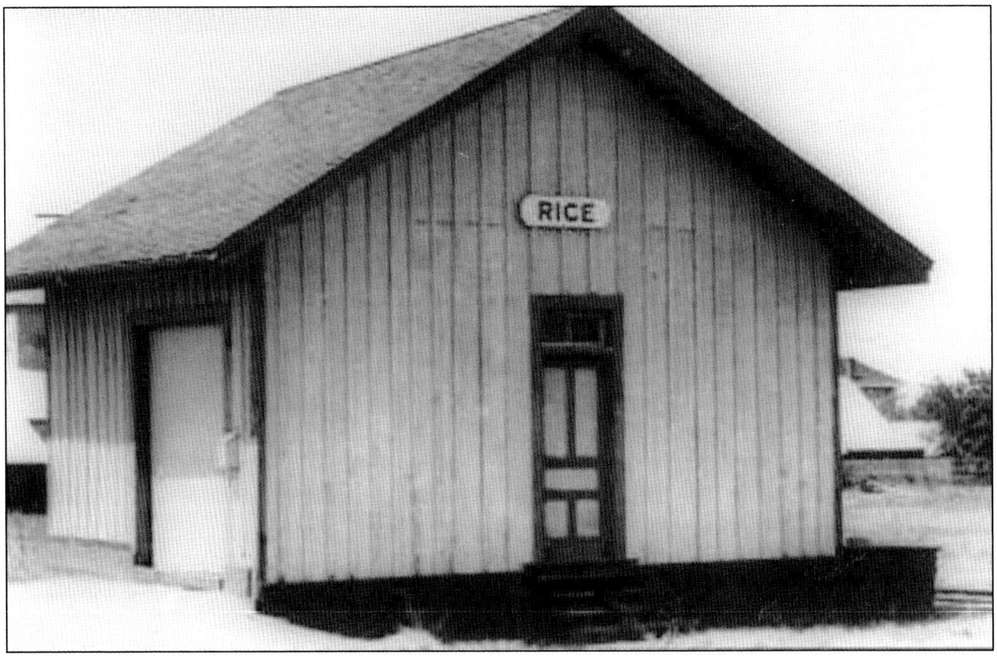

The Texas and New Orleans (H&TC) Railroad Depot in Rice, pictured above around 1920, was located on Calhoun Street. In October 1899, John Lipscomb of Hearne, an engineer for the Houston and Texas Central Railroad, was mistakenly shot by the Rice H&TC Depot night watchman, not recognizing Lipscomb as a railroad employee. Lipscomb died later that day from his injuries. (Courtesy of Jerry Herring.)

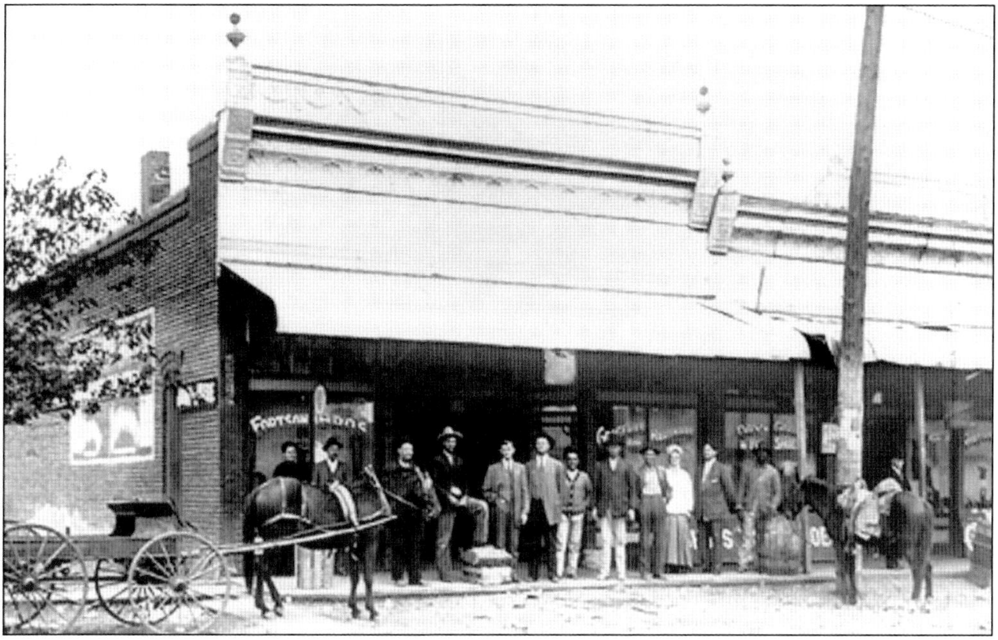

Like many small communities, the businesses in Rice grew around the railroad tracks and depots. The Fortson Brothers Grocery and Hardware Store (above at left) and the Fortson Brothers Dry Goods Store (to its right), pictured around 1907, were right across from the depot and loading platform. Also the owners of a local gin, the office for the gin was at one time located in the back of the grocery. (Courtesy of Jerry Herring.)

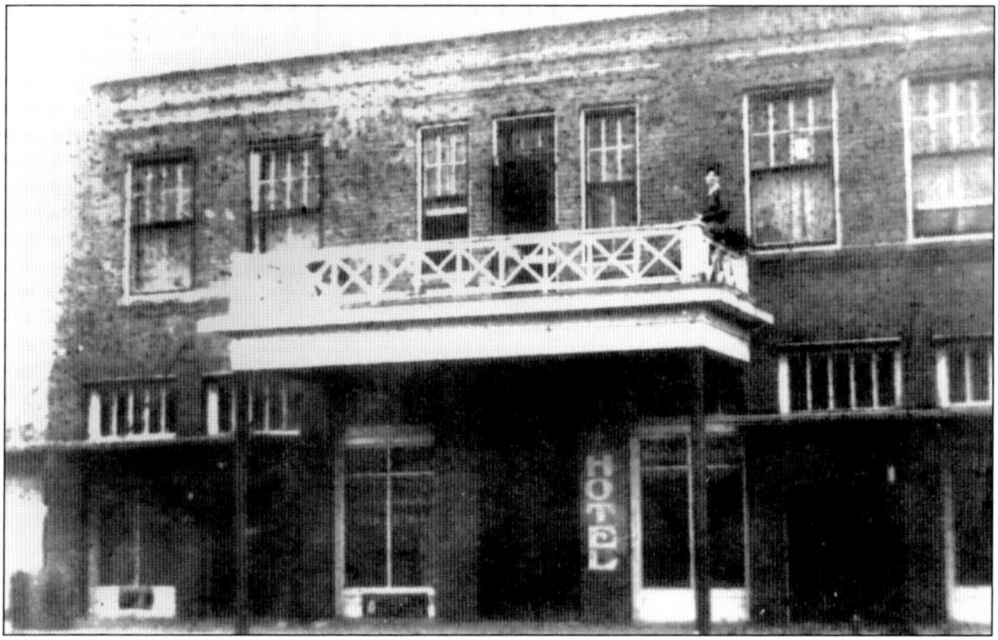

The Gatlin Hotel of Rice stood less than 200 feet from the Houston and Texas Central Railroad platform. The hotel was located on the southeast corner of Calhoun Street, across the alley from the depot. The hotel rooms were on the second floor of the redbrick building, and the first floor housed the variety store owned by the family of Joe Holland. (Courtesy of Jerry Herring.)

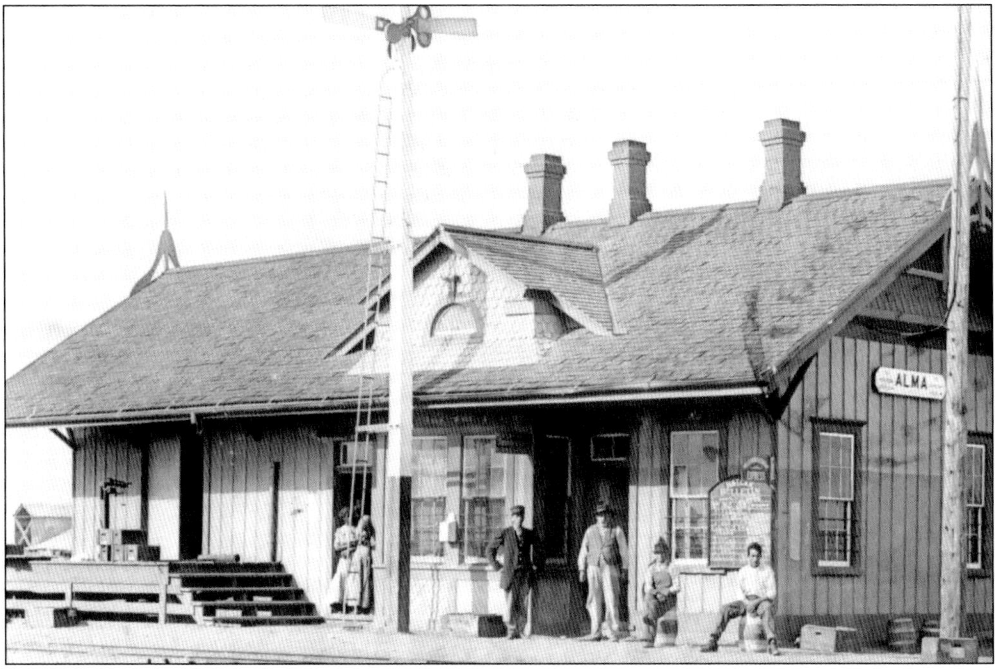

The Houston and Texas Central Railroad arrived in Alma in 1872. The depot, pictured above around 1909, provided both freight and passenger service. The freight depot is to the left with the loading platform. The Alma Business District was located to the west of the rail, pictured below in the 1890s. The second building from the right is the G. W. Collard General Merchandise Store. Collard and his wife, Sally Ruffin Collard, were pioneers of the community. (Both, courtesy of Ellis County Museum.)

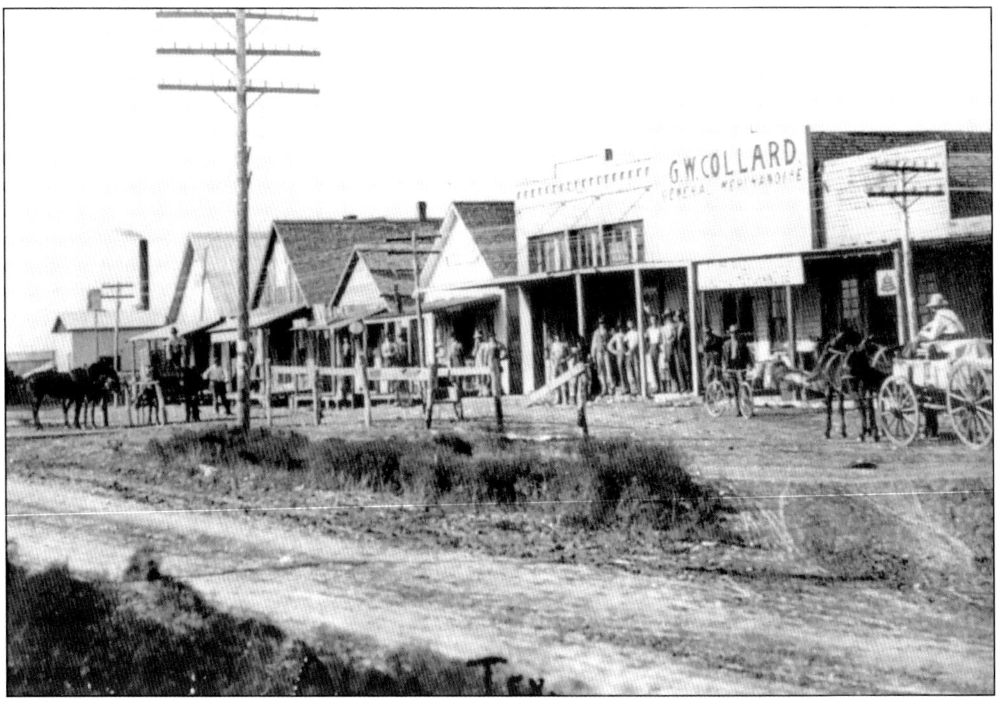

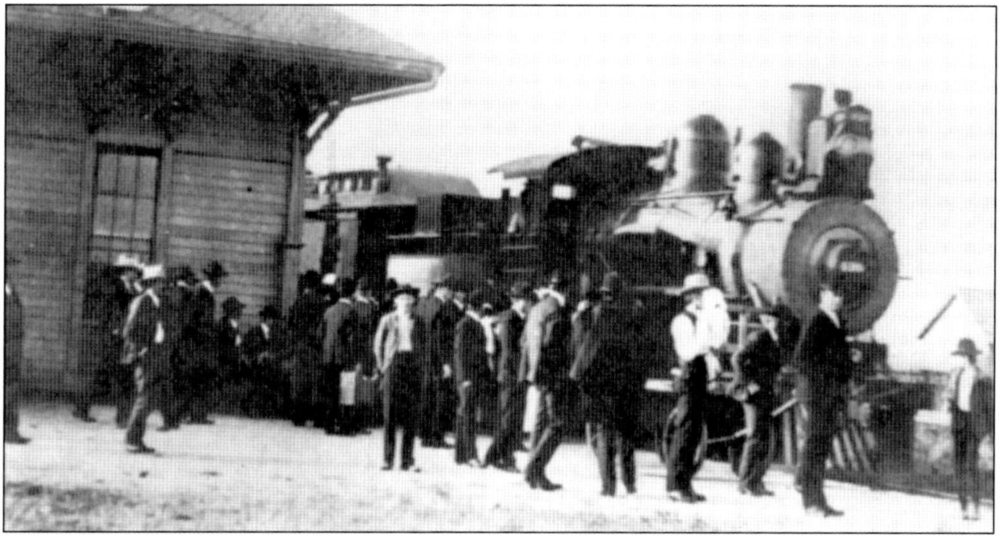

The Houston and Texas Central Railroad named the town of Garrett for the original landowners, Claiborne and William Garrett, who gave the right-of-way to the railroad in 1894. Early on Garrett was a junction for the main line of the H&TC and the Waxahachie Tap. Mail and freight was transferred in Garrett for all points west. Pictured above is a Houston and Texas Central passenger train at the Garrett depot around 1910. Among those early Garrett residents that worked for the railroad were C. P. Groves, B. H. Poe, J. L. Poe, E. C. Rawlins, Leslie Rawlins, and John Slagle. Pictured below is a H&TC child's ticket from Garrett to Hutchins from 1910. (Above, courtesy of Joe V. Pool; below, courtesy of Dane Williams.)

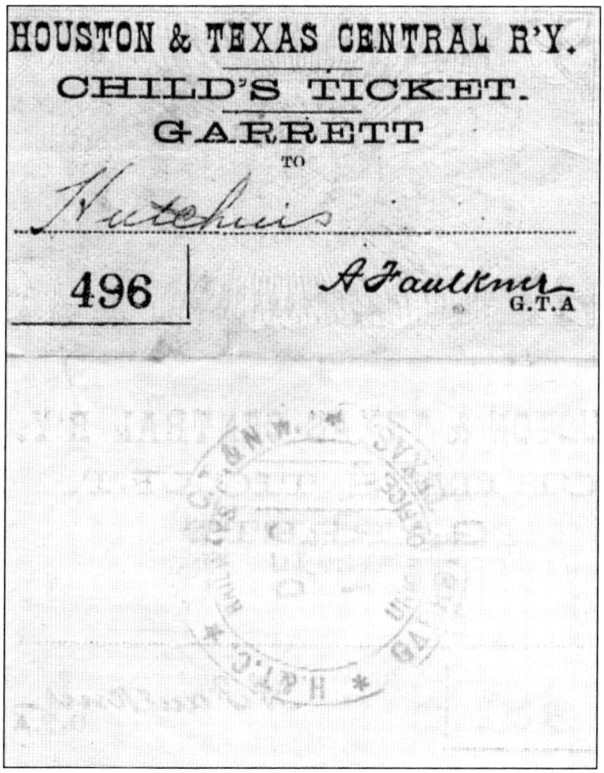

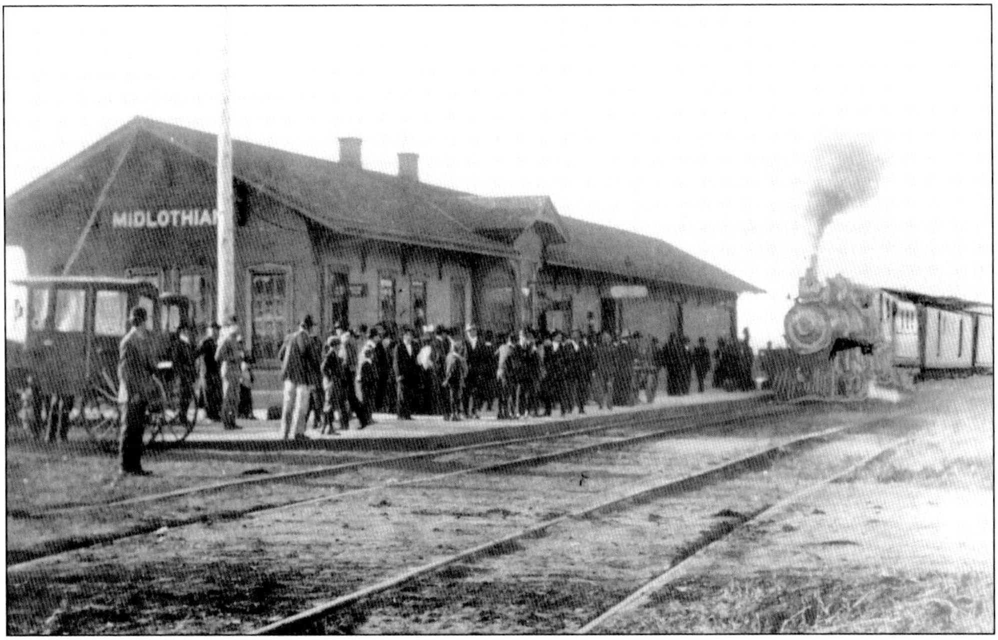

Midlothian's first depot was built in 1883 after the Gulf-Colorado–Santa Fe Railroad purchased the railroad line from the Chicago, Texas, and Mexican Central Railroad in 1882. Pictured above in 1919 are family members of Robert Lee Massey waiting for the train carrying the deceased Massey. A hearse can be seen to the left. Below, a northward view of Breckinridge Street in Ennis is pictured in January 1918, with Texas Midland Railroad tracks covered in snow running down the center. Pictured to the left of the tracks are (from left to right) Mary Joly, Ida Joly, Celesta Joly, and "Ol Dan." At a distance in the upper right hand corner the distinctive roofline of the Texas Midland depot can be seen. (Above, courtesy of Ellis County Museum; below, courtesy of the A. L. Bohanon Jr. family.)

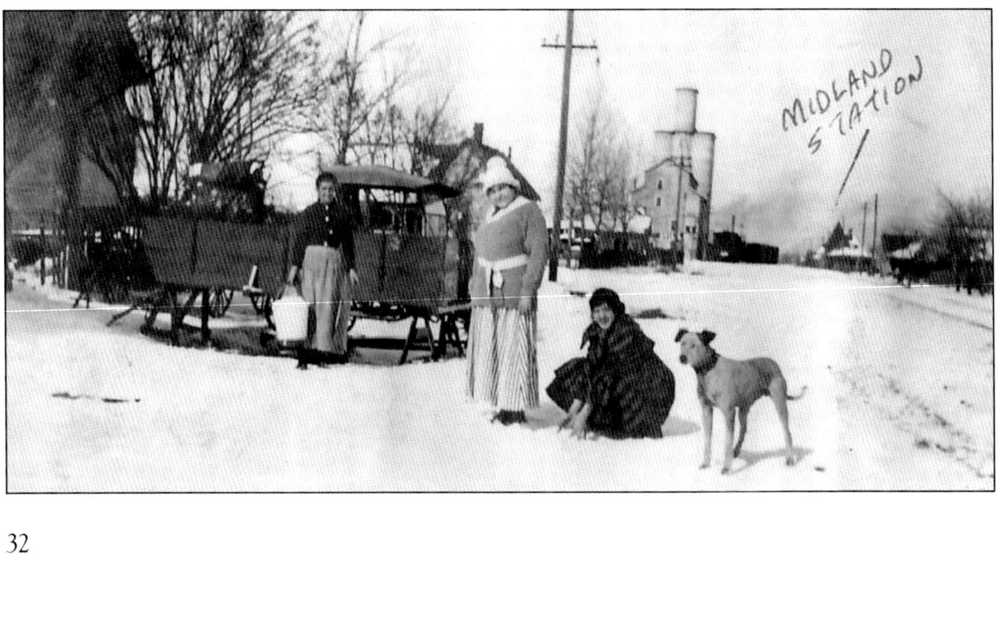

Three

COTTON AND THE RAIL

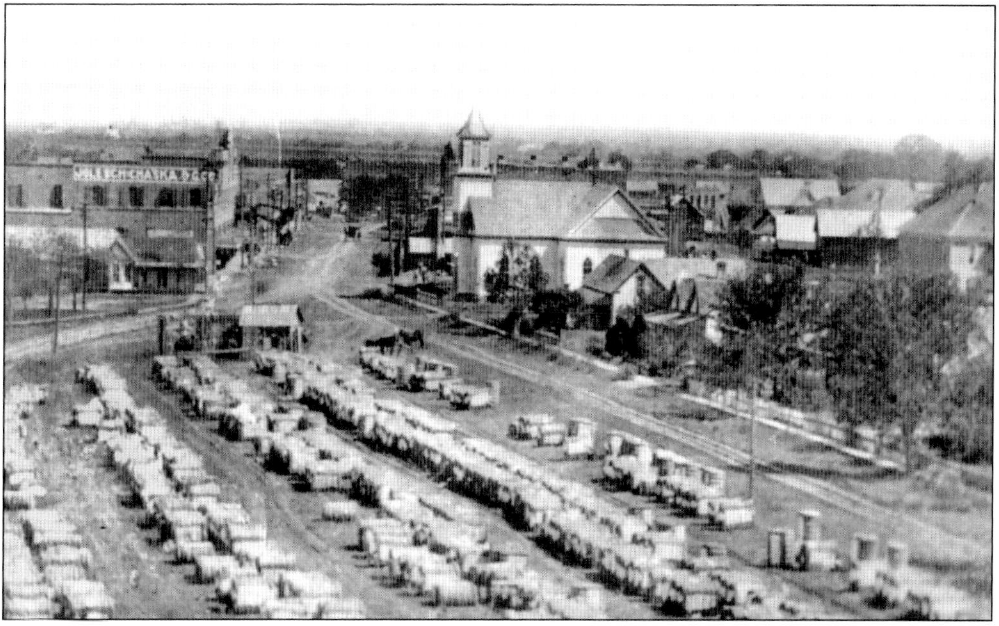

The Missouri-Kansas-Texas Railroad arrived in Italy in 1890. Its passenger and freight depot was built to the east of the railroad at the end of First Street. The International Great Northern Railroad came through in 1901, running along the west side of the city. The passenger and freight depot were built soon after and were located on Church Street, south of Main Street. Within a decade of the arrival of the rail, Italy had several gins, including the A. Mosely and Son Gin, the Farmer's Union Gin Company, the Italy Ginning Company, and the Ward and Wolaver Gin. The town was also home to the Italy Cotton Oil Company, the Italy Compress Company, and the Italy Cotton Yard. The year's cotton harvest is pictured above around 1895. In the background to the left of the photograph, the Jolesch and Chaska Store sign can be seen. (Courtesy of Ellis County Museum.)

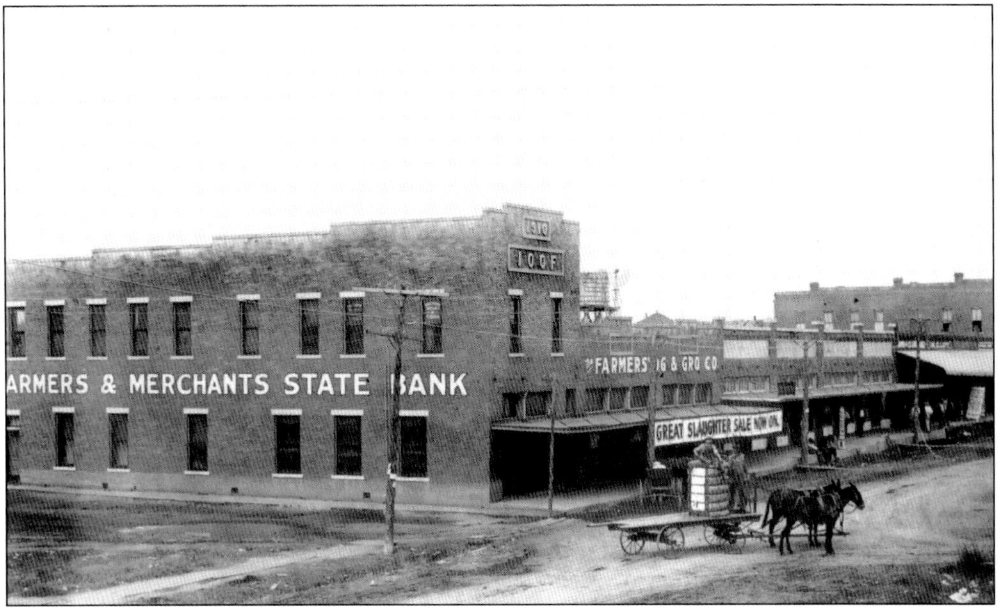

In 1903, Maypearl shipped more than 1,600 bales of cotton. In November 1913, the gin, built by C. E. Ingle, was destroyed by fire. Pictured around 1913 is a horse-drawn wagon carrying bales of cotton down Main Street. The Farmers and Merchant Bank was destroyed by fire in 1915 and was rebuilt in 1916. The banner on the Farmers Grocery beside it advertises "Great Slaughter Sale Now On." (Courtesy of Ellis County Museum.)

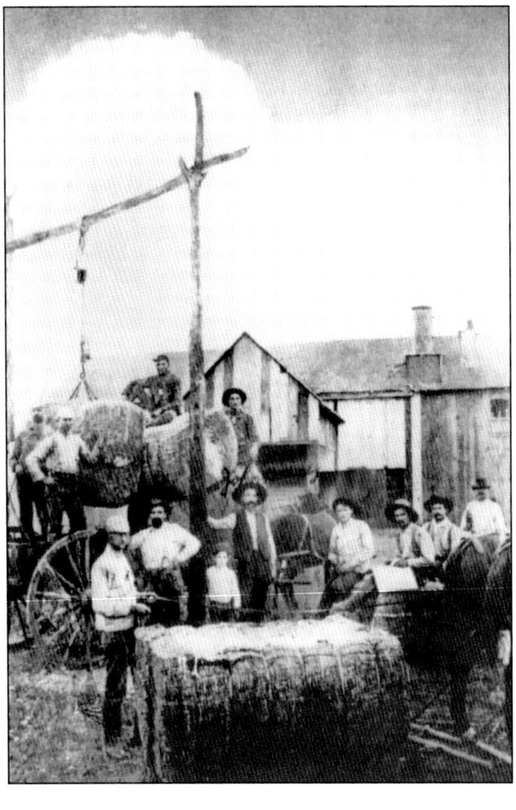

One of the oldest towns in Ellis County, Ovilla had a cotton gin by the early 1880s. While the town was bypassed by the railroads, its proximity to Red Oak, Midlothian, and Waxahachie provided the means to market their cotton. The Ovilla Cotton Gin is pictured at left around 1885, with John Billingsley, an early pioneer of the town, in the lower center of the photograph, wearing a vest and with his hand against the pole. (Courtesy of Ellis County Museum.)

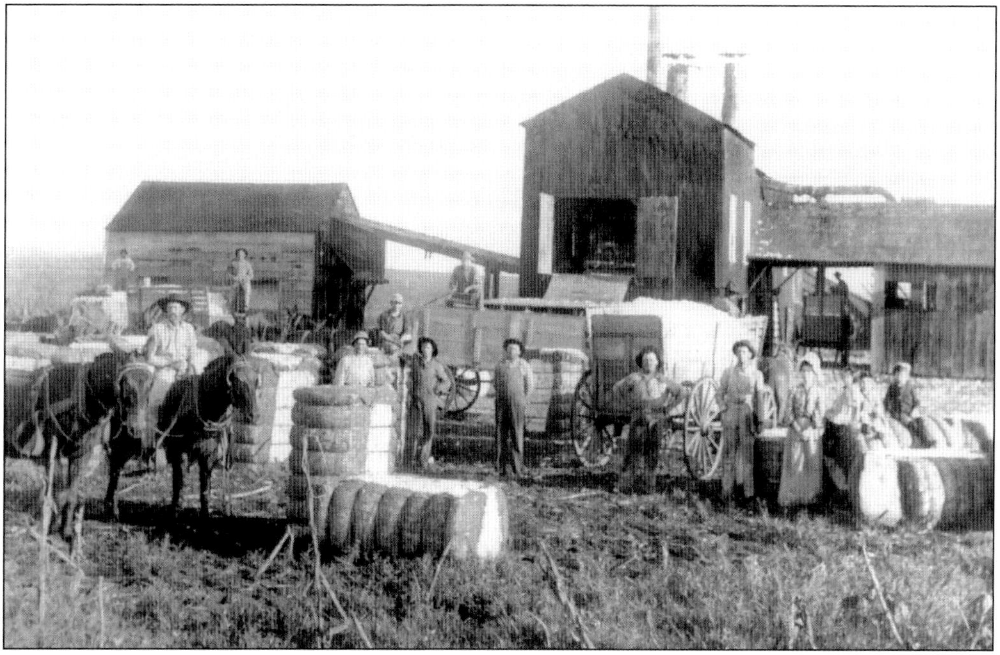

In May 1899, residents of Midlothian gathered and organized a joint stock company to build a cotton gin and oil mill, planned at that time to be called the Midlothian Cotton Oil Company. Several years later, in 1903, farmers gathered and organized a cooperative effort, the Farmers' Gin Company. Pictured above, workers can be seen among the equipment and bales of cotton at a steam-operated gin in Midlothian in the mid-1890s. The gin was located on Avenue G and Eighth Street, west of the railroad tracks and the downtown area. Pictured below, with Perry's Hardware Store in the background, horse-drawn wagons loaded with bales of the season's cotton harvest make their way through Midlothian's downtown around 1898. (Both, courtesy of Ellis County Museum.)

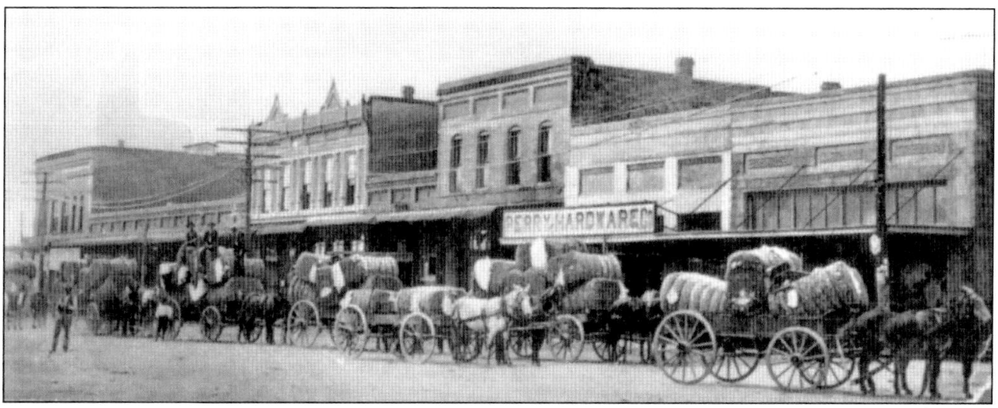

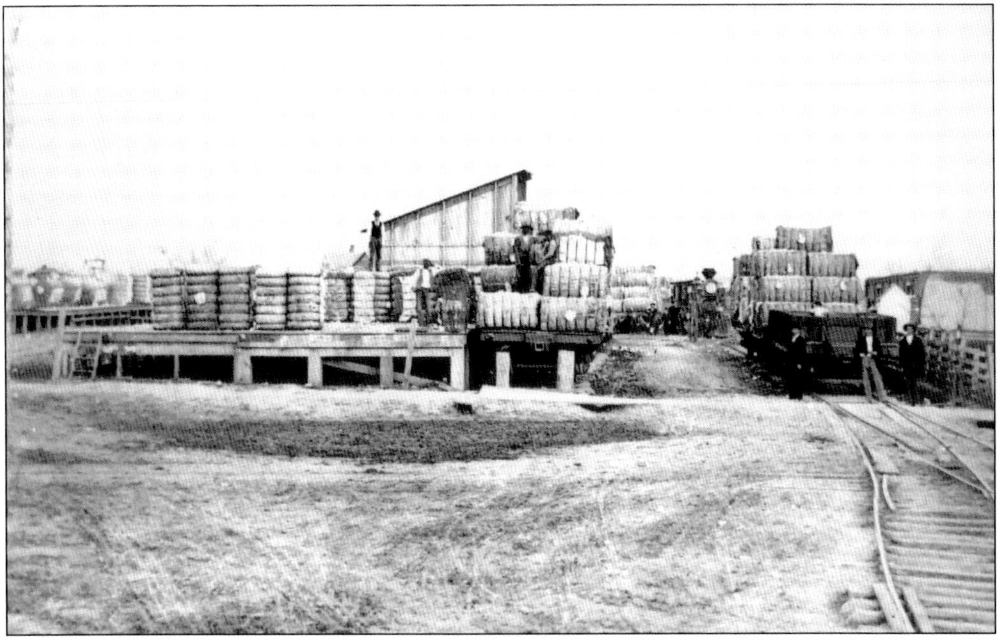

The Waxahachie Cotton Yard was located between North College and North Jackson Streets on the rail line. A Waxahachie Tap Railroad car can be seen at the yard, around 1881, as workers are loading cotton bales onto the train car. (Courtesy of Ellis County Museum.)

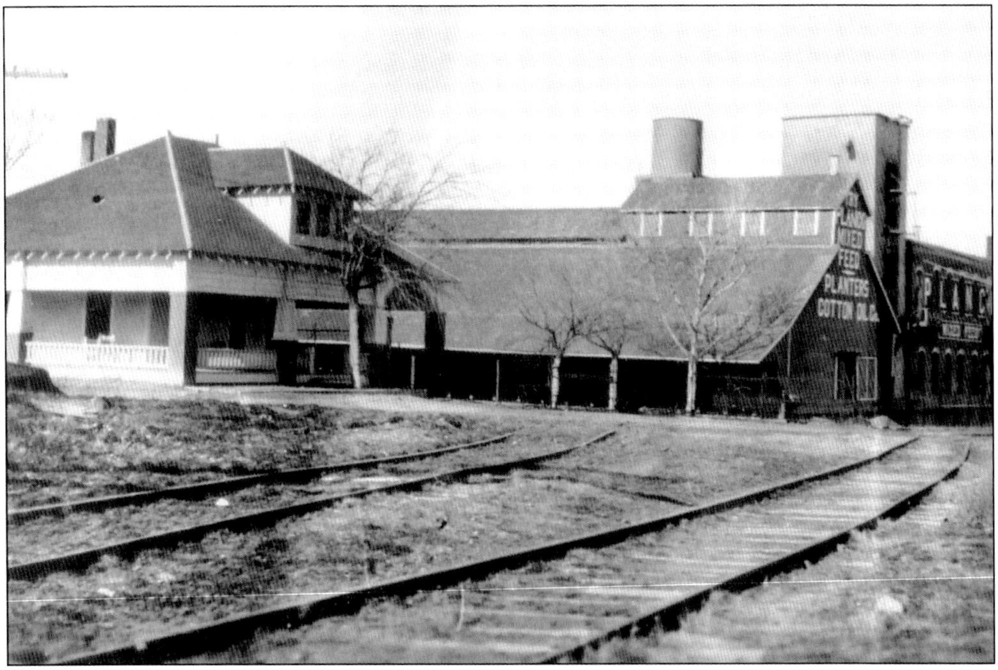

Prior to its closing in 1934, the Planters Cotton Oil Company of Waxahachie provided another source of revenue for the community from its staple crop, cotton. Located beside the Missouri-Kansas-Texas Railroad track, the company is pictured above to the right in a view looking across the track. (Courtesy of Ellis County Museum.)

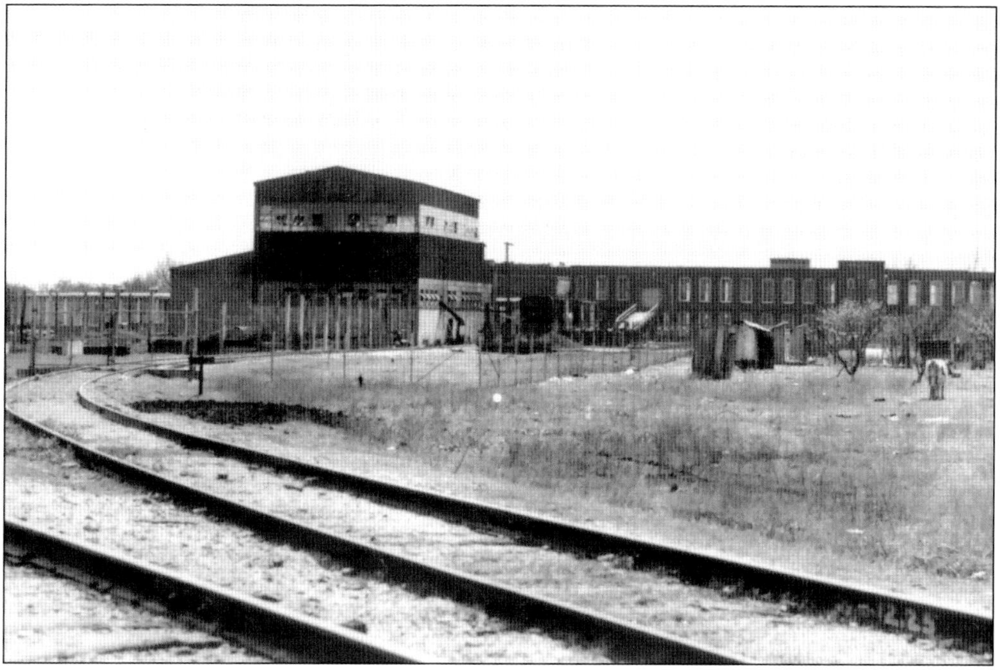

The Waxahachie Cotton Mills Company was built in large part through the funds raised from the local citizens of Waxahachie. Construction began in 1899, and by 1901, the mill was operating with 500 spindles and 150 looms. Located on the west side of town, the railroad tracks came right to the mill property, as pictured above in the early 1900s. Pictured below, a train can be seen stopped at the mill, where the cotton products could be loaded directly from the cotton mill to the train cars. In early August 1900, part of the first bale of cotton brought to Waxahachie that year, raised by A. J. Hogan on the Clint Sanderson farm near Byron, was kept to start off production in the Waxahachie Cotton Mill, which was still under construction. (Both, courtesy of Ellis County Museum.)

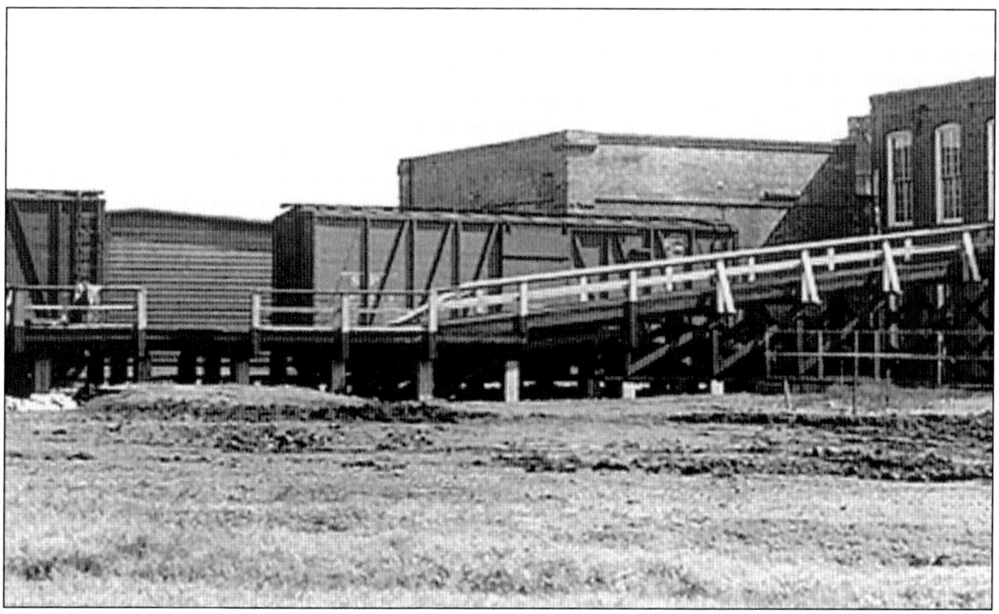

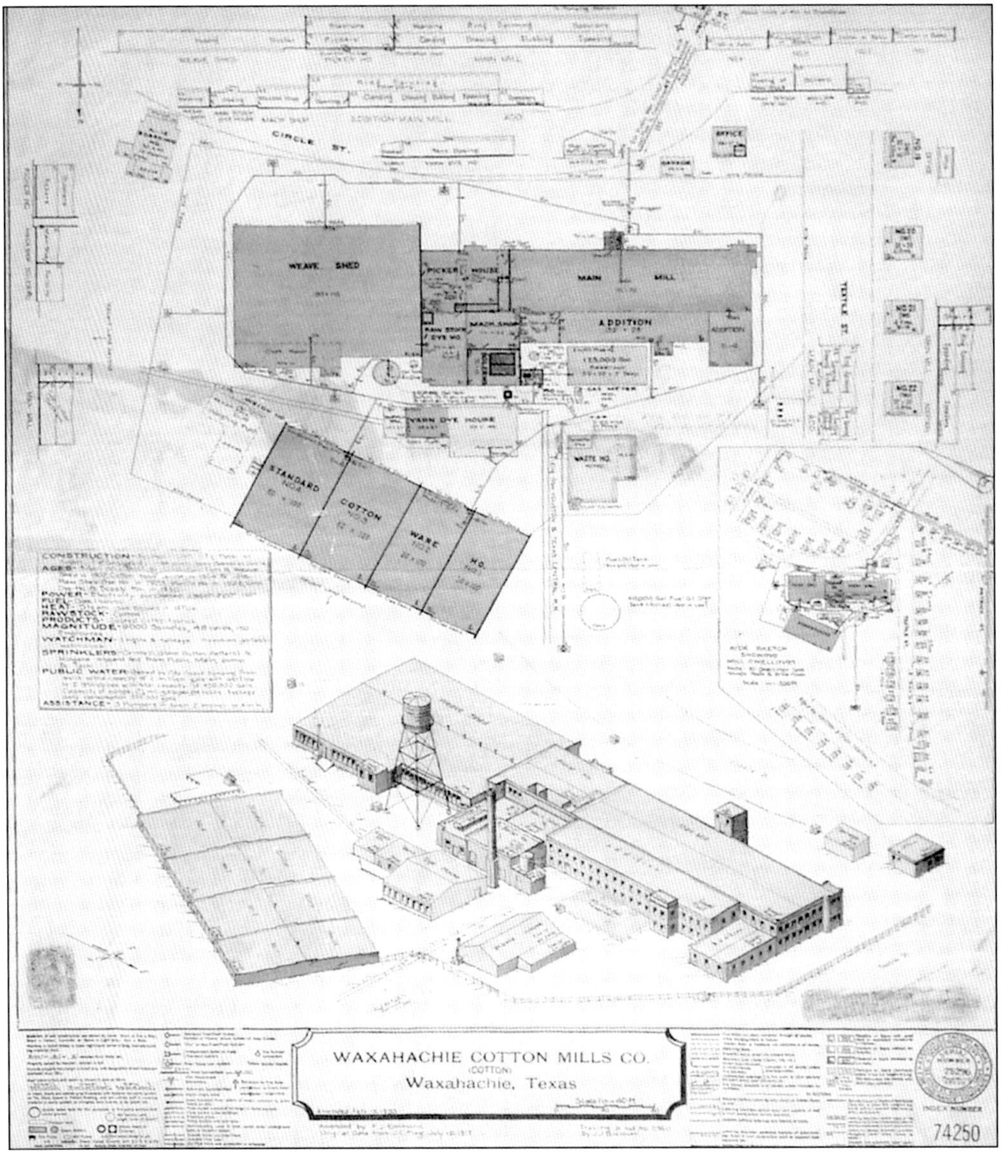

The Waxahachie Cotton Mill and all its related facilities occupied 20 acres of land to the west of the city. The Houston and Texas Central Railroad ran right up to the mill, as seen in the photograph's center. While an aerial view of the mill is provided in the lower edge of the photograph, a diagram of the interior of the mill is provided along the upper edge. Along the backside of the diagram, from left to right, the mill was comprised of a weave shed, a picker house, and the main mill to the right of the building. Below the mill diagram to the left of the railroad line depiction is the yarn dye house, and below it on a diagonal is the standard cotton warehouse. At the right of the photograph in the center is an inset that depicts the entire property, illustrating the many small frame buildings, located behind the mill, that housed the mill's employees. This area, which also included a large boardinghouse, was known as the Cotton Mill Village. (Courtesy of Ellis County Museum.)

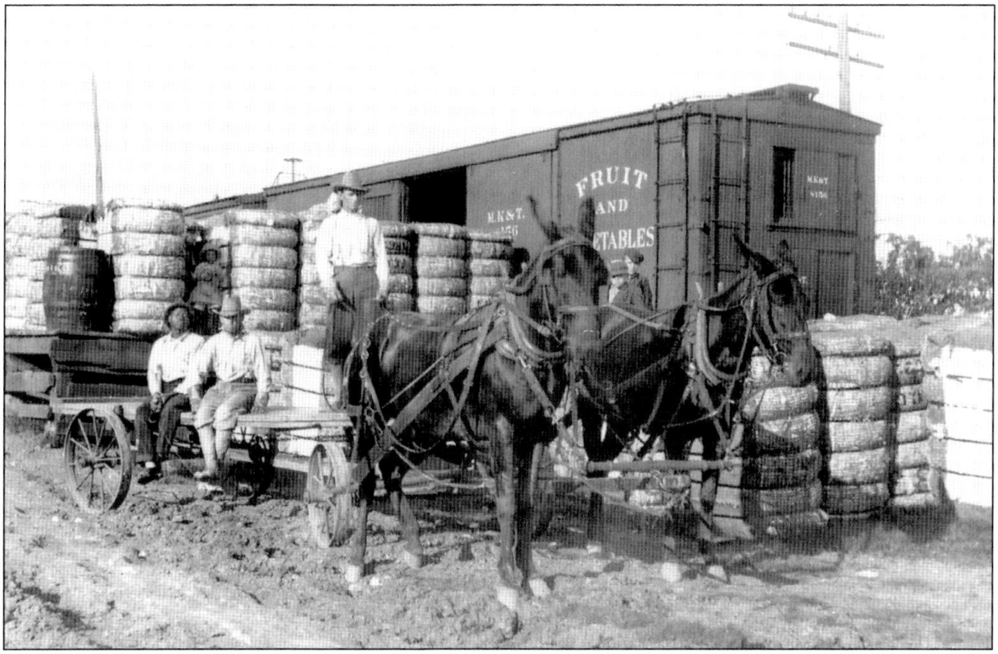

Ferris dealt with numerous gin fires in the early years, including the G. L. Norman Gin fire in November 1891, the Cole and Wickens Gin fire in November 1900, and the Ferris Gin Company Seed House fire in August 1902. Pictured above around 1900, with a Missouri-Kansas-Texas Railroad car in the background, are Sam Duff (sitting on wagon, second from left) and J. H. Duff (standing in wagon), along with several unidentified individuals. (Courtesy of Ellis County Museum.)

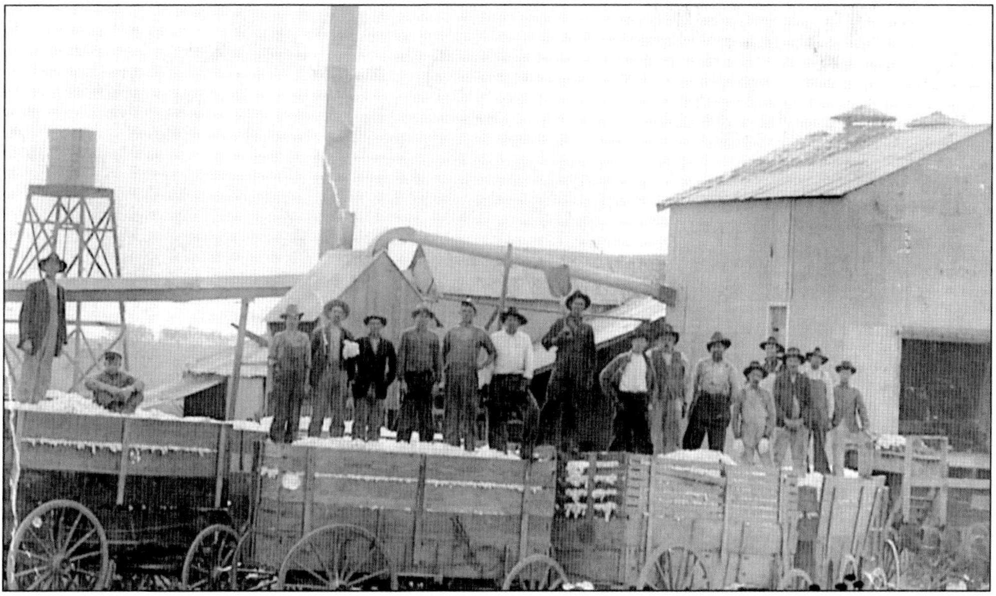

The Alma Gin, at one time owned by T. G. Wright, is pictured in the late 1890s. Several men, including T. G. Wright, are seen on wagons filled with cotton, with the gin in the background. In early September 1905, the gin, owned by Stringer and Linuille, was destroyed by fire. Also destroyed were the seed house and bales of old cotton still stored at the gin. (Courtesy of Ellis County Musuem.)

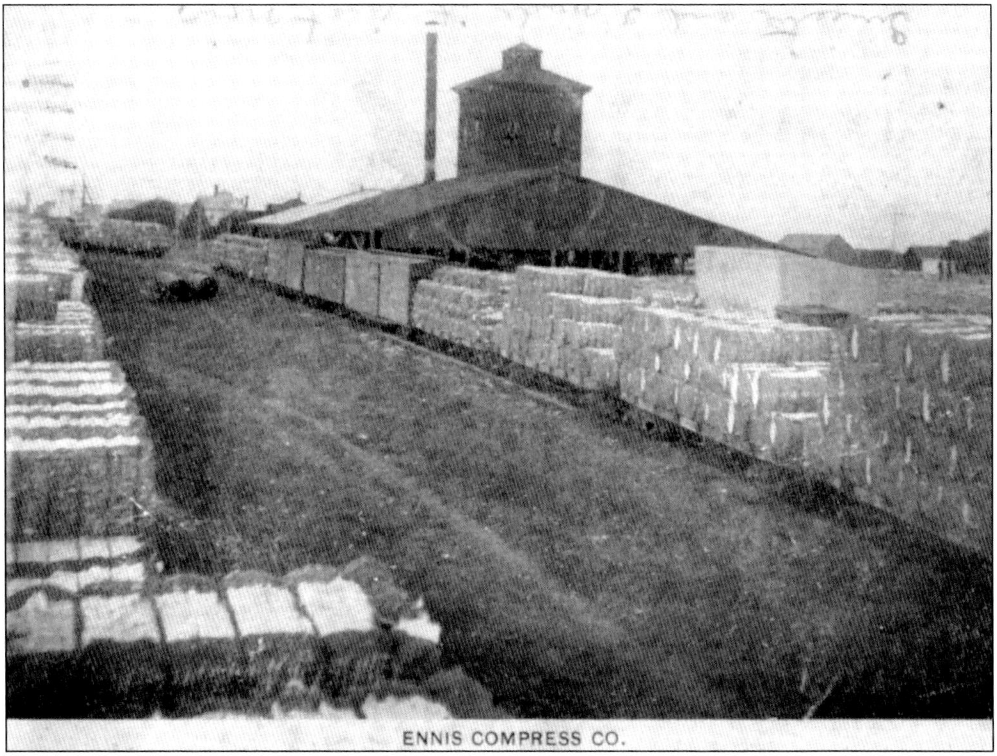

The Ennis Cotton Compress was established in 1885 on the south side of East Lampasas Street and occupied the area south to Burnett Street. It was built and was operated by J. Nalle. It was later purchased in the mid-1890s by another Ennis pioneer, Joseph Baldridge. The cotton compress had two spur tracks coming off the main line. Views of the compress were taken around 1900. On the east side of the compress, the spur track came off the main line in the curve running to the east of the compress along Breckinridge Street. It crossed both Ennis Avenue and Knox Street to the railroad switch near where Ennis Tag was located along Knox Street. (Above, courtesy of Reta Gadberry; below, courtesy of City of Ennis.)

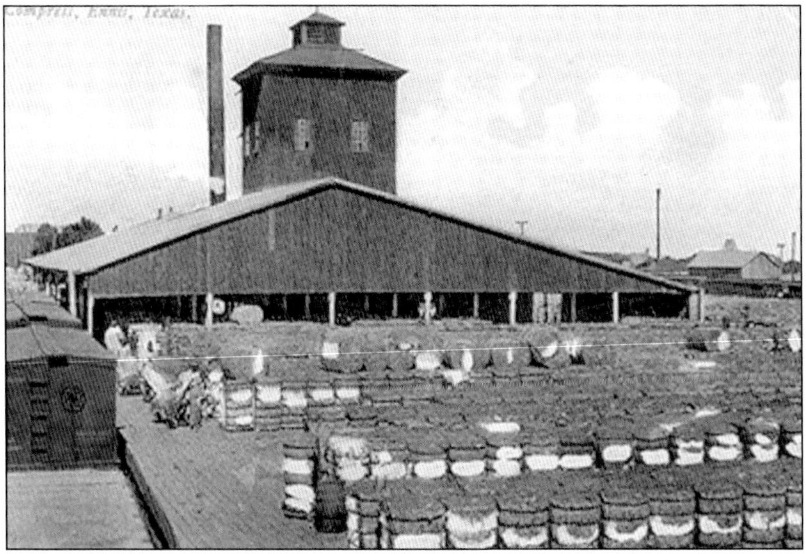

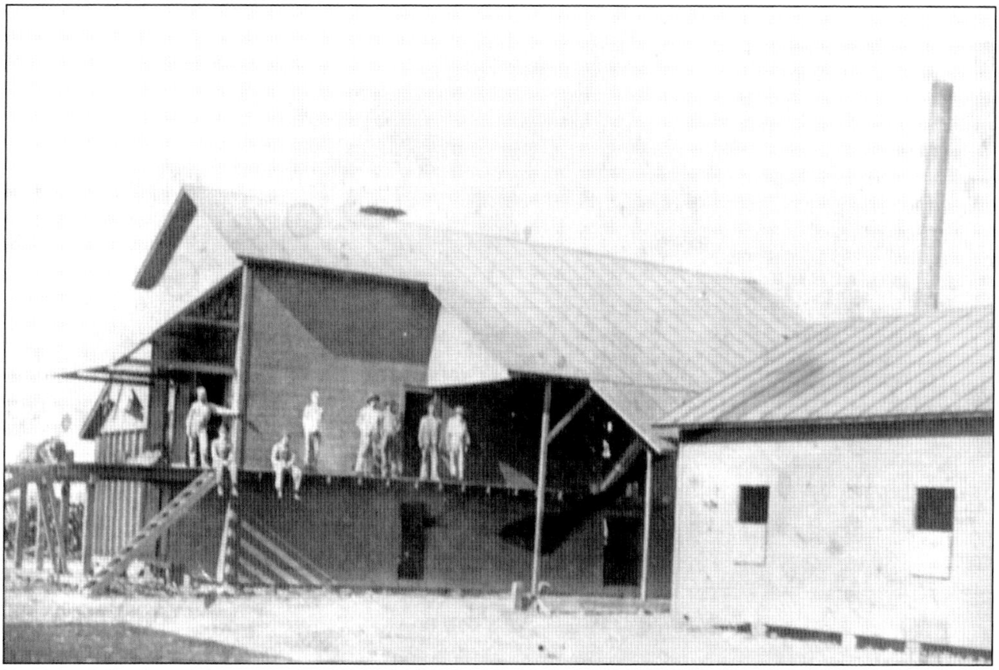

Forreston had two cotton gins, one of which is pictured above around 1900. In November 1891, the Kennedy and Sisk Gin was significantly damaged by fire, including the loss of 10 bales of cotton stored there at the time. In June 1909, farmers of the Forreston area organized to build a Farmers' Gin Company through subscription of stock. (Courtesy of Ellis County Museum.)

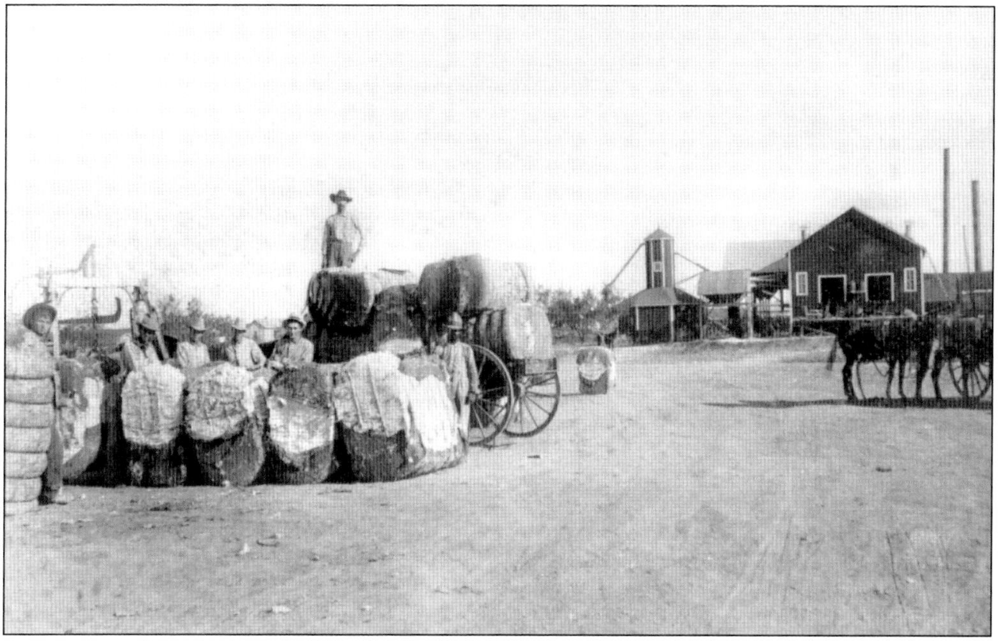

At one time, the community of Bardwell, just to the west of Ennis, had three cotton gins. Pictured around 1910 is the J. W. Bartlett Cotton Gin, which was located south of the railroad tracks. It continued in operation until it was destroyed by fire in 1963. Bardwell also had a cotton seed oil mill, which was built in 1912 and was run by Dr. J. W. Tolleson. (Courtesy of Joe V. Pool.)

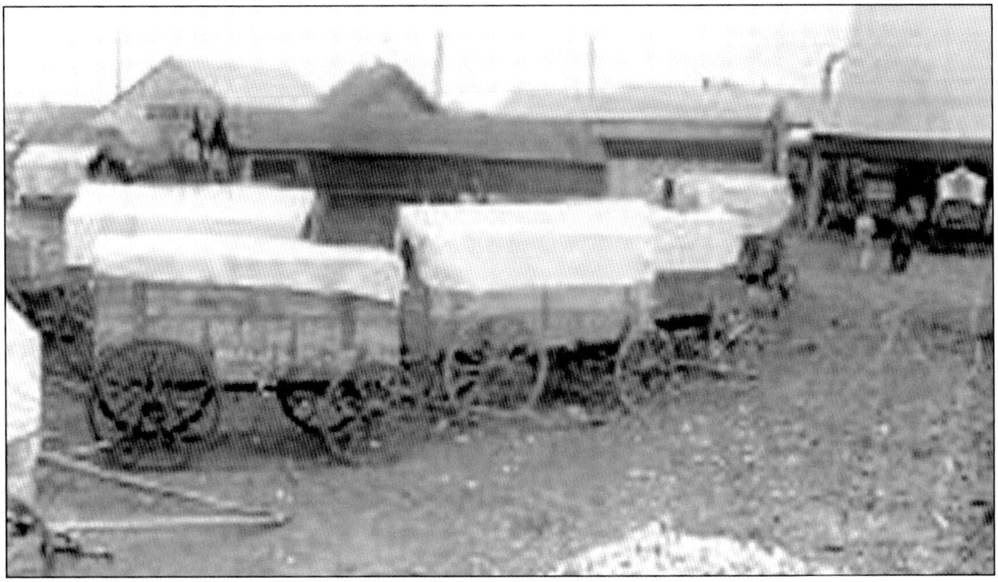

Located right on the edge of Navarro and Ellis Counties, the community of Rice was built around the railroad. By the early 1900s, the city had several gins. They included the Fortson Brothers Gin, which was to the east of the railroad tracks between Camden and Jefferson Streets, the Farmers Union Gin located at Marshall and McKinney Streets, and the H. C. Noel Gin, which was to the east of McKinney Street on Gilmer Street. To the north of the Noel Gin along McKinney was the Rice Cotton Yard and Warehouse. Pictured are two of Rice's cotton gins around 1910. In October 1921, the electric gin, owned by H. C. Noel, suffered major fire damage. A lack of sufficient firefighting equipment at the gin hampered efforts to put out the flames. (Both, courtesy of Jerry Herring.)

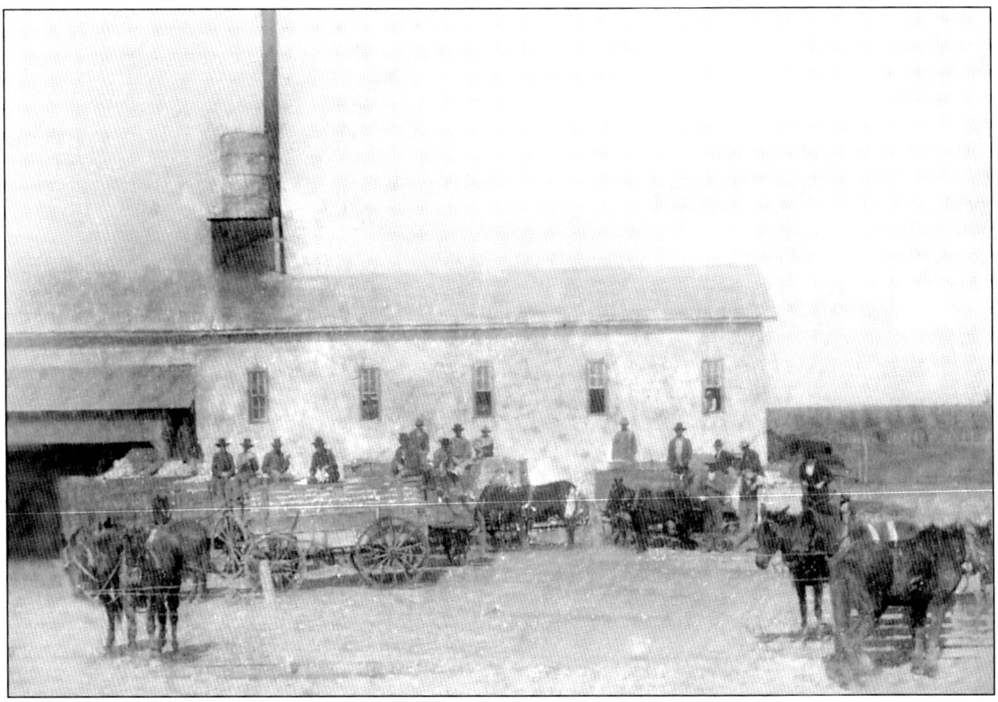

Four

Ennis Named Division Headquarters

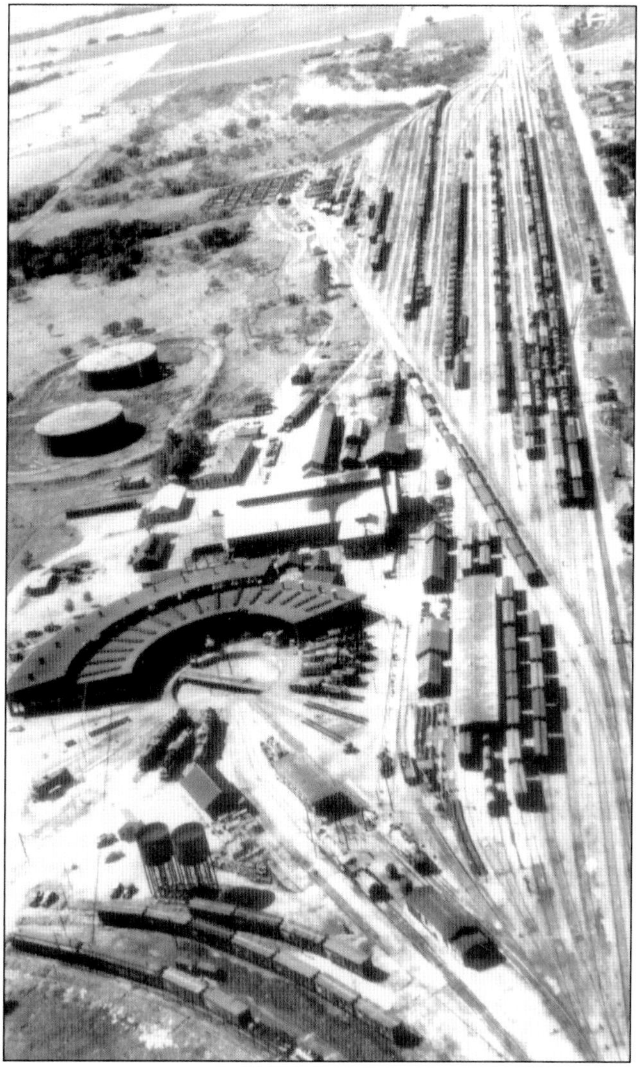

Construction on the Ennis roundhouse and machine shops began in the late 1890s. Houston and Texas Central Railroad officials, including S. Tuzzle, superintendant of locomotive power, travelled to Ennis often to consult with local railroad representatives such as J. J. Doran, chief clerk Jeff N. Miller, and Lawrence Daffan to work out all the details before construction began. In 1898, the contracts on the roundhouse and machine shops were signed and excavation began in December. The roundhouse was to be 90 feet deep and made of pressed brick covered with slate; more than 400,000 bricks were used for the walls. Plans were made that would allow three engines on the blocks at one time and for six fires to be maintained at once. The machine shops were to be equipped with all that would be needed to provide the necessary items to make repairs, with the exception of boilers. The estimated cost of construction at the time was $40,000. The facility is pictured here in a 1949 aerial view. (Courtesy of City of Ennis.)

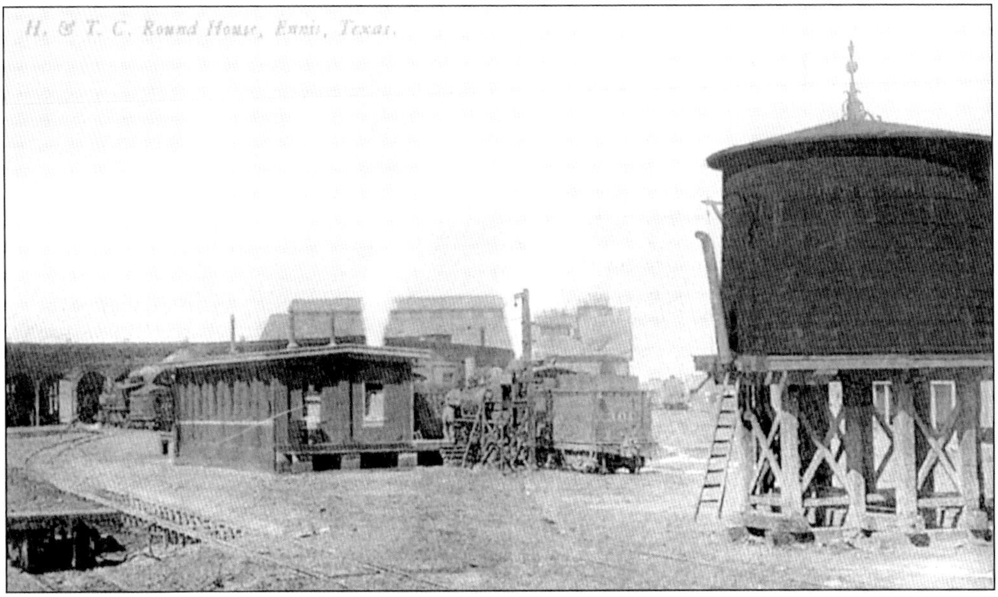

The roundhouse and machine shops are pictured here around 1910. Houston and Texas Central Railroad officials estimated that from the onset 100 to 200 jobs would be created. Many city leaders, including Joe Baldridge, Capt. Mark Latimer, Pete Freeman, Dr. J. C. Loggins, Louis Cerf, and J. Blakey, travelled to Houston to meet with Houston and Texas Central Railroad officials. These gentlemen were instrumental in obtaining the contract for Ennis to become a division point with the railroad. As part of the agreement, the city raised the $25,000 bonus required, donated 90 acres of land, and built the first of three lakes to provide the water needed by the railroad facility. In April 1912, assistant superintendent John F. Sugrue of the H&TC announced plans for a new turntable and six new turntable pits for the Ennis Roundhouse. (Both, courtesy of City of Ennis.)

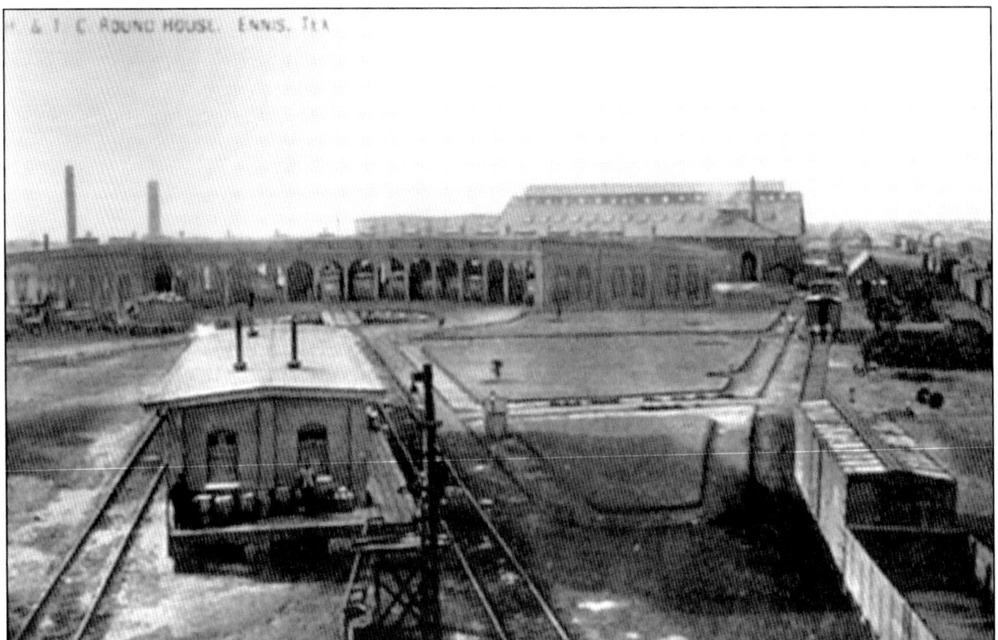

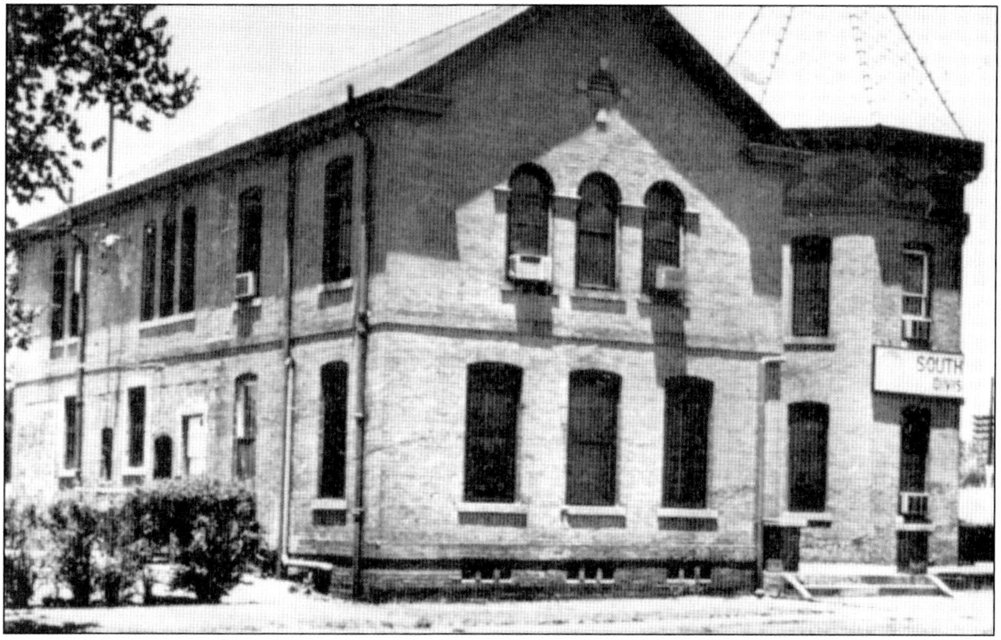

In April 1900, F. B. Shipp of the Young Men's Christian Association of St. Louis met with Ennis businessmen. The meeting resulted in plans to build the YMCA at Southwest Main and Baylor Streets. The railroad agreed to provide the land, cash for construction, and contributions to the operating expenses. Joseph Baldridge was named chairman of the finance committee for the project. Plans for the facility at that time included a library, a game room, a bowling alley, and a lecture hall. In 1932, it became the Houston and Texas Central Railroad Division headquarter offices and later the Southern Pacific Railroad headquarters until it closed in 1965. The building is pictured above along Baylor Street and pictured below from east Baylor Street with the main line in the foreground. (Above, courtesy of George Graves, part of the Ford Curry Collection; below, courtesy of Ralph and Ruby Essary.)

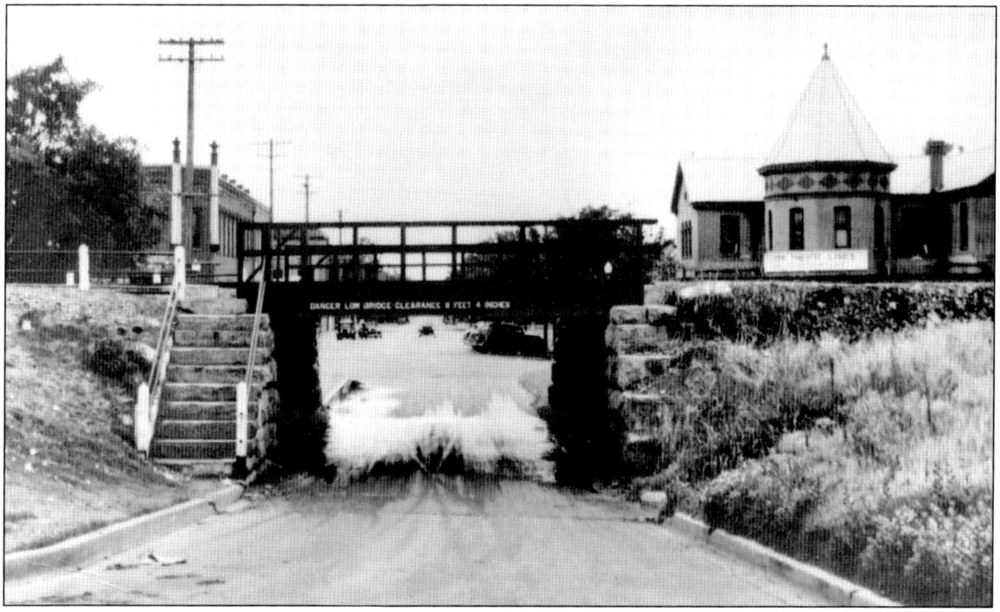

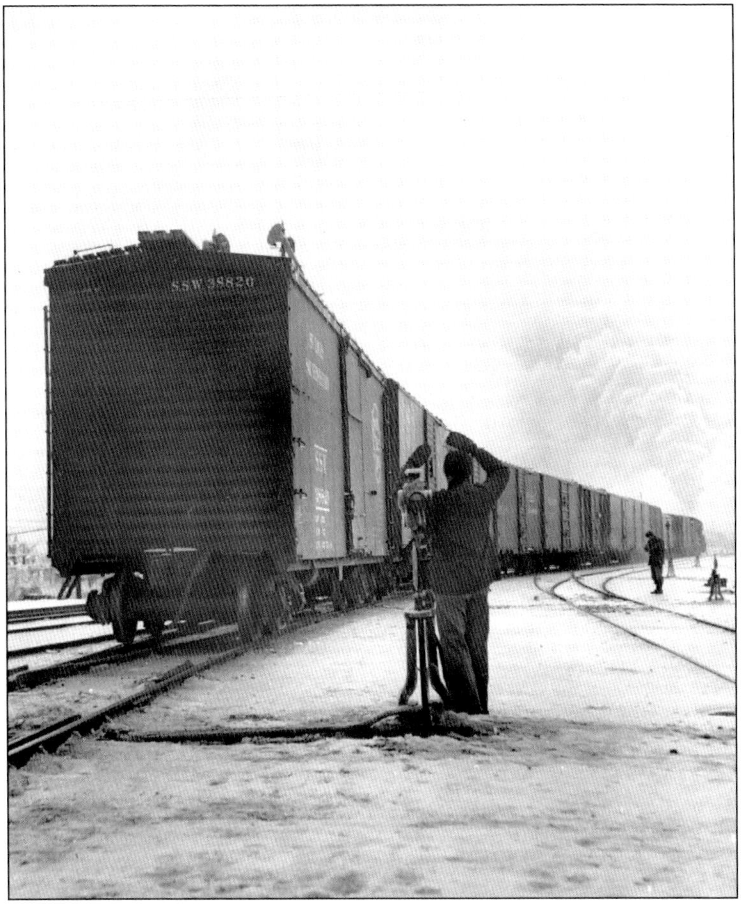

With the switch open to the RIP (Repairs in Progress) tracks, a switchman can be seen signaling stop with his hands up in January 1949. RIP tracks can be seen to the right. (Courtesy of Dane Williams, part of the Ford Curry Collection.)

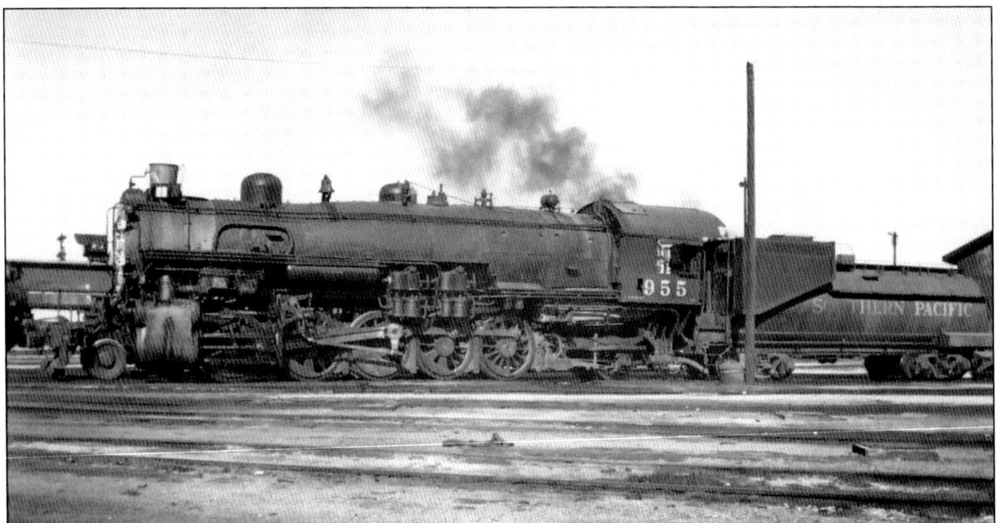

With three RIP tracks (Repairs in Progress) in the foreground, engine No. 955 is on the inbound track of the Ennis roundhouse in the 1940s. The pole to the right appears lowered to re-sand the engine. (Courtesy of Dane Williams, part of the Ford Curry Collection.)

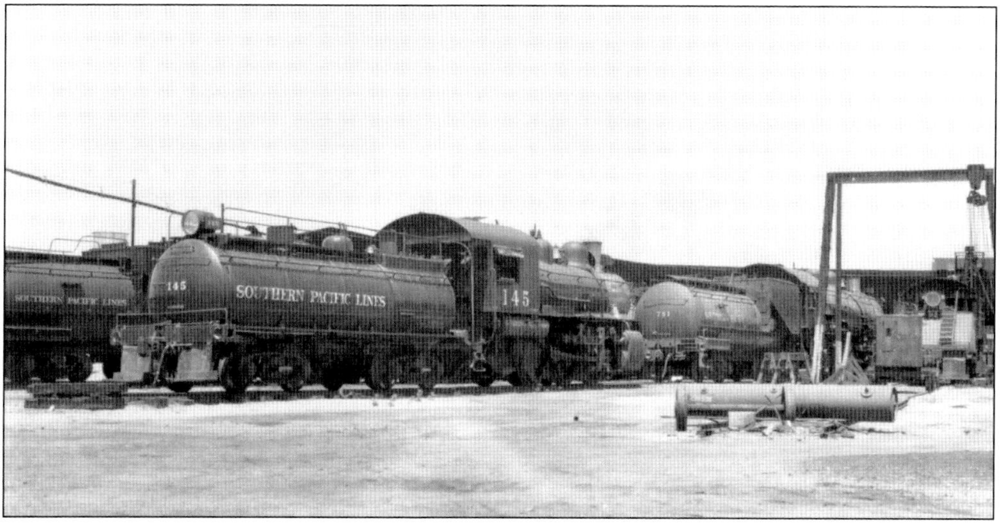

Engine No. 145 is on the inbound track of the Southern Pacific shop yards. To its right is a hoist used for lifting wheels. The Ennis roundhouse can be seen in the background. (Courtesy of Ennis Public Library.)

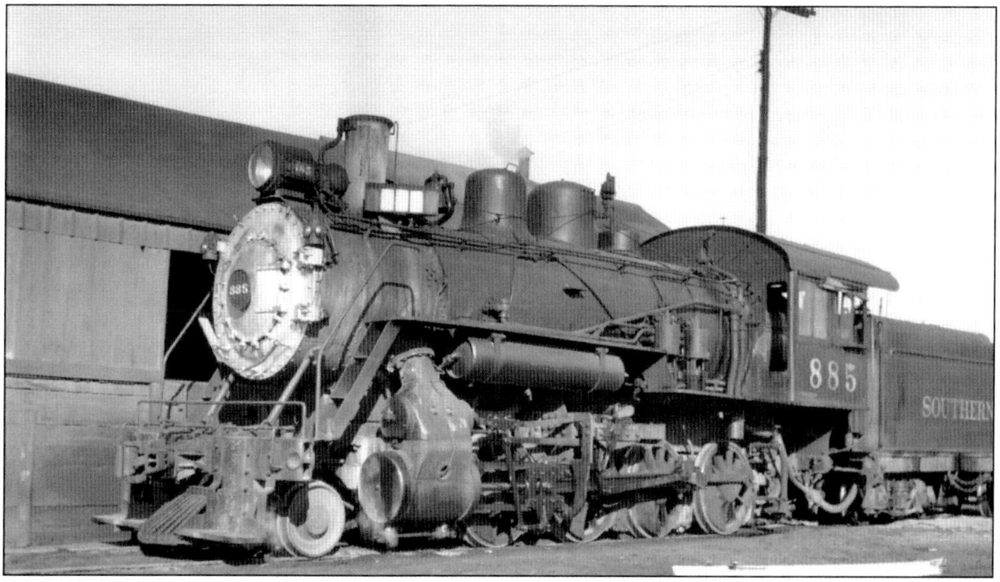

With the Ennis roundhouse in the background, engine No. 885 is pictured on the outbound track. On July 1, 1921, in the early hours of the morning, Houston and Texas Central Railroad fireman E. D. Estes was robbed of $135 and a pistol while going to the Ennis roundhouse. He was not injured but could not provide authorities with a description of the assailant. (Courtesy of Dane Williams, part of the Ford Curry Collection.)

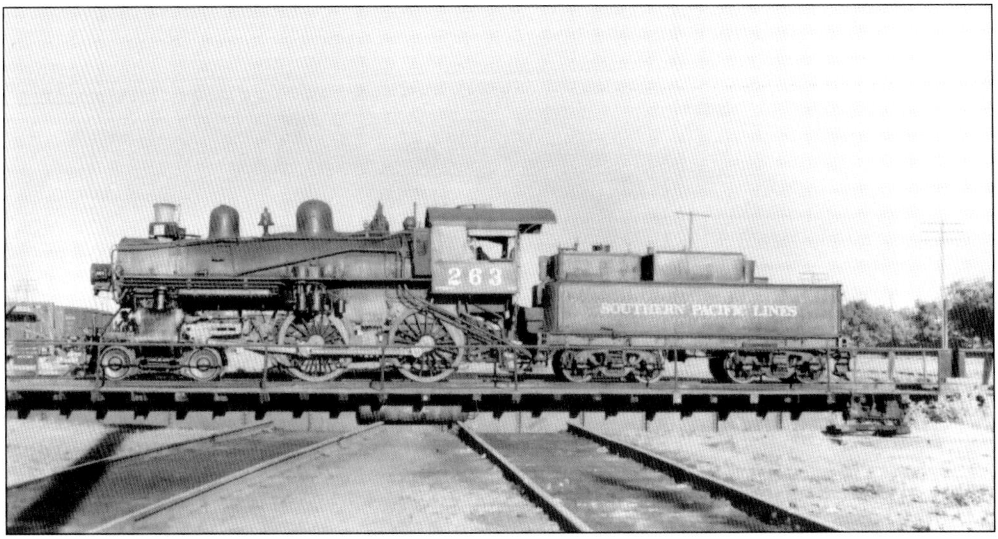

Southern Pacific Railroad engine No. 263 is seen on the Ennis roundhouse turntable in the 1940s. Below the turntable are the roundhouse inbound (right) and outbound tracks. (Courtesy of Ennis Public Library.)

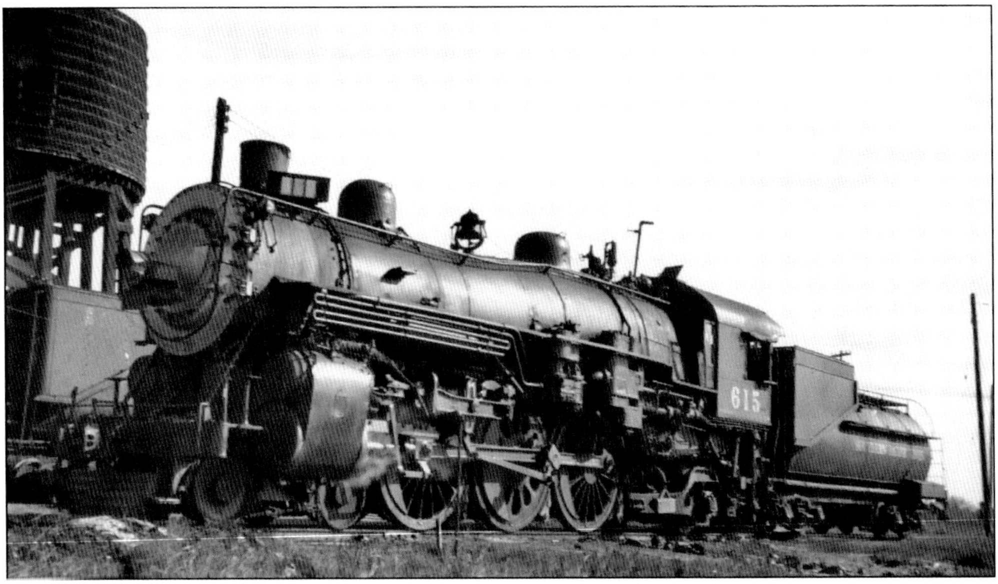

Steam engine No. 615, is pictured above at the Ennis roundhouse in the 1940s. On November 16, 1909, Lytle Wade, an engineer with the Houston and Texas Central Railroad of Ennis, was scalded while taking his engine out of the roundhouse. Reports stated that a steam pipe burst, and the majority of the injuries were to both his feet. (Courtesy of Dane Williams, part of the Ford Curry Collection.)

With snow on the ground and the old Ennis roundhouse sandhouse to the right, dozens of spare wheels can be seen lining the area next to the RIP track pictured at right around 1949. Below, Southern Pacific engine No. 691 sits on the turntable at the Ennis roundhouse in June 1952. In July 1909, Houston and Texas Central Railroad assistant superintendent John F. Sugrue announced from Ennis that the railroad company would be using about 20 tank cars to haul water to the roundhouse and machine shops of Ennis. This was in response to low water levels at the city lake as well as low reserve levels at stations along the line. (Both, courtesy of Dane Williams, part of the Ford Curry Collection.)

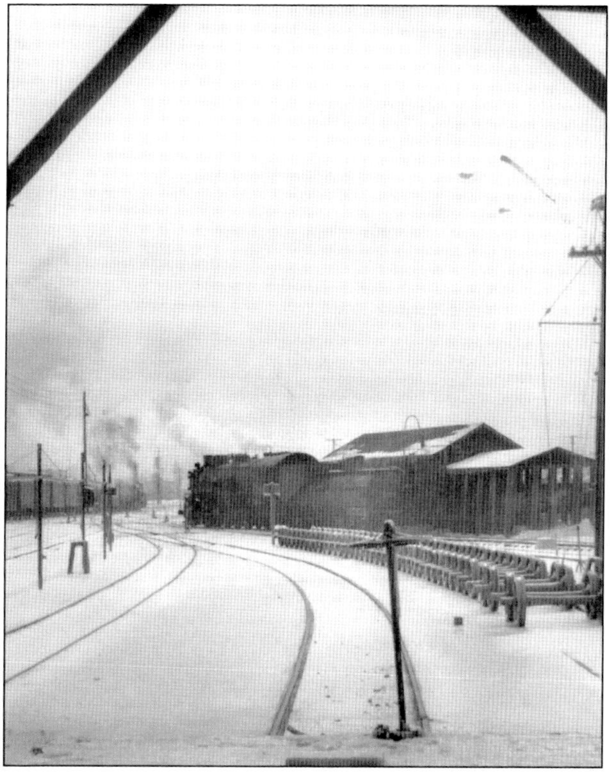

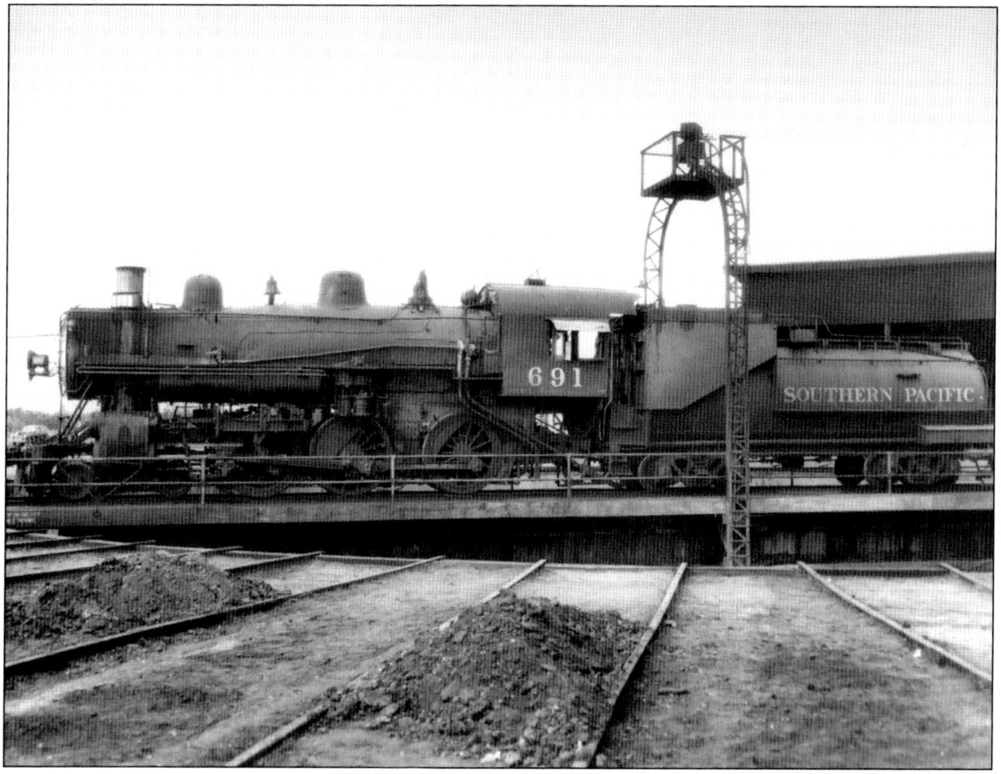

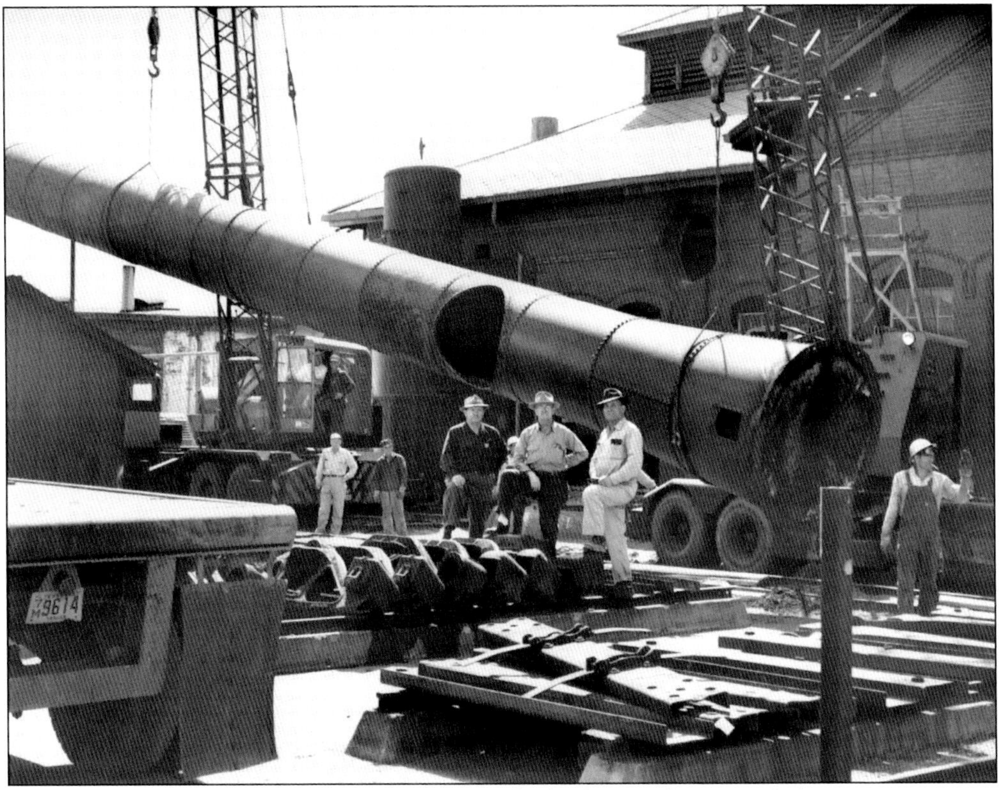

A rear portion of the Ennis roundhouse is in the background, pictured above, as a crane is lifting and maneuvering the base of a floodlight being installed between the roundhouse and the machine shops around 1950. Of the three men standing toward the fore of the photograph, George Hedrick, general foreman at the time, is at the far left. Southern Pacific Railroad Sunbeam No. 650 is pictured below at the Ennis roundhouse. (Above, courtesy of Dane Williams, part of the Ford Curry Collection; below, courtesy of Joe V. Pool.)

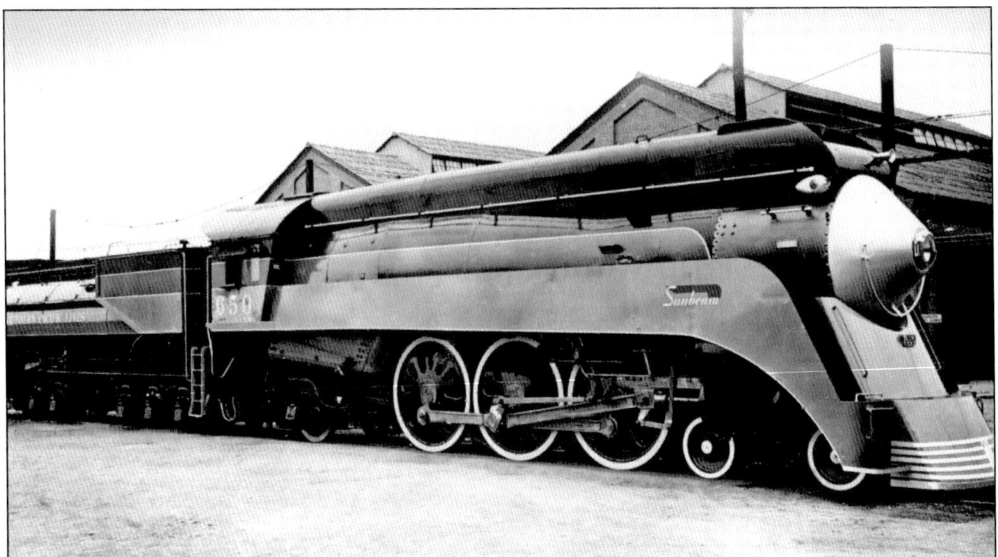

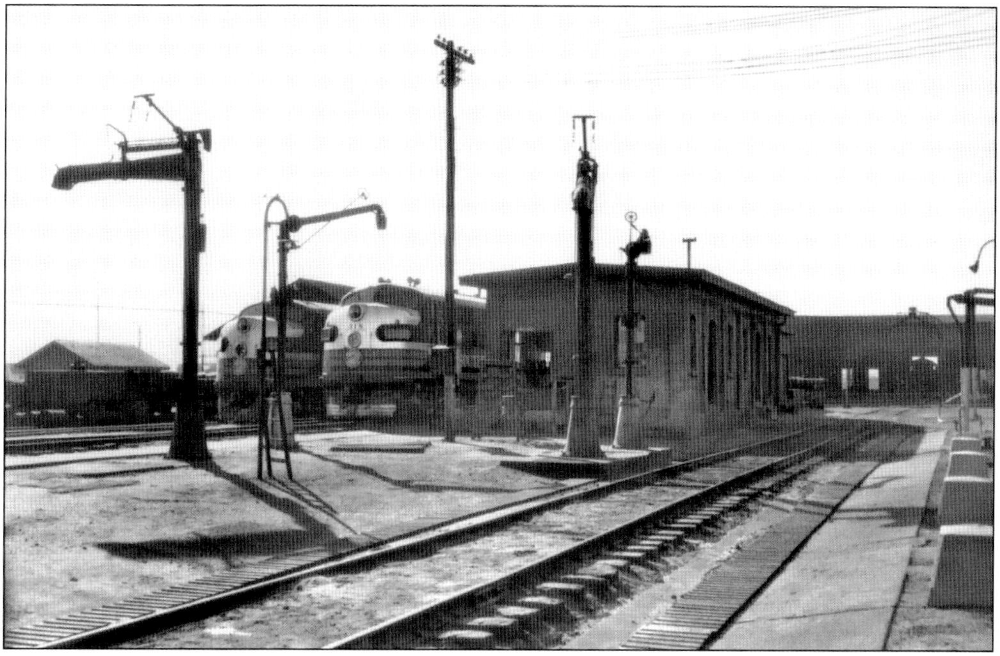

Water and oil were essential to the operation of a steam engine. A water spout is visible to the left of the photograph, while the center of the photograph shows the oil room, where lubricants for the steam engines were stored at the Ennis roundhouse. (Courtesy of Dane Williams, part of the Ford Curry Collection.)

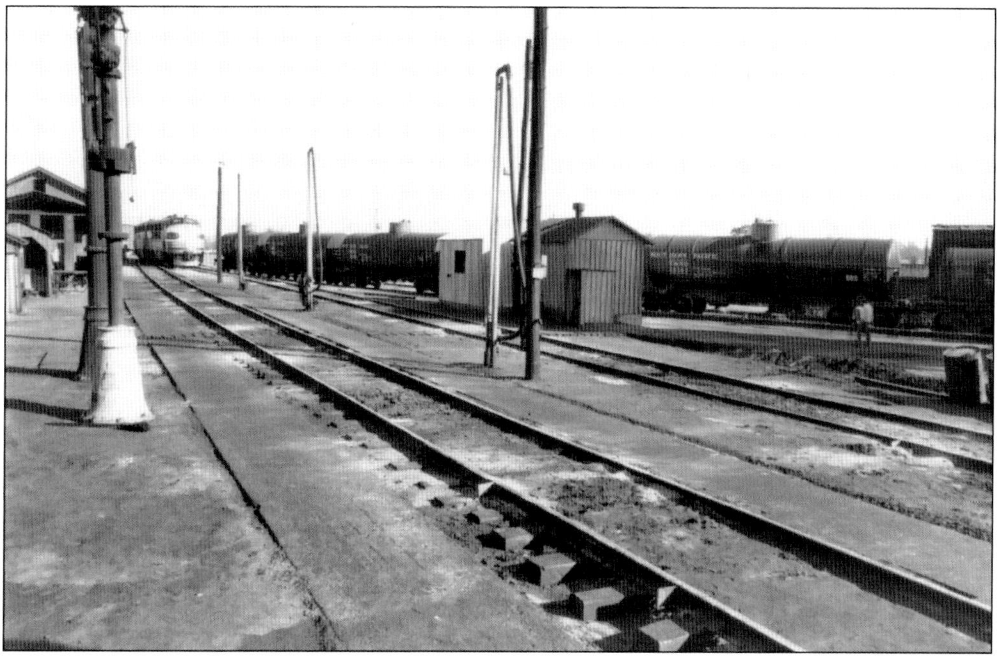

An EMD F-unit diesel engine can be seen in the background of this photograph. The No. 1 switch track at the Ennis roundhouse can be seen with the sandhouse, located to the left in the upper portion of the photograph. The gas station is located to the right of the track toward the center of the photograph. (Courtesy of Dane Williams, part of the Ford Curry collection.)

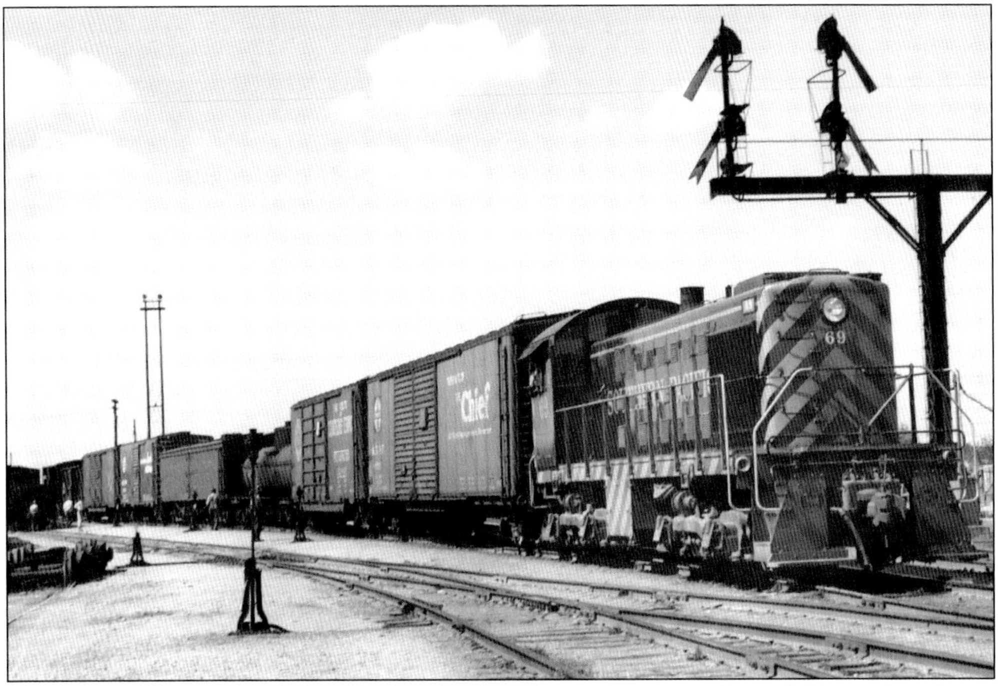

Engine No. 69 was one of the first diesel switch engines that came through Ennis. It is shown sitting on the main track at the roundhouse in September 1950. (Courtesy of Dane Williams, part of the Ford Curry Collection.)

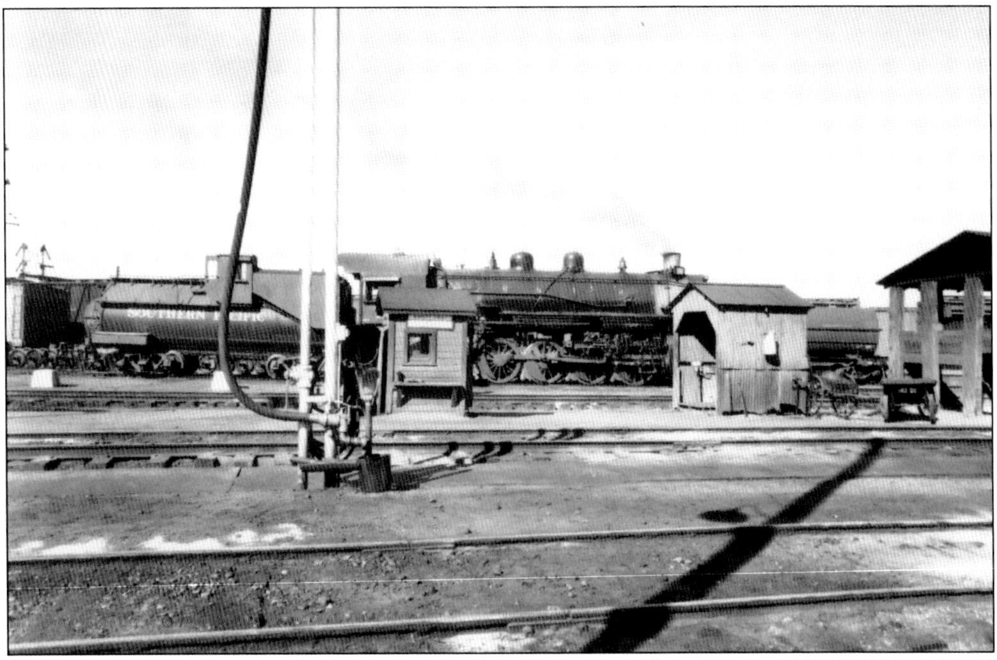

A steam engine can be seen on the fuel track of the Ennis roundhouse around 1940. Also referred to as the cinder-pit track, it allowed for work to be done underneath the train. The inbound track is pictured in the foreground, with the outbound track directly behind it. (Courtesy of the Ennis Public Library.)

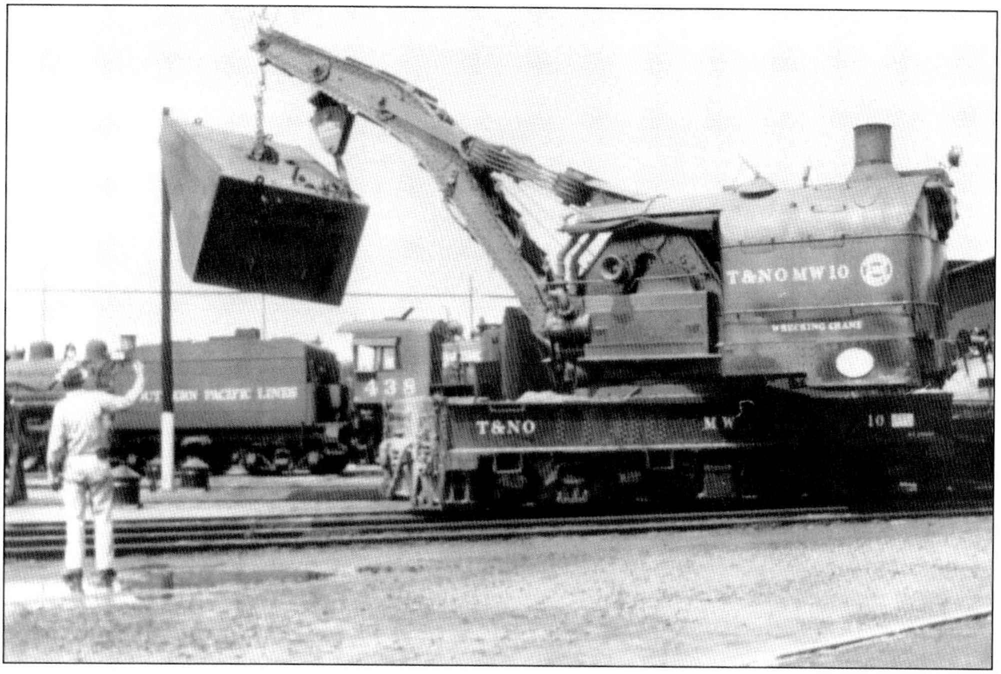

A Texas and New Orleans wrecking crane is pictured in the foreground of engine No. 438 at the Ennis roundhouse around 1950 as the process of picking up the remains of a wreck is undertaken. No. 438 was, at one time, part of the Texas Midland Railroad before the company was bought out by the Southern Pacific Railroad in 1928, then leased to the Texas and New Orleans Railroad. The south side of the roundhouse is pictured below in the 1930s. (Above, courtesy of Dane Williams, part of the Ford Curry Collection; below, courtesy of Eddie Luksa.)

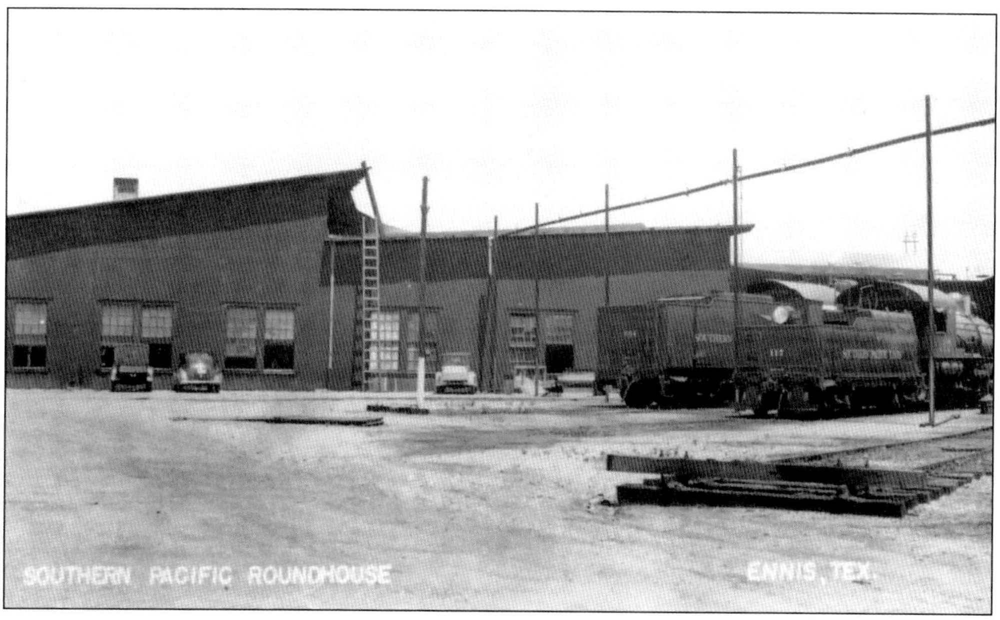

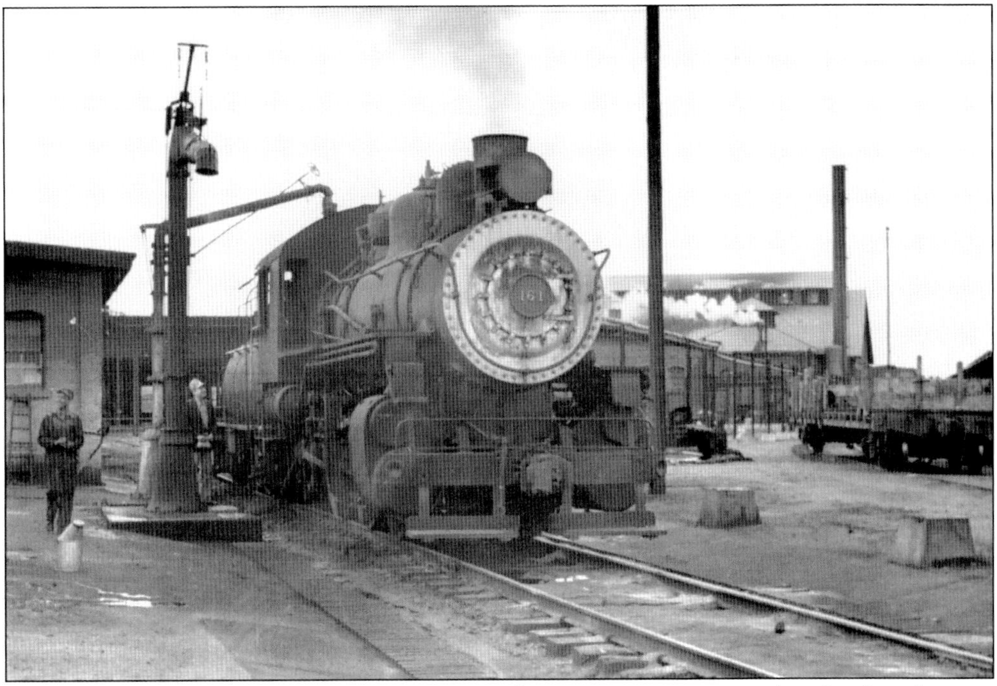

Switch engine No. 161 is seen at the Ennis roundhouse in 1948 positioned under the oil spout. Below the oil spout on the same pole, the water spout for the earlier steam engines can be seen. (Courtesy of Dane Williams, part of the Ford Curry Collection.)

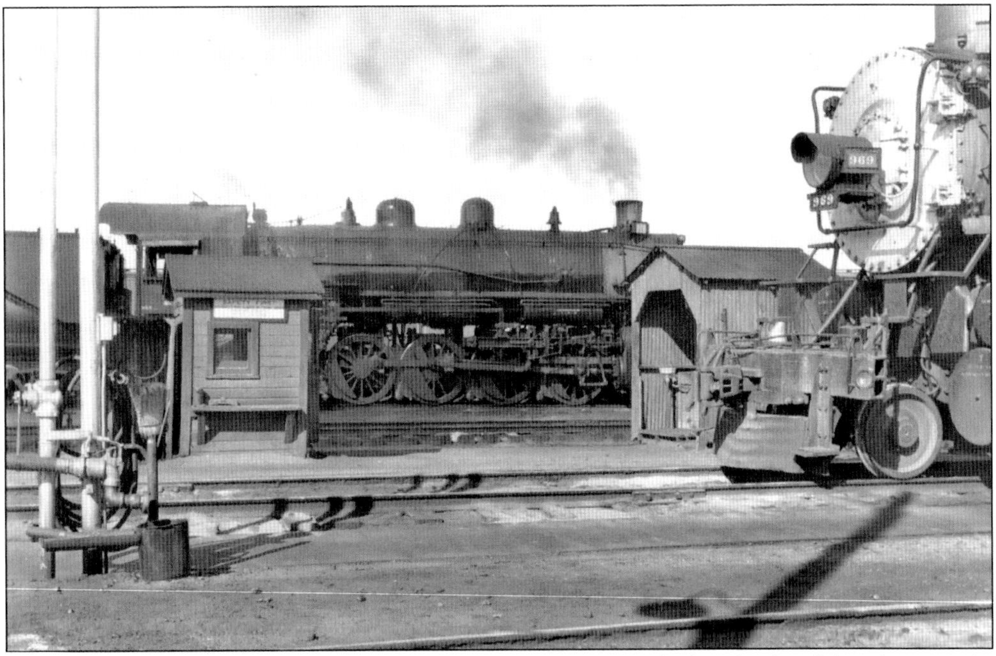

Engine No. 969, with its cowcatcher, can be seen along the right-hand side of the photograph. Another unidentified engine is positioned behind the diesel hookup at the left-hand side of the photograph in April 1952. This was when many engines were converting from steam to diesel. (Courtesy of Dane Williams, part of the Ford Curry Collection.)

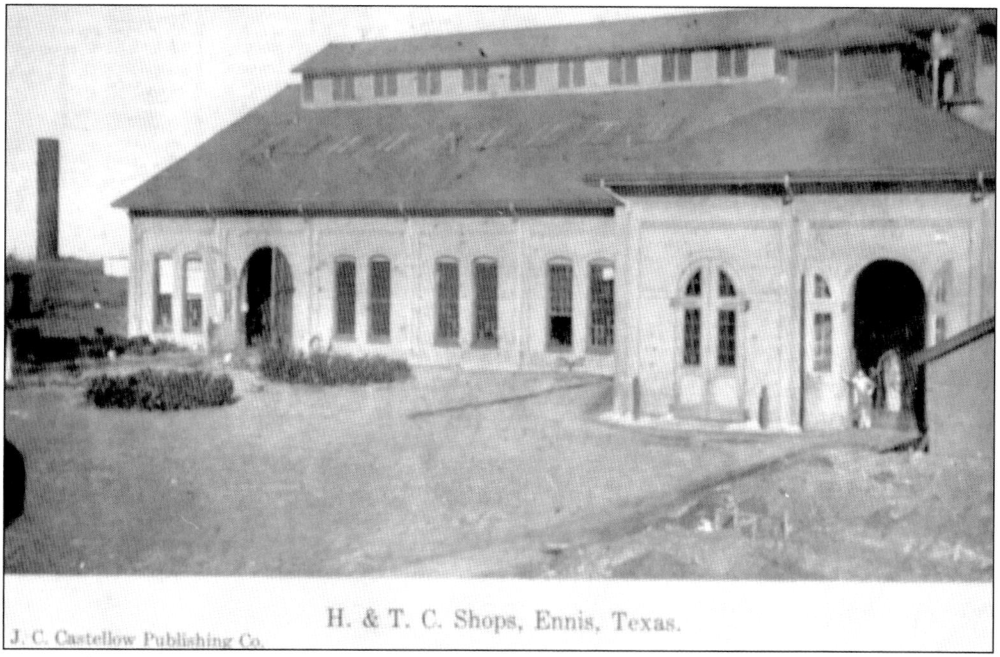

An unidentified individual can be seen standing in the doorway of this 1908 view of the Ennis roundhouse. Craftsmen of every kind brought their skills to the roundhouse. Boiler makers, crane operators, hostlers, locomotive carpenters, machinists, pipe fitters, turntable operators, and track support operators for sanding and fueling are some of those that used their skills to rebuild and repair steam engines. (Courtesy of Joe V. Pool.)

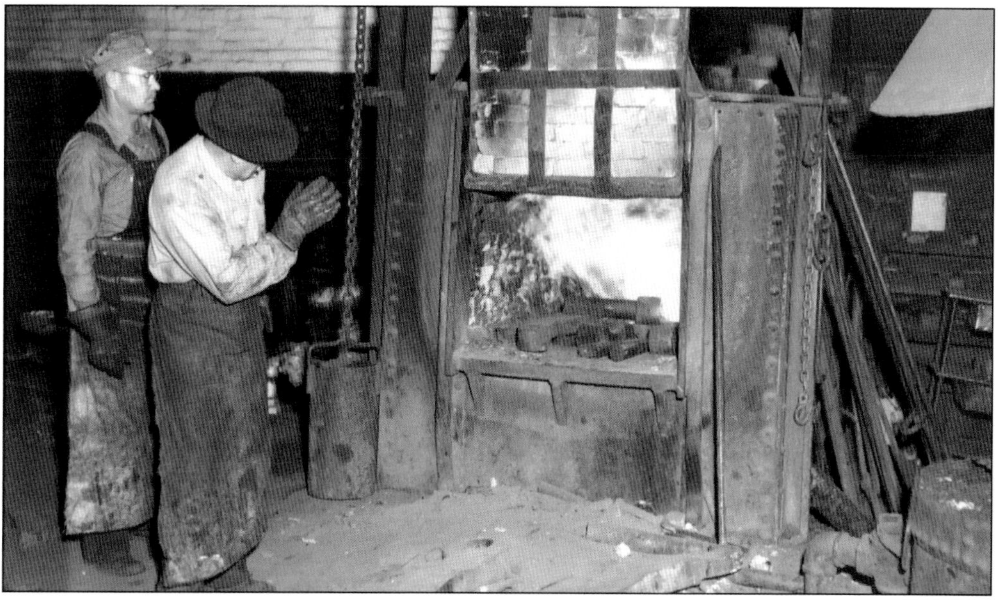

Inside the Ennis roundhouse blacksmith shop Ronald C. Percival (left) and an unidentified worker stand by the old forge, where brake shoes were made and tested for endurance to heat. The 1931 expansion of the roundhouse and machine shops by Southern Pacific Railroad included new machinery and electrical equipment to repair locomotive driving wheels faster. It also included a new water system and electric drop pit. (Courtesy of the Ennis Public Library.)

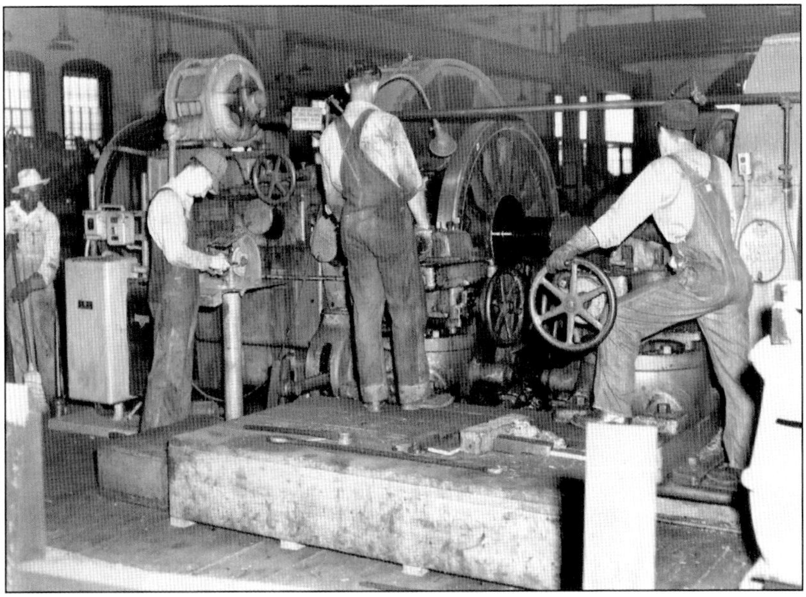

Inside the Ennis roundhouse in May 1951, men are shown working on steam engine wheels. J. L. Smith is pictured below to the right. Some of the earliest employees that worked at the shops in 1910 also included many that began with the railroad in the early 1870s and were among the earliest settlers of Ennis. These men included W. E. Boren (clerk), J. J. Connor (general foreman), Tom Crocker (car carpenter), J. K. Donnall (engine herder), Jim George (car repair foreman), A. A. Gidden (storekeeper's assistant), H. M. Hefner (clerk), W. E. Irwin (car carpenter), Bill Lawson (car carpenter), D. B. McNamara (chief clerk), E. Newman (car inspector), W. H. Nichols (general airbrake inspector), John Spitzmiller (roundhouse foreman), C. W. Tilley (machine shop foreman), M. A. Townsend (machinist), J. W. Tullous (car repairer), and B. Wood (storekeeper.) (Both, courtesy of Dane Williams, part of the Ford Curry Collection.)

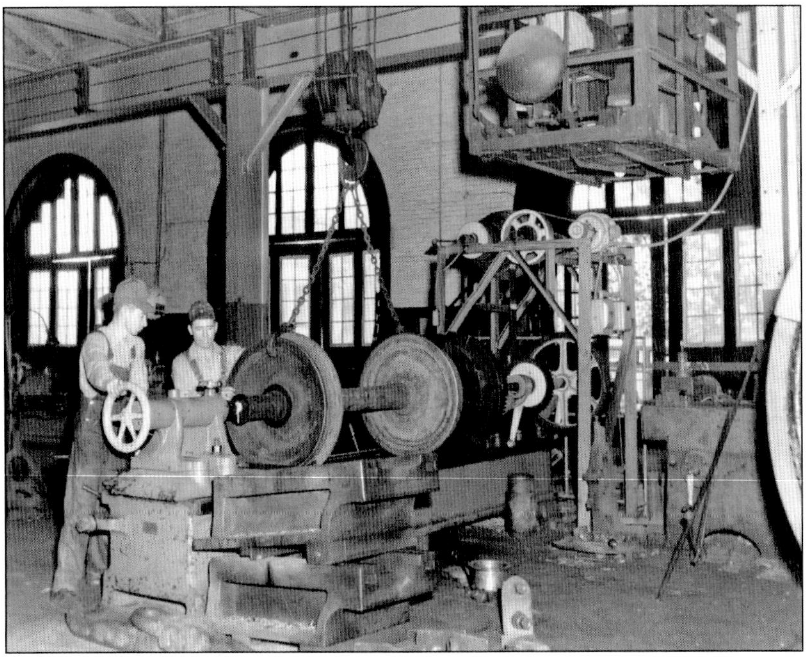

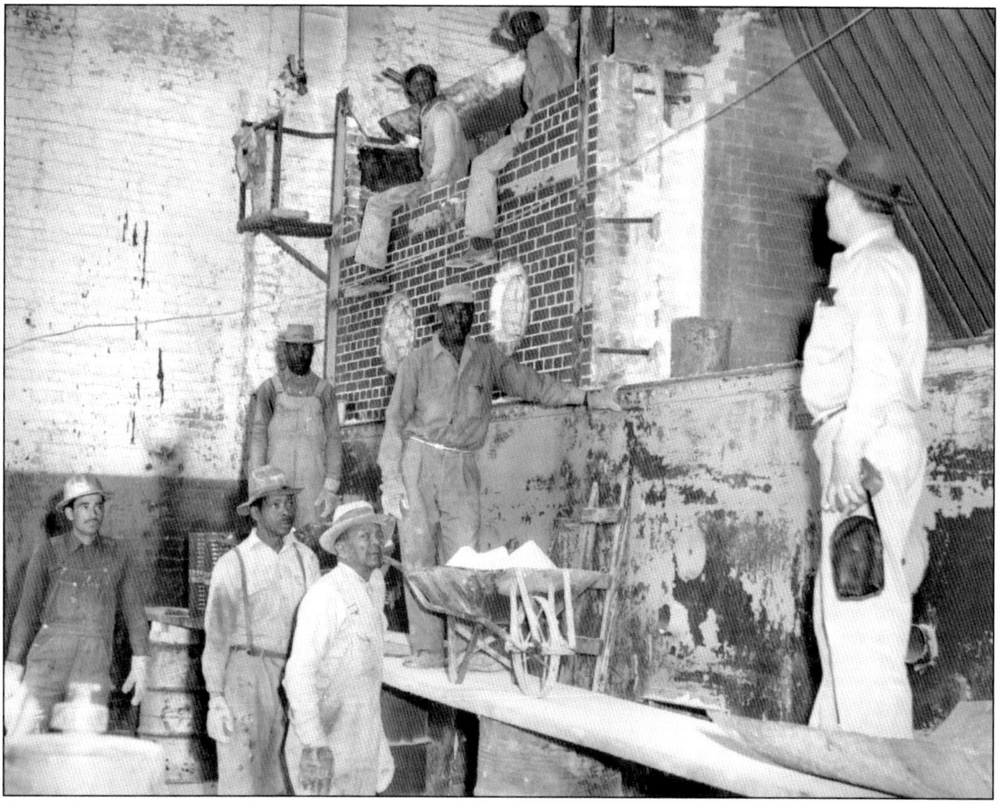

With the transition to diesel engines, the roundhouse had to be expanded to accommodate the larger engines, as pictured above in the late 1940s. Decades earlier, in 1931, Southern Pacific Railroad expanded the Ennis roundhouse to 15 stalls, 10 of which could accommodate the new "900" engines. The railroad also installed a new $40,000, one-hundred-foot turntable to accommodate the larger locomotives being placed into service at that time. (Courtesy of Ennis Public Library.)

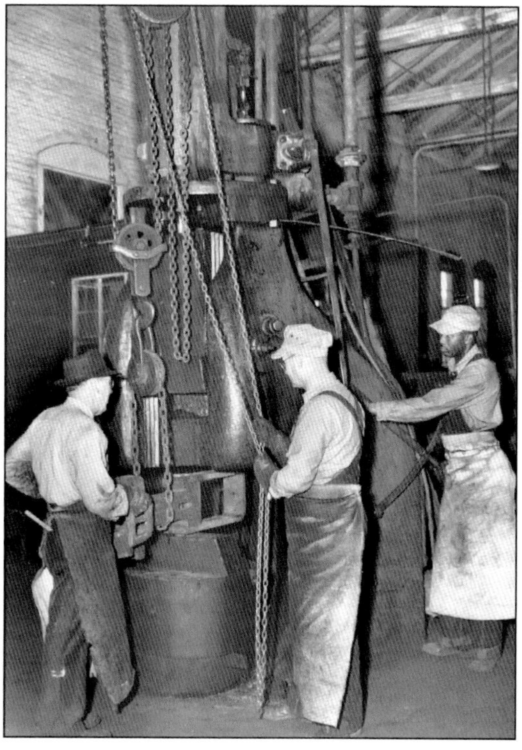

At the Southern Pacific Railroad Machine Shops just north of Ennis, Ronald C. Percival, hammersmith for the railroad, operated a 3,500-pound steam hammer. Despite the enormous power of the steam hammer, it was so controlled that it could crack a pecan without crushing the meat within the shell. Pictured at right around 1950 is R. C. Percival (center) with two other railroad employees. (Courtesy of Ennis Public Library.)

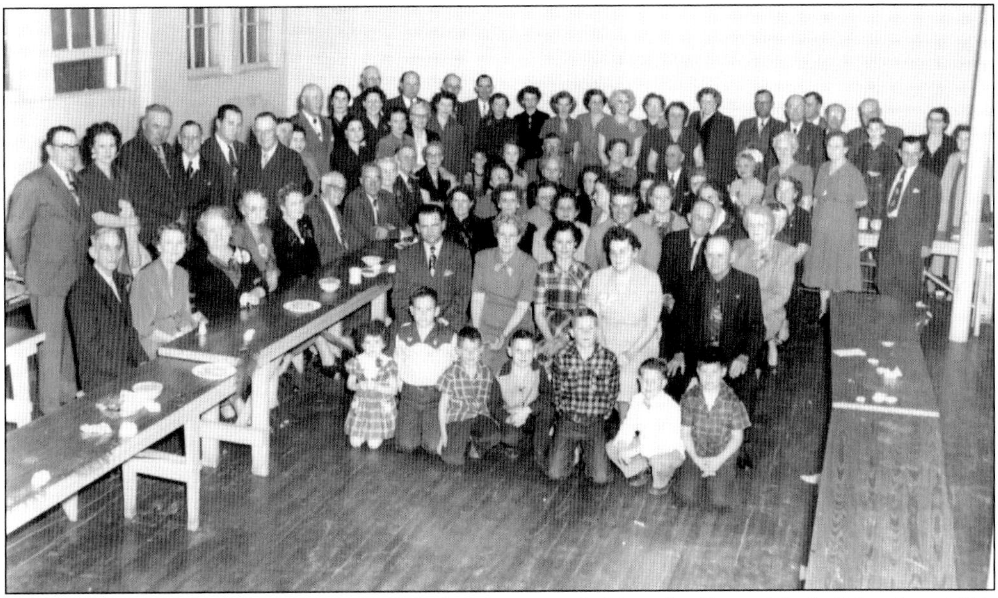

The Southern Pacific Railroad engineers banquet was held at the Ennis High School in 1951. Among those pictured above are Lee Templin and Mickey Harrison, wife of engineer J. T. Harrison. Pictured below is the retirement of Joe Schramek. From left to right are (kneeling, first row) two unidentified and Joe Jamrog; (kneeling, second row) Claudie Terrell, Henry Campbell, August Bus, T. F. Lindle, unidentified, and Joe Schramek; (sitting) Loyd Smith, Lester Sledge, and Hearne Watts; (kneeling, third row, behind Henry Campbell) Dean Wilson; (standing, first row) ? Ward, Tom Collier, unidentified, Johnny Kouba, John Jurica, Gus Hernandez, two unidentified, Mike Sweeney, George Bolen, George Hedrick, ? Percival, F. E. Hoefer, W. H. Vick, and Tom Workman; (standing, second row) Byrne Cooke, four unidentified, Billy Jack Hart, ? Ferris, unidentified, and John Thompson. (Both, courtesy of Ennis Public Library.)

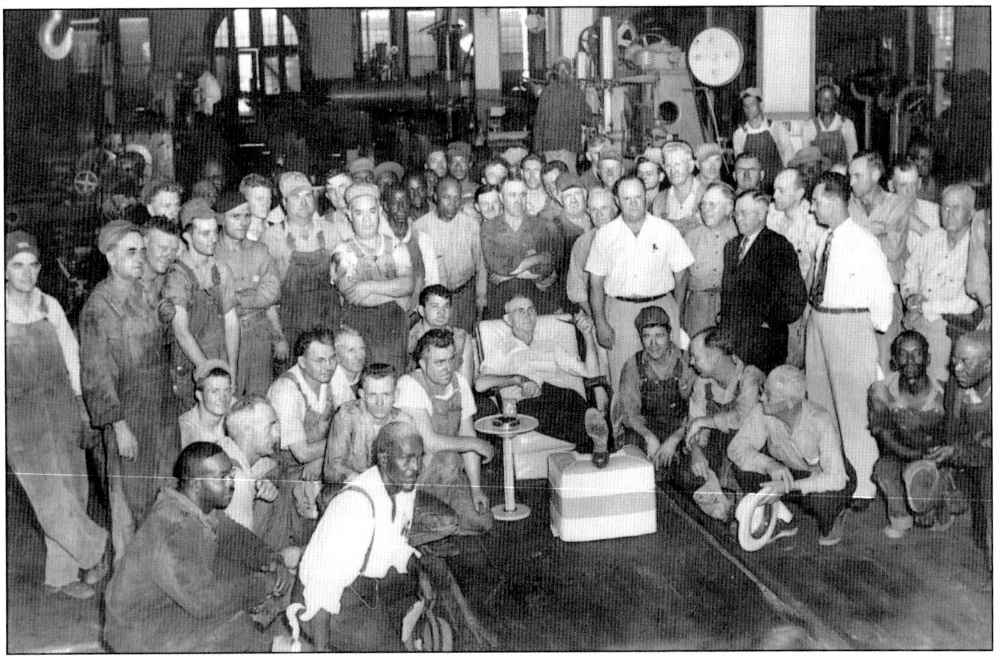

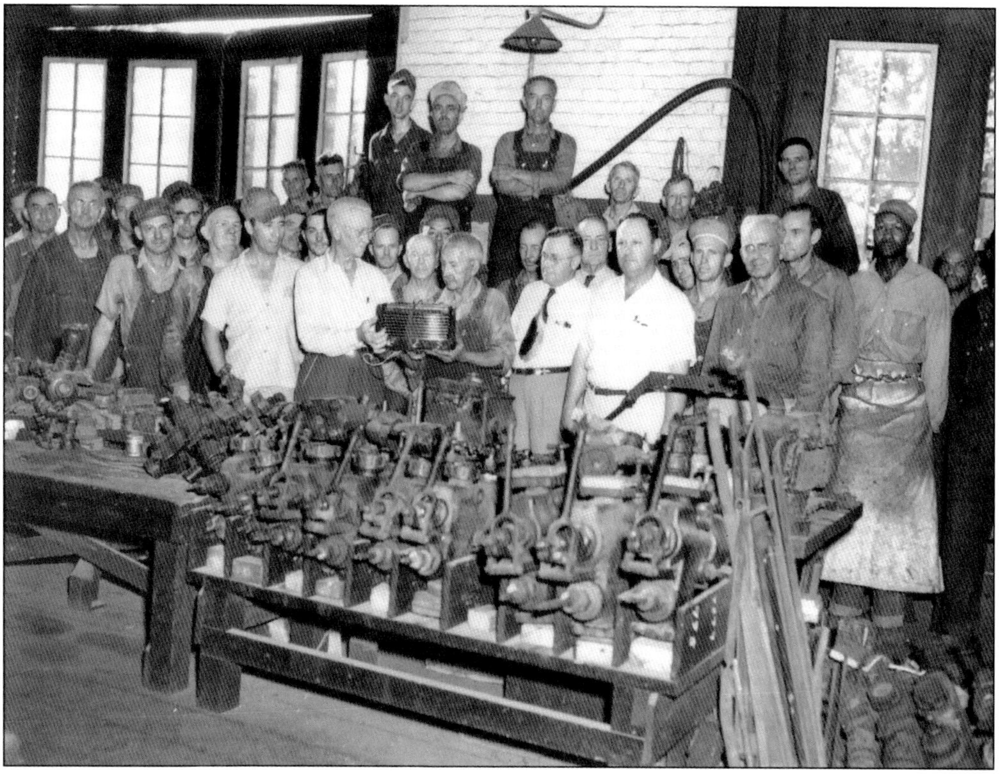

Employees at the Ennis roundhouse and machine shops gather for the retirement of Joe Malevear in 1948. Injectors for steam engines can be seen on the table. Pictured above from left to right are (first row) Tom Collier, Joe Schramek, August Bus, Mike Sweeney, Loyd Smith, Hearne Watts, Bill Davey, Joe Malevear, F. E. Hoefer, Doug Hedrick, and Tom Workman; (second row) Victor Mach, Eddie Luksa, two unidentified, Raymond Kudelek, Gus Hernandez, Lester Sledge, J. E. Frels, Barney Tolar, Bud Harris, ? Thompson, and unidentified; (third row) Bill Petterman, ? Mikula, unidentified, H. Clark, Henry Campbell, T. F. Lindle, Everett C. Turner, and Johnny Kouba. Pictured below is a Southern Pacific Railroad employee awards ceremony held at the City Auditorium in 1949. (Both, courtesy of Ennis Public Library.)

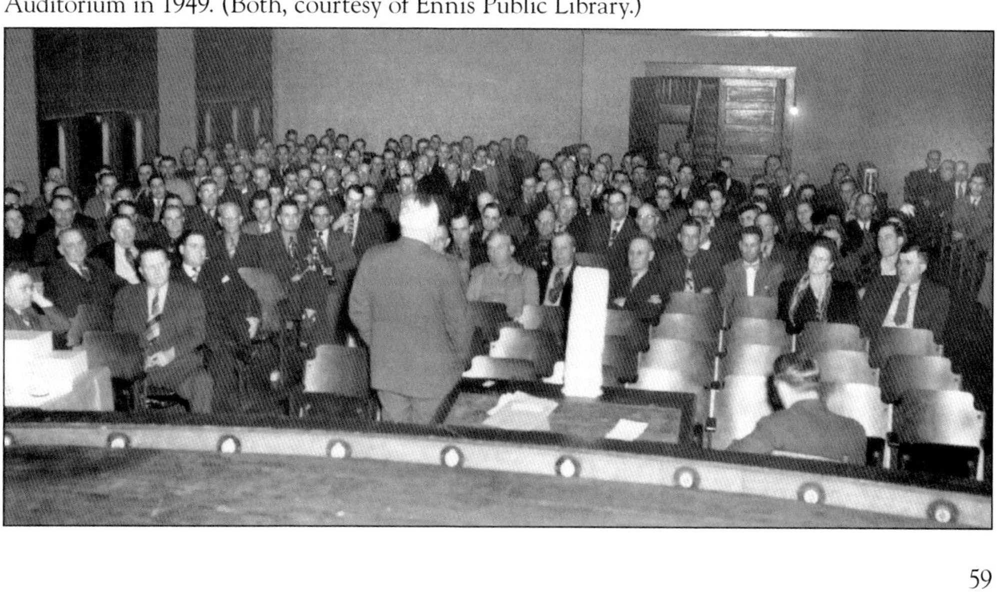

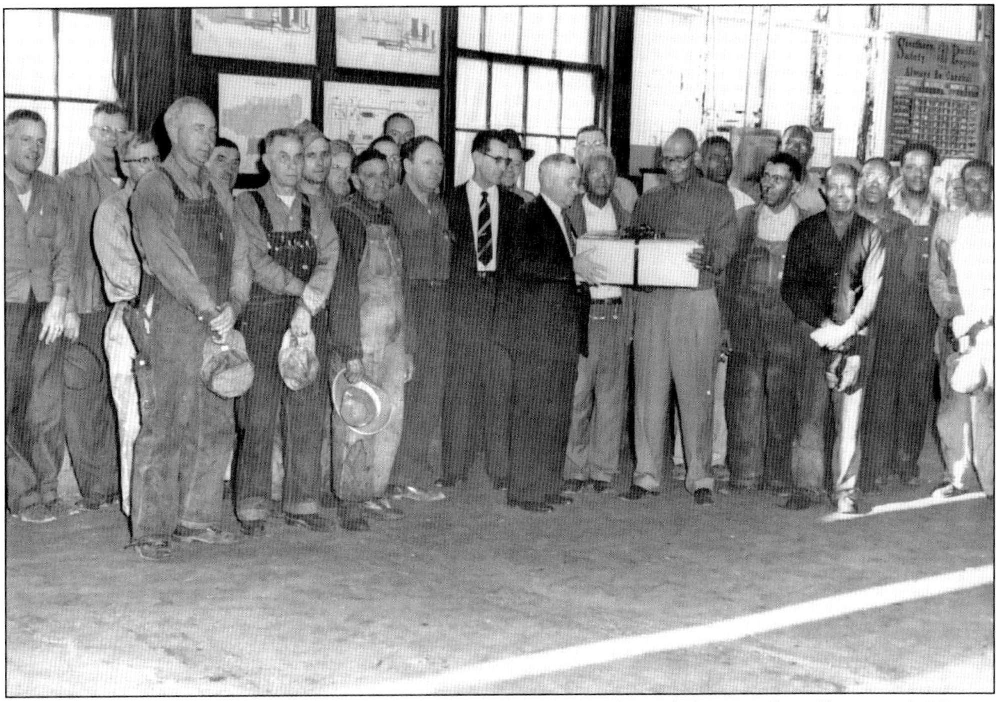

Among those pictured above at a retirement event are, from left to right, (first row) Henry Campbell, Bill Petterman, unidentified, George Hedrick, W. H. Vick, and F. E. Hoefer; (second row) Byrne Cooke, unidentified, Jim Pavelka, Johnnie Kouba, two unidentified, John Thompson, and Joe Massengill. Pictured below are many of those that attended a Southern Pacific luncheon on October 18, 1954. From left to right are (first row) Owen Satterfield, Byrne Cook, unidentified, Ray Telfair Sr., ? Hickman, J. V. Pool, and unidentified; (second row) Floyd Casebolt, unidentified, L. G. Wood, Albert Toth, J. Harrison, two unidentified, Roy Brown, and Joe Mitchell. (Above, courtesy of Ennis Public Library; below, courtesy of Eddie Luksa.)

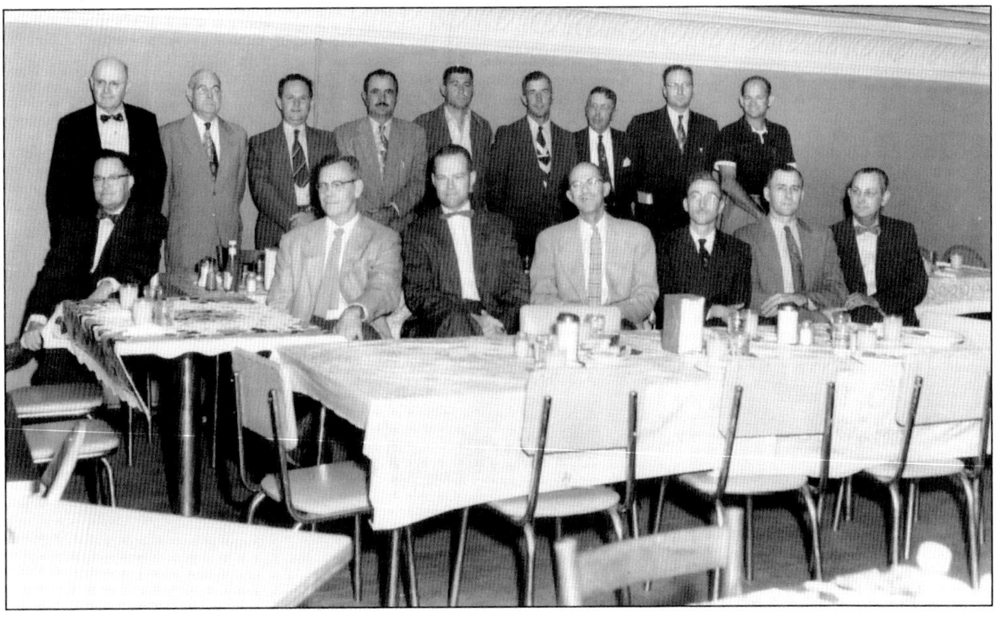

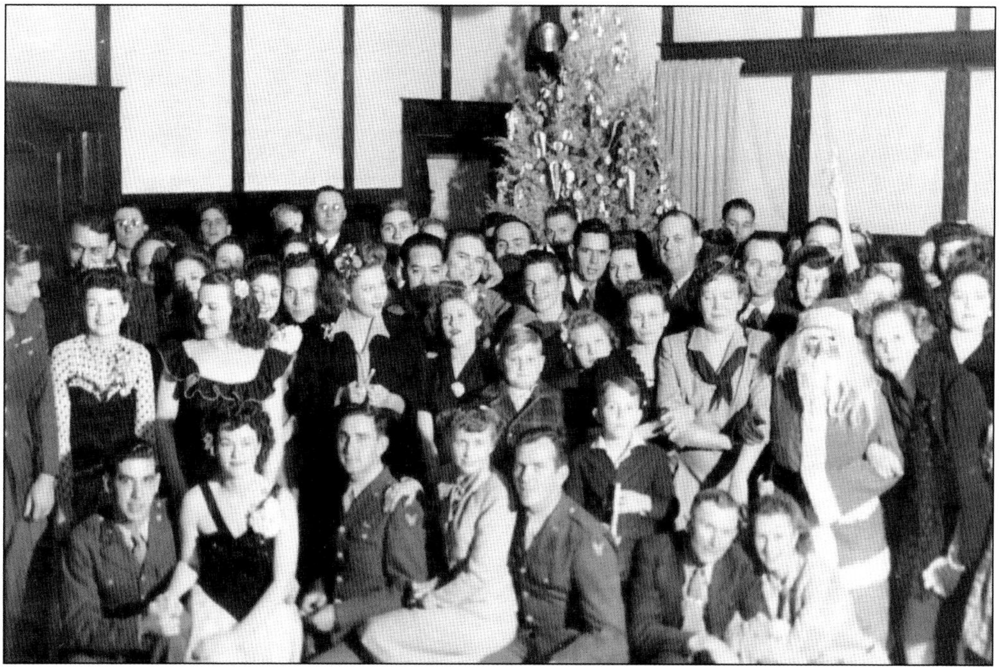

This Christmas party in the 1940s was given by the Southern Pacific Service Club. It was held at an unknown country club in Dallas. Among the many division headquarters railroad employees and their wives pictured are Dorothy Comiskey (second row, second from left) and Martha Ann Boothe (second row, third from left). (Courtesy of City of Ennis.)

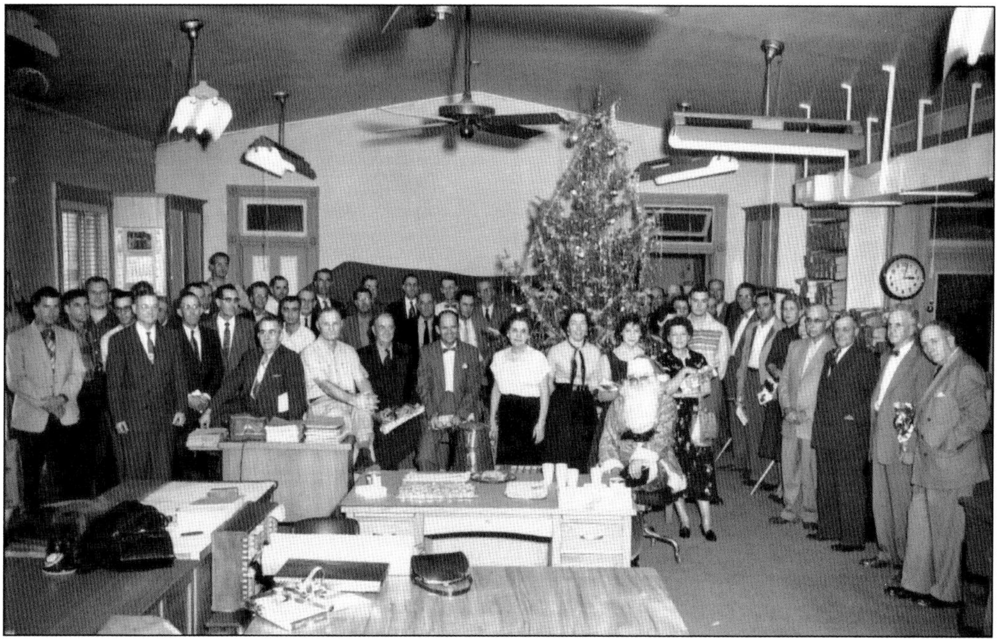

Gathered around a Christmas tree and Santa Claus, Southern Pacific Railroad employees enjoy their Christmas party in 1955 at division headquarters in Ennis. Among those along the first row are ? Kulhanek, H. H. Lummus, Joe Mitchell, and Carolyn Latimer. (Courtesy of Ennis Public Library.)

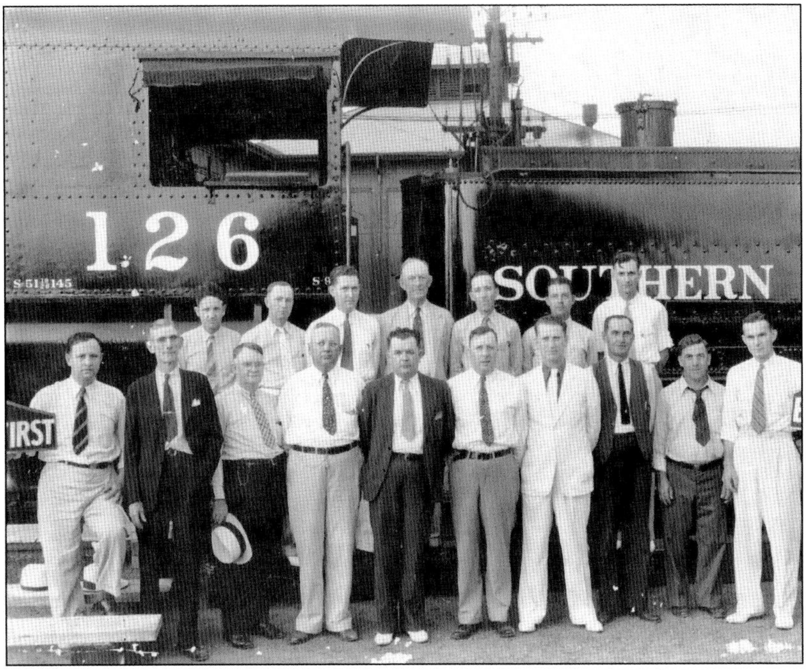

Southern Pacific Railroad employees gather in front of engine No. 126 at the Ennis roundhouse in the 1930s. Pictured from left to right are (first row) George Hedrick, ? Donahue, Alfred T. Rawlins, T. M. Spence, Gordon Lyons, William Percival, John B. Ensor, Martin Rogala, T. Leatham, and A. McKeever; (second row) J. V. Taylor, Walter Owens, Earl W. Woods, John Simpson, Alvin E. Mahan, Lou Baldridge, and Henry Cloud. Almost 40 years earlier, also on the roundhouse grounds, hundreds gathered at the opening of the Houston and Texas Central Shops in Ennis in 1892, pictured below. On the occasion of the 75th anniversary of the rail's arrival to Ennis in 1947, the *Ennis Daily News* commemorated the event with a special section that included this 1892 image. (Above, courtesy of Joe V. Pool; below, courtesy of *Ennis Daily News*.)

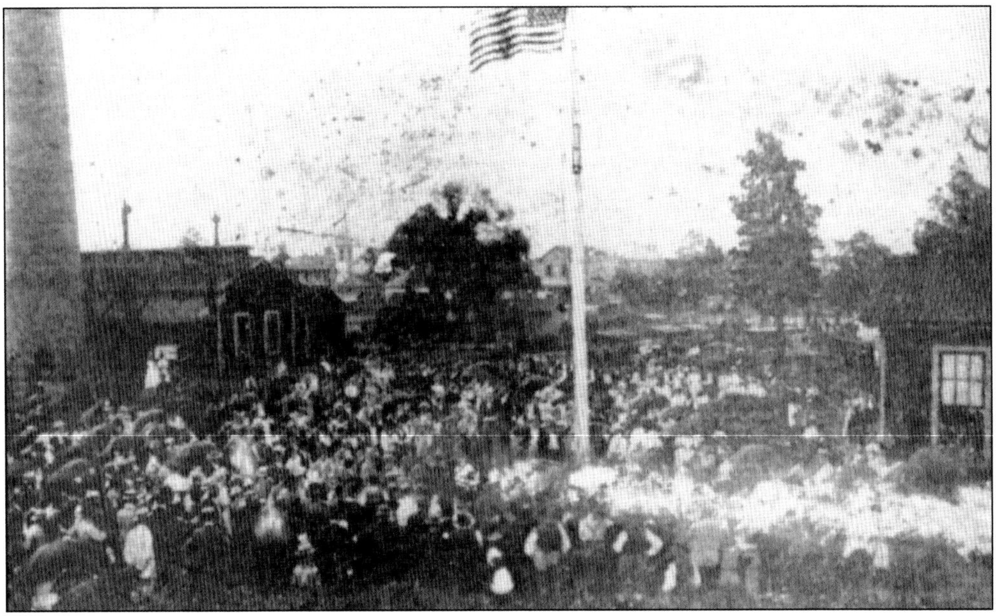

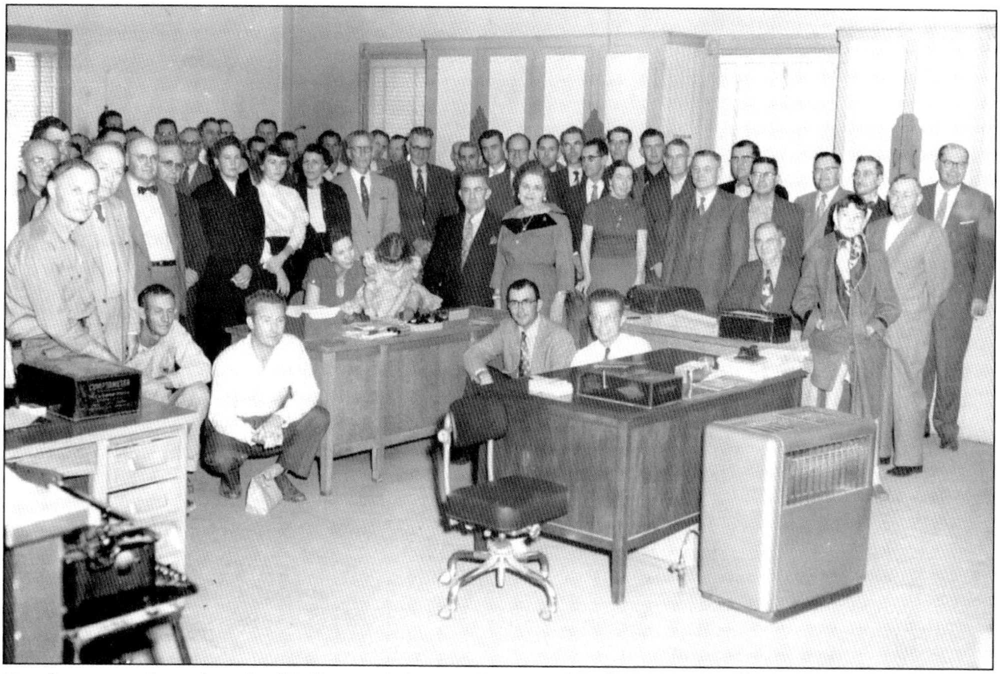

Employees gathered at the Dallas and Austin division headquarters at the Ennis superintendent main office on December 24, 1954. Pictured from left to right are (first row, squatting) ? Sinclair, George Graves Jr., Olen Bailey, and Jack Burkhead, (second row, sitting) Bennie Stokes, unidentified child, H. H. Lummus, and Betty Moore (standing), Carolyn Schanewerk (standing), C. Oats, and ? Satterfield, (third row, standing) Frank Mach, P. Lockhart, Floyd Casebolt, unidentified, Jerry Lahon, Mrs. Mike Kelly, Jenny Glaspy, Earl Morgan, Bob Williams, B. Test, Fred Zapletal, Joe Mitchell, A. Grant, Walter McElhaney, W. H. Vick, D. Miller, unidentified, Bryan Adams, Julius Kulhanek, ? Howard, Lou Baldridge, Owen Satterfield, ? Hickman, F. E. Hoefer, and unidentified. A flag-raising ceremony is pictured below at the Ennis roundhouse in the 1940s. Pictured from left to right are Tom Leatham, E. Norman, and Jessie Byars. (Above, courtesy of George Graves; below, courtesy of Ennis Fire Department.)

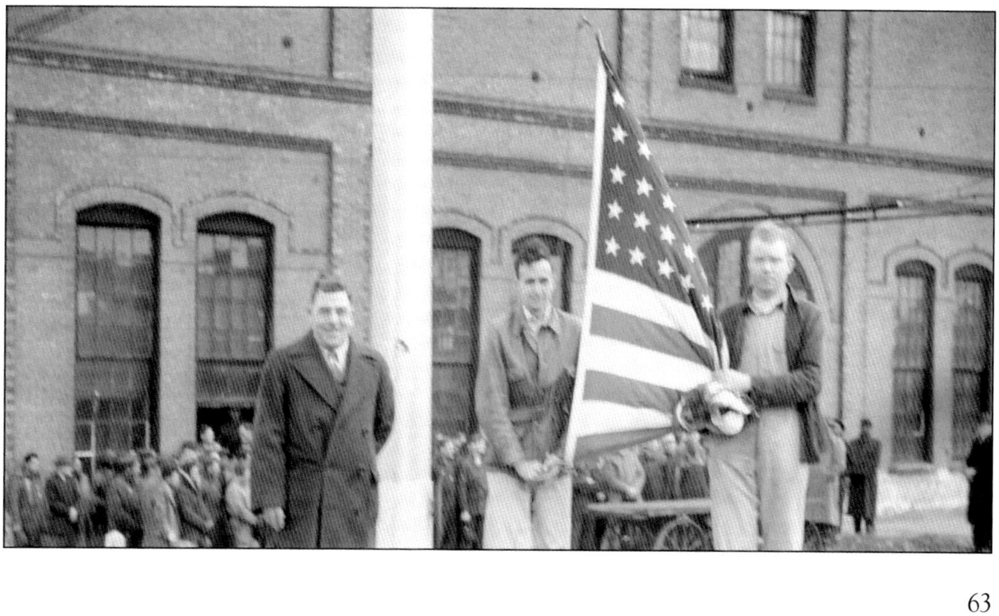

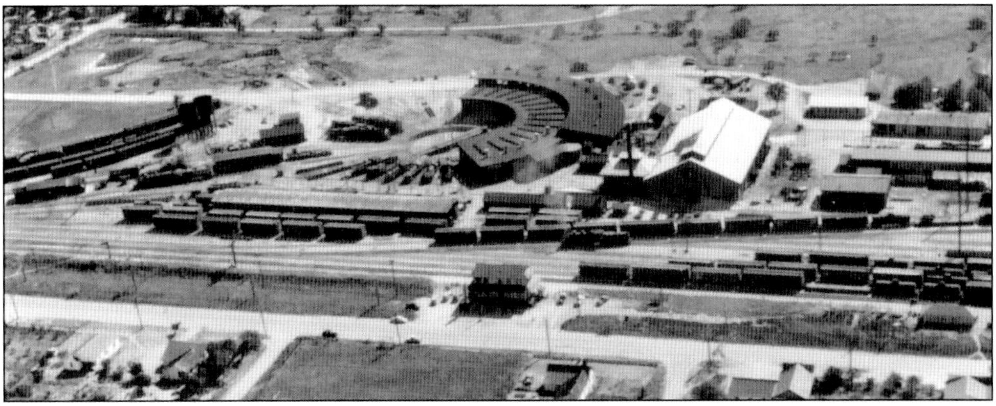

The majesty of the Ennis roundhouse and rail yards, located 1 mile north from the heart of the city, was beyond description. Pictured above in August 1948, the Southern Pacific shops were a place of constant activity. The silence that came with the demolition of the facility was as huge as the suddenly bare acres of land. Lee Templin, a retired Southern Pacific locomotive engineer, is pictured below standing in the midst of what was once the rail yards of the Ennis roundhouse facility. The roundhouse, machine shops, and then the rail yards themselves, all an intricate part of the city's history, were demolished and removed. Only the main line and three yard tracks remained at the time of this photograph in February 1988. (Above, courtesy of Joe V. Pool; below, courtesy of Jim and Helen Templin.)

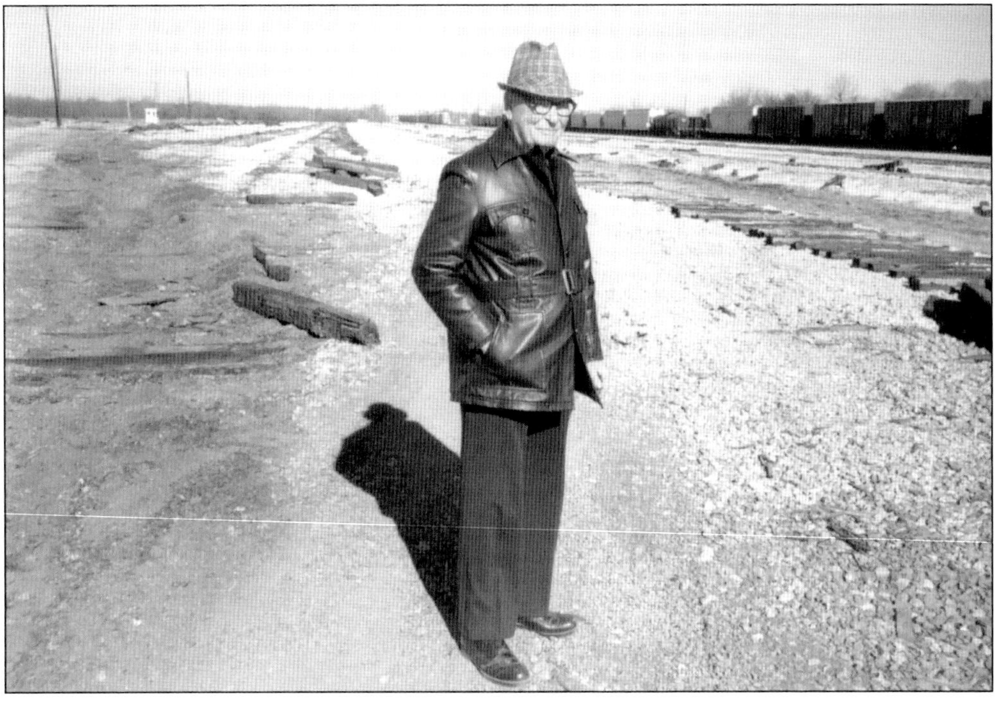

Five

The Interurban

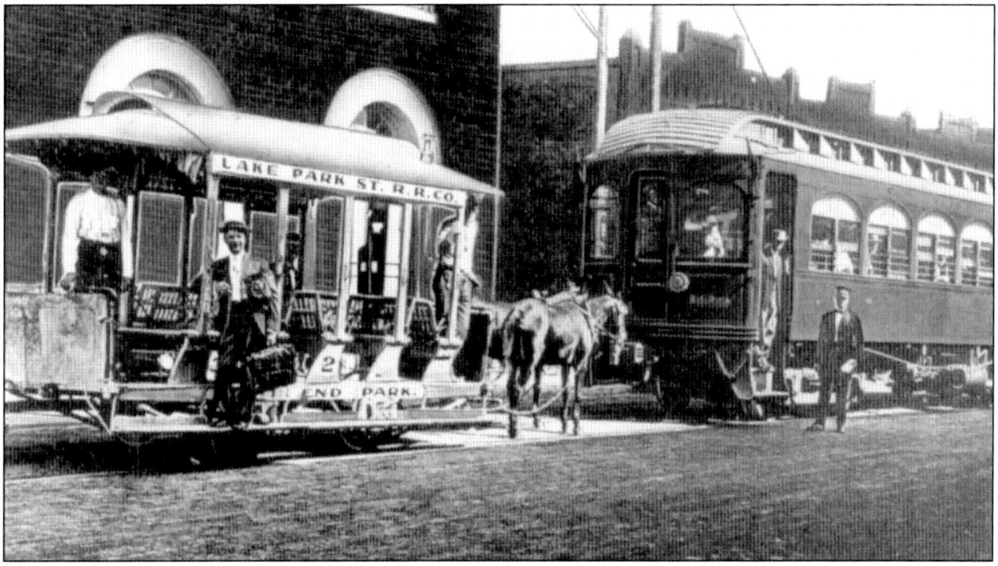

J. F. Strickland, along with Osce Goodwin and M. B. Templeton, all of Waxahachie, began promoting an electrical railway between Dallas and Sherman in the early 1900s. The inaugural trip of that line was in June 1908. In 1909, Strickland, a founder of the Texas Traction Company, bought controlling interests of the Denison and Sherman Electric Railway, and in 1911, that railway was sold to the Texas Traction Company. In 1912, Strickland formed the Southern Traction Company, and that same year, work on the line between Ferris and Dallas began. At that same time, a competing company, the Dallas Southern Traction Company, began work on the line from south Dallas to Waxahachie. With the arrival of the Texas Electric Interurban to Ellis County, the Lake Park Street Railroad mule-drawn streetcars were about to become a thing of the past. With the backside of Curlin's Pharmacy in the background at the left, a mule-drawn streetcar and an interurban car with their drivers standing beside them are pictured around 1915. (Courtesy of Ellis County Museum.)

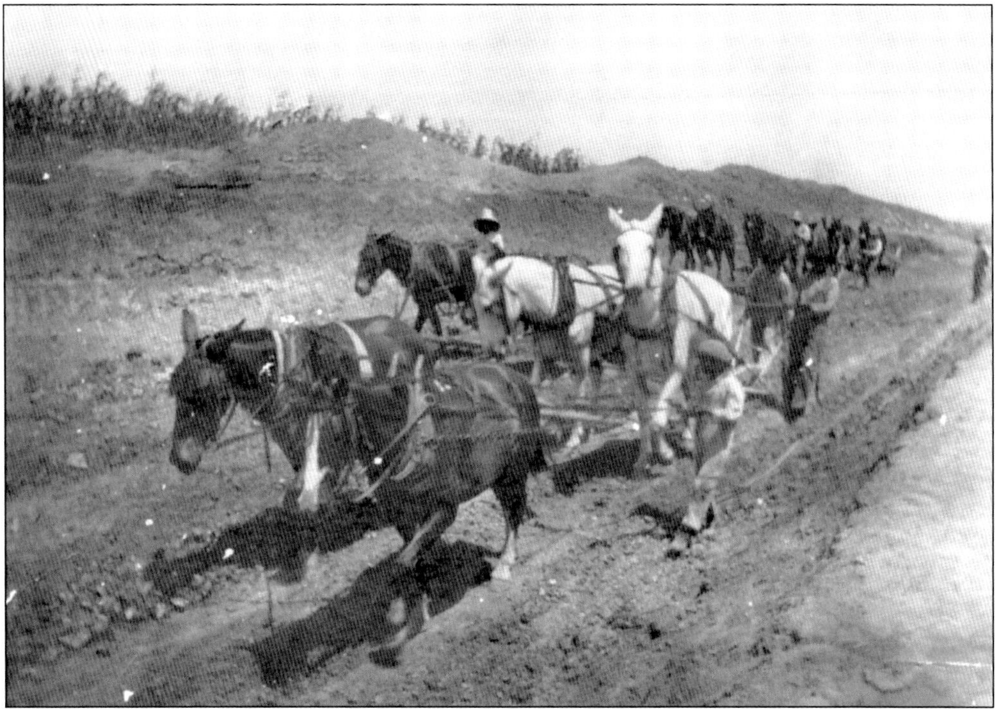

Hundreds of miles of right-of-way had to be cleared for the Texas Electric Railway in Ellis County. Much of it was through terrain between communities as pictured above, where men work on the line that would connect Ennis to Corsicana in Navarro County. Years later, a 1926 map, pictured below, details the plans to eliminate just over 7 miles of railroad tracks in Ellis County between Ferris and Palmer. (Above, courtesy of Ennis Public Library; below, courtesy of Ellis County Museum.)

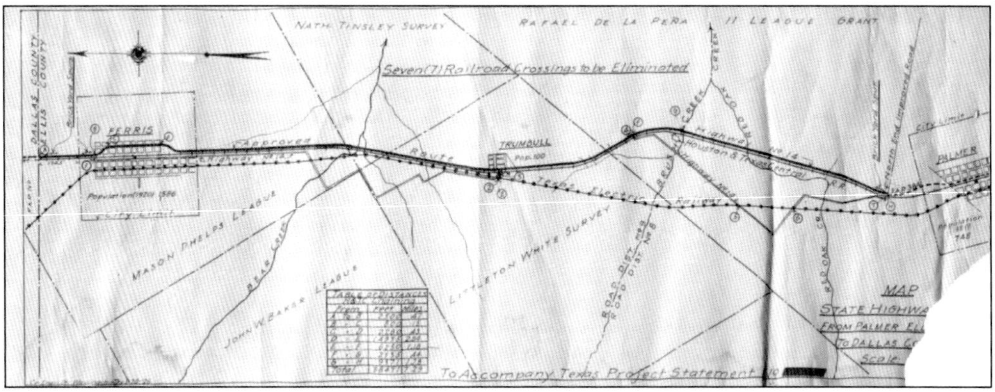

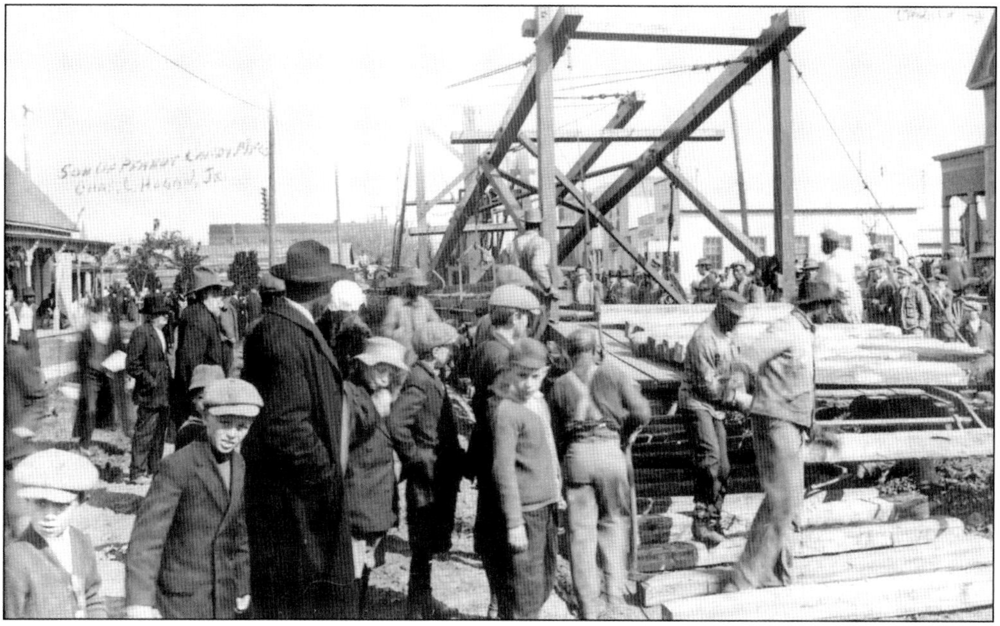

It took tremendous manpower to lay the track of the Texas Electric Railway. This is seen above as the track is being laid on South Dallas Street near Crockett Street in Ennis in April 1913. Schools were suspended for a time during that day to allow for students to be taken to the site to see the work being done. Ethel Herrington is pictured at right, standing beside the interurban track in a southward view along Dallas Street in Ennis around 1918. (Above, courtesy of Ennis Fire Department; right, courtesy of the A. L. Bohanon family.)

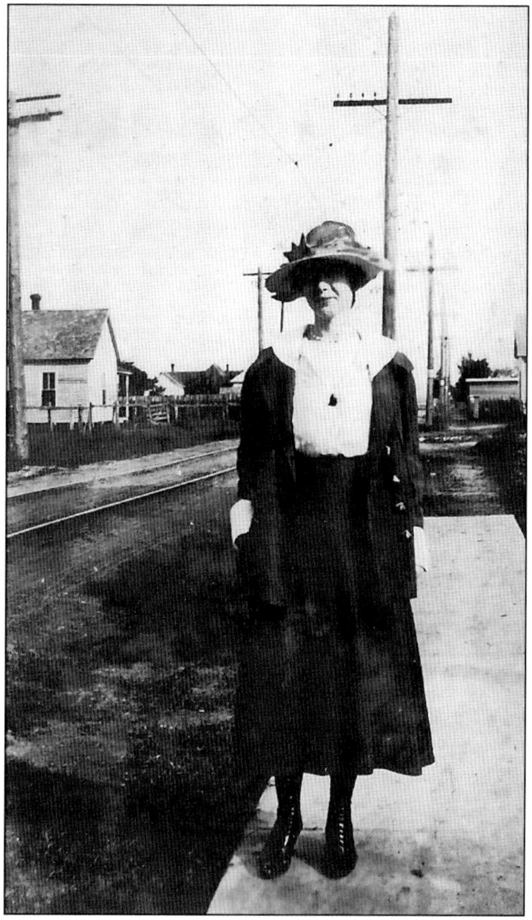

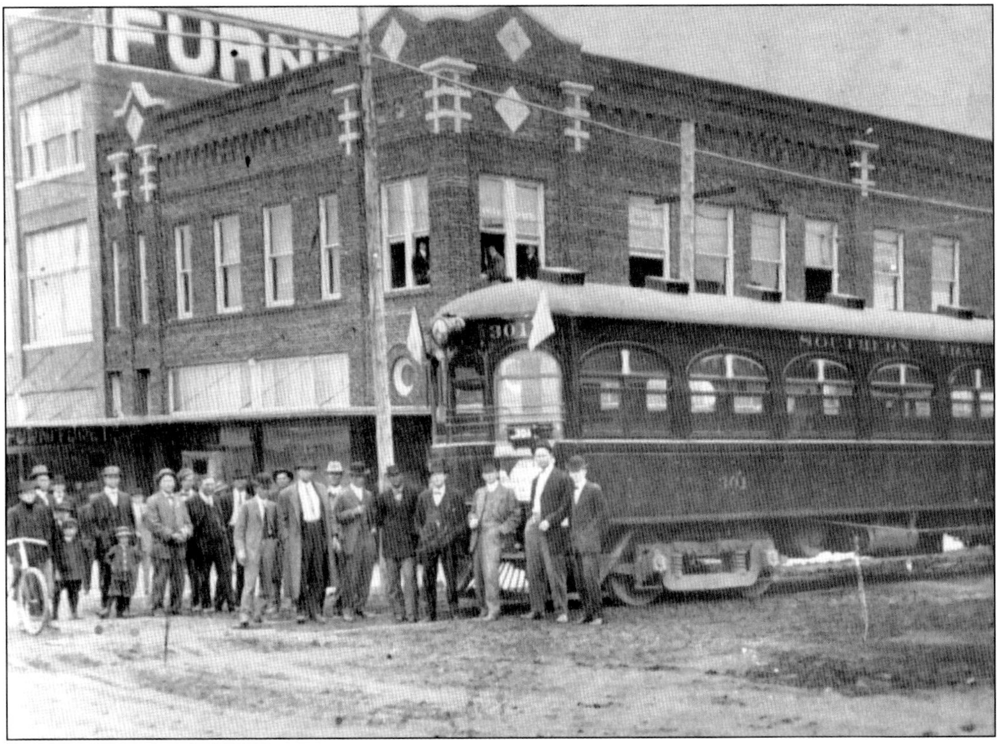

On October 13, 1913, the first Texas Electric Railway interurban car departed from Ennis to Corsicana. The inaugural trip was commemorated with a gathering of city and community leaders, as well as Texas Electric Railway Company officials, pictured above at Ennis Avenue and Dallas Street. Pictured below is the interurban car as it makes its first trip to Alma from Ennis. From the north, the interurban came into Ennis on McKinney Street, turned east on Baylor Street, then south again on Dallas Street as it went out of Ennis south to Alma. (Both, courtesy of Ennis Public Library.)

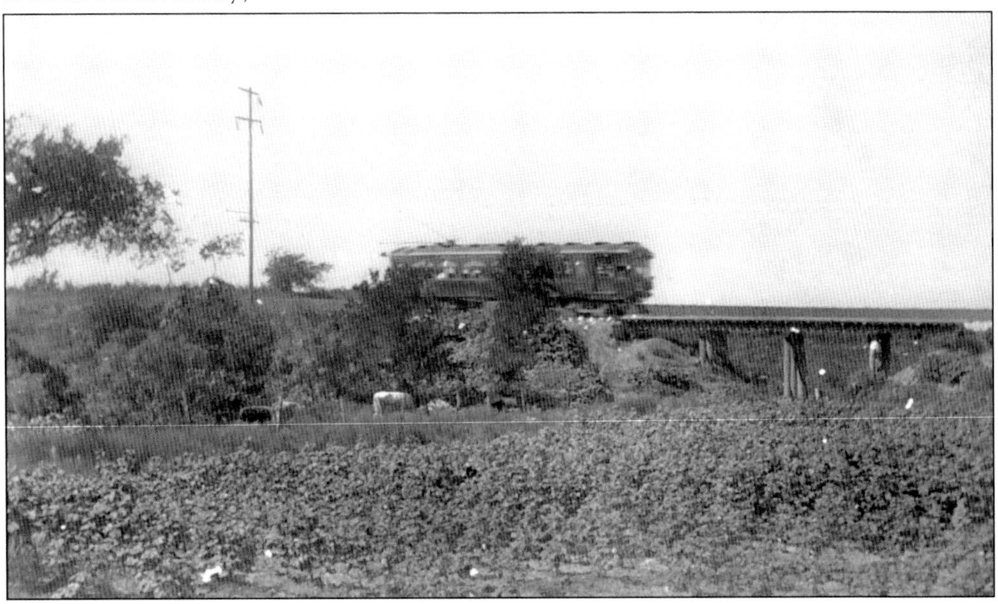

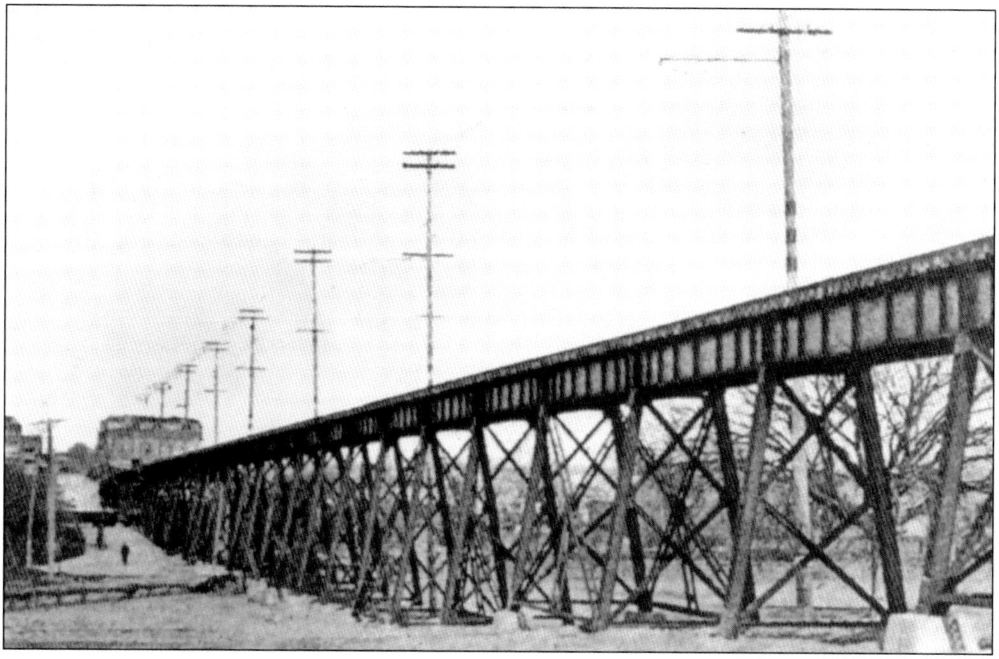

The Waxahachie steel overpass trestle, pictured above around 1925, was 800 feet long and 40 feet high. It crossed over the Waxahachie Creek as well as two steam railroad tracks, the Missouri-Kansas-Texas Railroad and the Burlington–Rock Island Railroad, before entering the town on South College Street. An interurban can be seen crossing the trestle, pictured below around 1940. The railroad crossing sign to the right is positioned just before the tracks, located approximately three blocks south of downtown Waxahachie. (Both, courtesy of Ellis County Museum.)

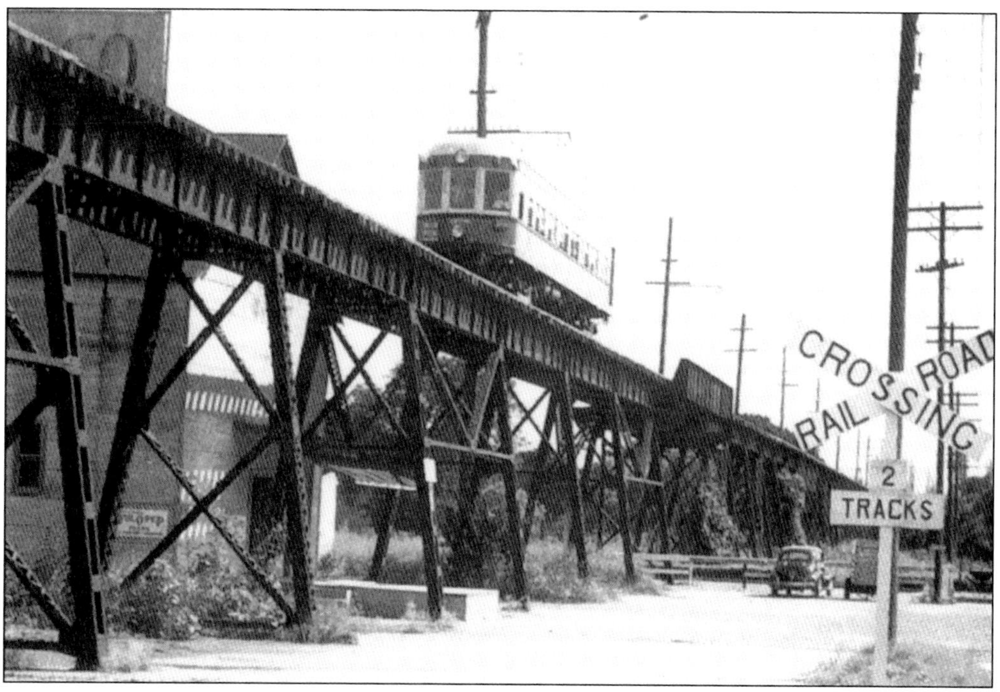

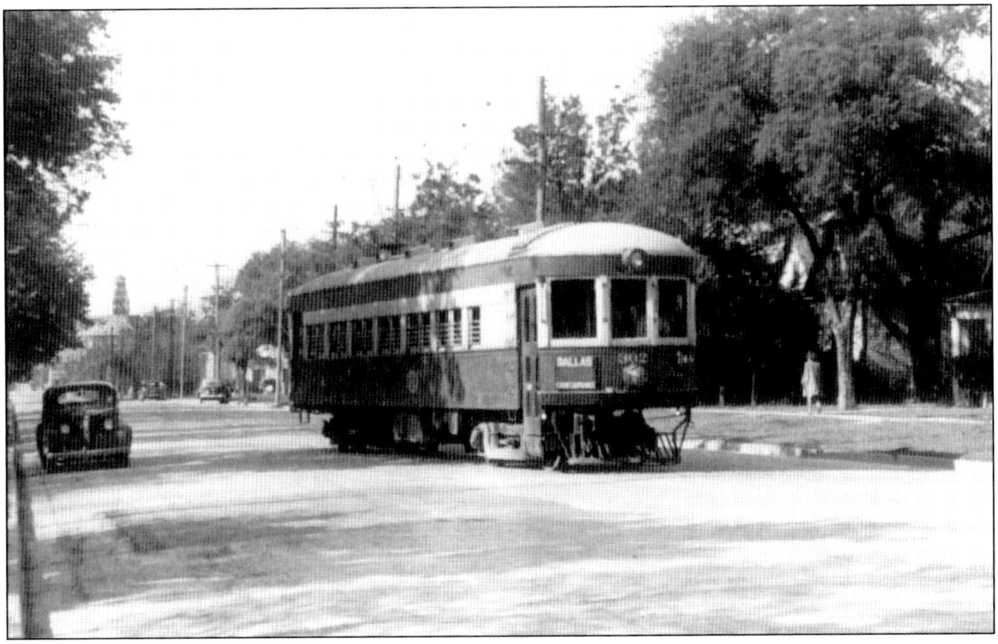

An interurban car travelling down North College Street is seen above around 1935. The Ellis County Courthouse can be seen in the background at the left side of the picture, on the other end of College Street. Another interurban passenger car, Southern Traction Company No. 313 en-route to Dallas, is pictured below on the tracks that ran down the middle of the streets in most cities serviced by the Texas Electric Railway. (Both, courtesy of Ellis County Museum.)

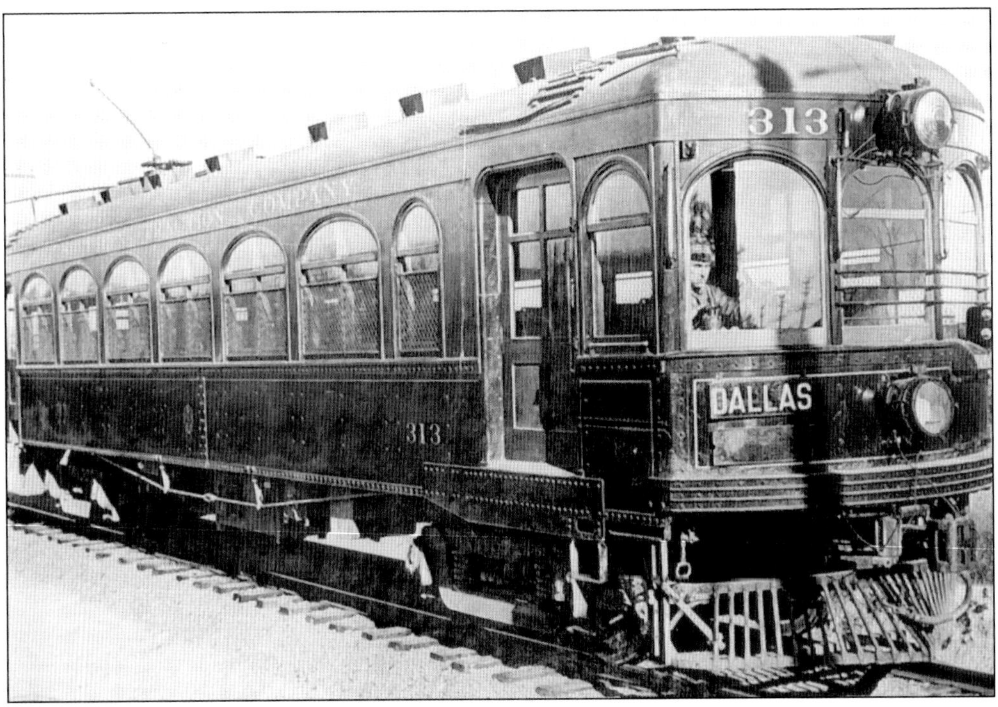

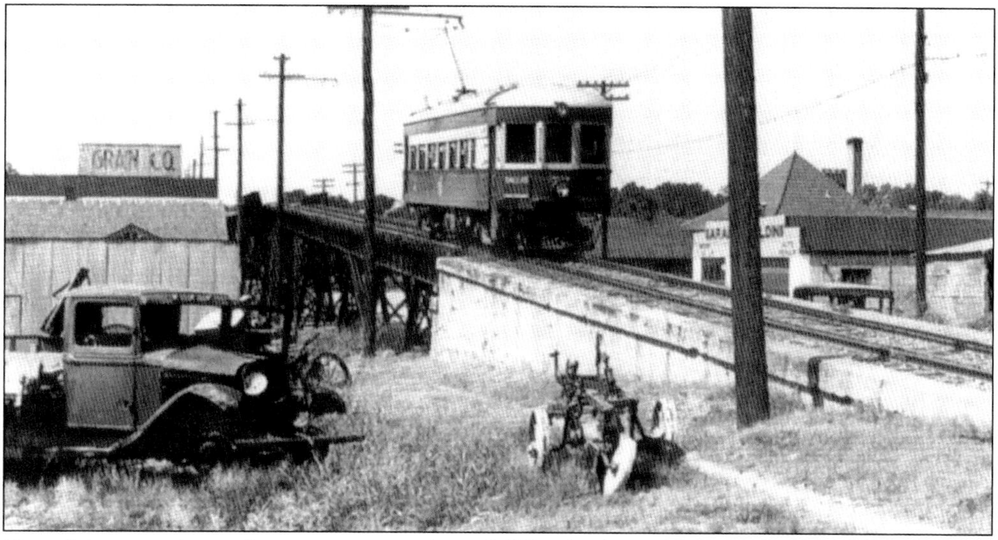

One of the many interurban trains to run through Waxahachie is seen traveling northbound just as it came off the trestle running over the Missouri-Kansas-Texas and Burlington–Rock Island Railroad tracks just south of downtown Waxahachie around 1940. (Courtesy of Ellis County Museum.)

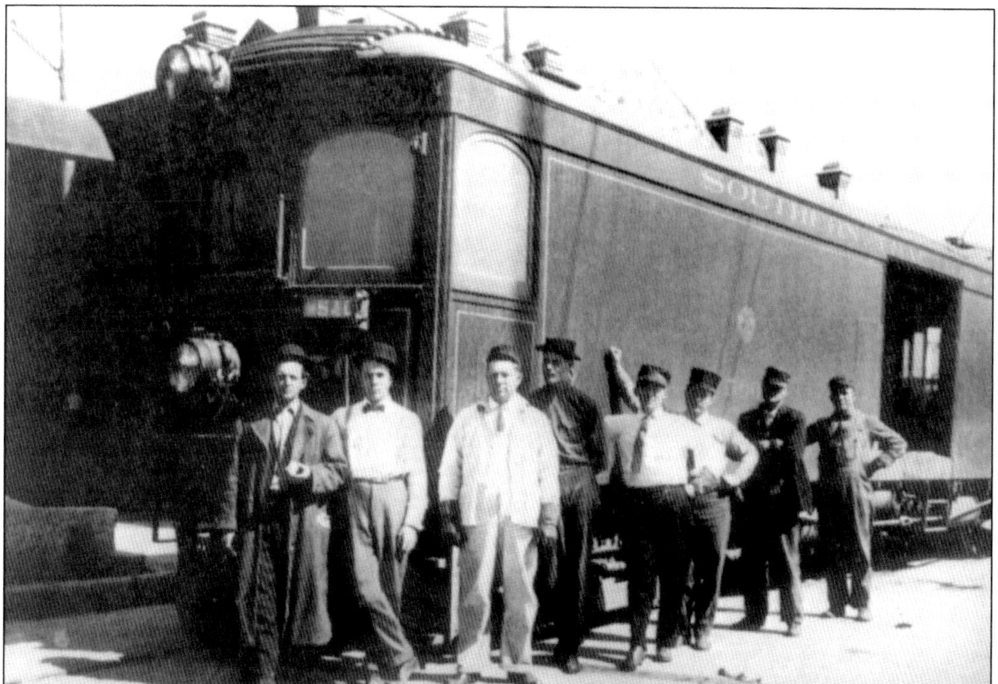

Several men can be seen standing in front of a Southern Traction Company interurban freight train on Franklin Street in Waxahachie in 1915. (Courtesy of Ellis County Museum.)

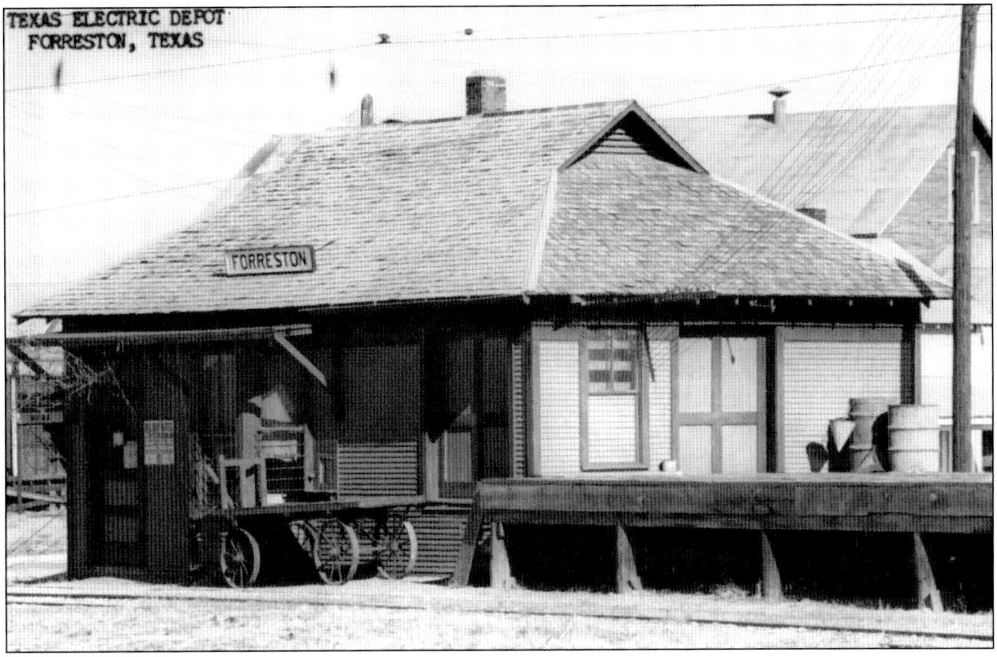

The Forreston Texas Electric Depot, pictured in December 1938, was located on what is now U.S. Highway 77 and situated between both the MKT and Texas Electric tracks. Behind the depot to the right of the photograph is a portion of one of the city's cotton gins, which is still standing. On the sign between the door and cart it reads "Holiday Rates." (Courtesy of John and Barbra Kaufman.)

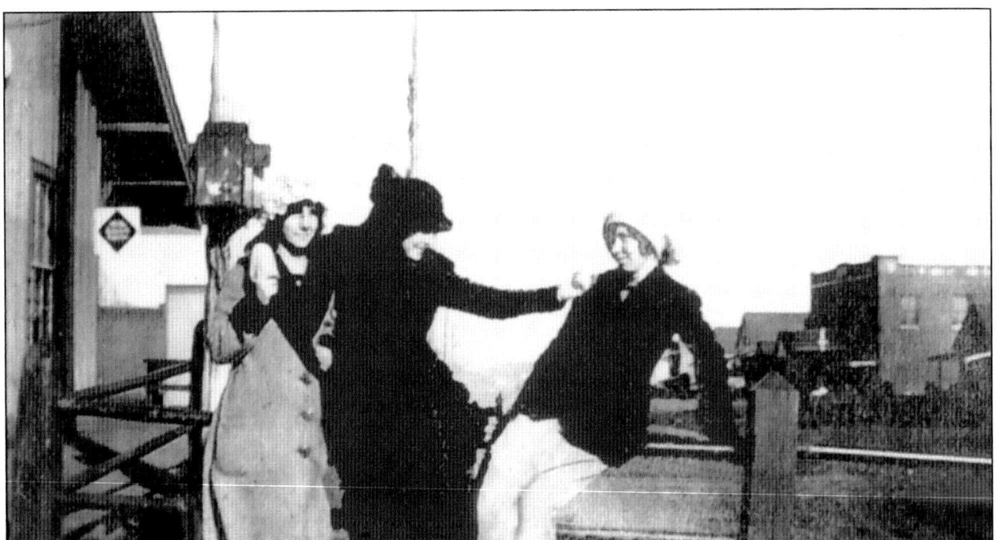

The interurban depot was located on South Calhoun Street in Rice along the railroad tracks, pictured above around 1915. Three young women are seen on the depot platform with the town in the background. (Courtesy of Jerry Herring.)

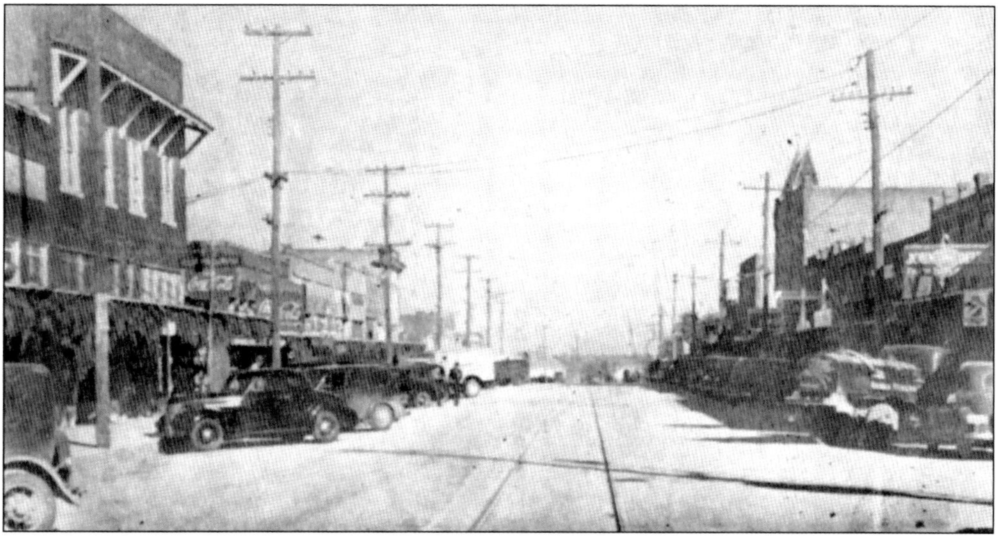

The Texas Electric Interurban came through Italy on both Clark and Main Streets before heading south to Milford and Hillsboro or north to Forreston and Waxahachie. The interurban tracks can be seen above in a view looking down Italy's Main Street in the 1940s. On September 30, 1913, on a special run for stockholders, a group of musicians from Italy were on the train from Hillsboro to Waxahachie, scheduled to perform at the spike-driving ceremonies there. Another train brought guests to the city from Dallas. An interurban car is pictured below in 1948 making one of the last trips through Italy, as the lines were in the process of being closed down. (Both, courtesy of Ellis County Museum.)

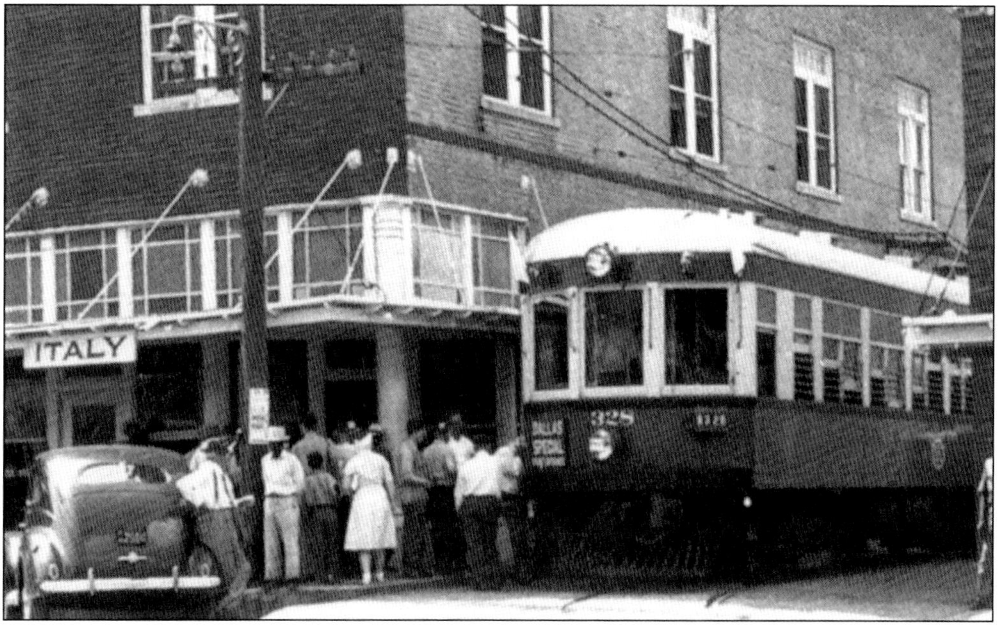

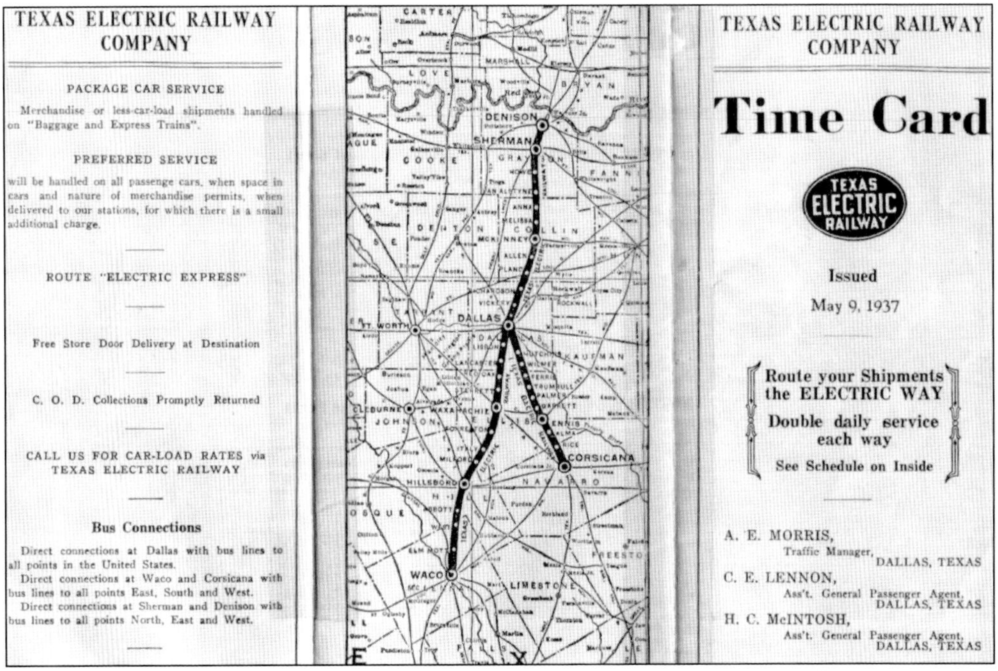

TEXAS ELECTRIC RAILWAY COMPANY

PACKAGE CAR SERVICE

Merchandise or less-car-load shipments handled on "Baggage and Express Trains".

PREFERRED SERVICE

will be handled on all passenge cars, when space in cars and nature of merchandise permits, when delivered to our stations, for which there is a small additional charge.

ROUTE "ELECTRIC EXPRESS"

Free Store Door Delivery at Destination

C. O. D. Collections Promptly Returned

CALL US FOR CAR-LOAD RATES via TEXAS ELECTRIC RAILWAY

Bus Connections

Direct connections at Dallas with bus lines to all points in the United States.

Direct connections at Waco and Corsicana with bus lines to all points East, South and West.

Direct connections at Sherman and Denison with bus lines to all points North, East and West.

TEXAS ELECTRIC RAILWAY COMPANY

Time Card

TEXAS ELECTRIC RAILWAY

Issued

May 9, 1937

Route your Shipments the ELECTRIC WAY

Double daily service each way

See Schedule on Inside

A. E. MORRIS,
Traffic Manager, DALLAS, TEXAS

C. E. LENNON,
Ass't. General Passenger Agent, DALLAS, TEXAS

H. C. McINTOSH,
Ass't. General Passenger Agent, DALLAS, TEXAS

In the late 1930s, it took just under two hours to travel from downtown Dallas to Corsicana by the Texas Electric Railway Interurban. The trains ran 12 times a day, throughout the day, Monday through Saturday. Stopping in a number of communities along the way, including Oak Cliff, Monroe, Hutchins, Wilmer, Ferris, Trumbull, Palmer, Garrett, Ennis, Alma, and Rice, the interurban provided a mode of transportation accessible to those cities as well as nearby communities through the late 1940s. Pictured are views of the 1937 time card of the Texas Electric Railway for the Dallas-to-Corsicana line. (Both, courtesy of Dane Williams.)

Dallas-Corsicana Division

TIME CARD NO. 118

Subject to change without notice **Effective June 17, 1934**

SOUTHBOUND—DALLAS TO CORSICANA (Read Down)

	Passenger Trains												Baggage and Express Trains	
TRAIN NUMBERS →	615	617	619	621	623	625	627	629	631	633	635	637	701	
STATIONS	AM	AM	AM	AM	PM	PM	PM	PM	PM	PM	PM	PM	AM	PM
Lv. Dallas	‡6 00	7 40	8 40	10 40	12 40	2 40	4 40	5 40	‡6 15	7 40	9 40	11 00	1 40	§12 40
" Oak Cliff Junction	‡6 10	7 50	8 50	10 50	12 50	2 50	4 50	5 50	‡6 25	7 50	9 50	11 10	1 47	§12 50
" Monroe	‡6 17	7 59	8 59	10 59	12 59	2 59	4 59	5 59	‡6 34	7 59	9 59	11 19	1 55	§12 59
" Hutchins	‡6 27	8 10	9 10	11 10	1 10	3 10	5 10	6 10	‡6 45	8 10	10 10	11 30	2 07	§1 10
" Wilmer	‡6 33	8 17	9 17	11 17	1 17	3 17	5 17	6 17	‡6 53	8 17	10 17	11 37	2 15	§1 17
" Ferris	‡6 41	8 25	9 25	11 25	1 25	3 25	5 25	6 25	‡7 01	8 25	10 25	11 45	2 37	§1 25
" Trumbull	‡6 48	8 30	9 30	11 30	1 30	3 30	5 30	6 30	....	8 30	10 30	11 50	2 43	§1 30
" Palmer	‡6 56	8 37	9 37	11 37	1 37	3 37	5 37	6 37	....	8 37	10 37	11 57	3 05	§1 37
" Garrett	‡7 02	8 43	9 43	11 43	1 43	3 43	5 43	6 43	....	8 43	10 43	12 03	3 11	§1 43
" Ennis	‡7 10	8 51	9 51	11 51	1 51	3 51	5 51	6 51	....	8 51	10 51	12 11	3 27	§1 51
" Alma	‡7 20	9 01	10 01	12 01	2 01	4 01	6 01	7 01	....	9 01	11 01	12 21	3 36	§2 01
" Rice	‡7 25	9 06	10 06	12 06	2 06	4 06	6 06	7 06	....	9 06	11 06	12 26	3 52	§2 06
Ar. Corsicana	‡7 49	9 30	10 30	12 30	2 30	4 30	6 30	7 30	....	9 30	11 30	12 50	4 15	§2 30
STATIONS	AM	AM	AM	PM	PM	PM	PM	PM	PM	PM	PM	AM	AM	PM

NORTHBOUND—CORSICANA TO DALLAS (Read Down)

	Passenger Trains												Baggage and Express Train
TRAIN NUMBERS →	612	614	616	618	620	622	624	626	628	630	632	634	702
STATIONS	AM	AM	AM	AM	AM	AM	PM	PM	PM	PM	PM	PM	PM
Lv. Corsicana	....	‡6 00	6 40	7 40	9 40	11 40	1 40	2 40	3 40	5 40	7 40	9 40	6 30
" Rice	....	‡6 19	6 59	7 59	9 59	11 59	1 59	2 59	3 59	5 59	7 59	9 59	6 54
" Alma	....	‡6 25	7 05	8 05	10 05	12 05	2 05	3 05	4 05	6 05	8 05	10 05	7 08
" Ennis	....	‡6 35	7 15	8 15	10 15	12 15	2 15	3 15	4 15	6 15	8 15	10 15	7 25
" Garrett	....	‡6 44	7 24	8 24	10 24	12 24	2 24	3 24	4 24	6 24	8 24	10 24	7 34
" Palmer	....	‡6 50	7 30	8 30	10 30	12 30	2 30	3 30	4 30	6 30	8 30	10 30	7 50
" Trumbull	....	‡6 56	7 36	8 36	10 36	12 36	2 36	3 36	4 36	6 36	8 36	10 36	7 56
" Ferris	‡6 35	‡7 01	7 41	8 41	10 41	12 41	2 41	3 41	4 41	6 41	8 41	10 41	8 05
" Wilmer	‡6 41	‡7 08	7 48	8 48	10 48	12 48	2 48	3 48	4 48	6 48	8 48	10 48	8 17
" Hutchins	‡6 49	‡7 15	7 55	8 55	10 55	12 55	2 55	3 55	4 55	6 55	8 55	10 55	8 24
" Monroe	‡7 03	‡7 27	8 07	9 07	11 07	1 07	3 07	4 07	5 07	7 07	9 07	11 07	8 36
" Oak Cliff Junction	‡7 10	‡7 35	8 15	9 15	11 15	1 15	3 15	4 15	5 15	7 15	9 15	11 15	8 45
Ar. Dallas	‡7 25	‡7 50	8 30	9 30	11 30	1 30	3 30	4 30	5 30	7 30	9 30	11 30	8 55
STATIONS	AM	AM	AM	AM	AM	PM	PM	PM	PM	PM	PM	PM	PM

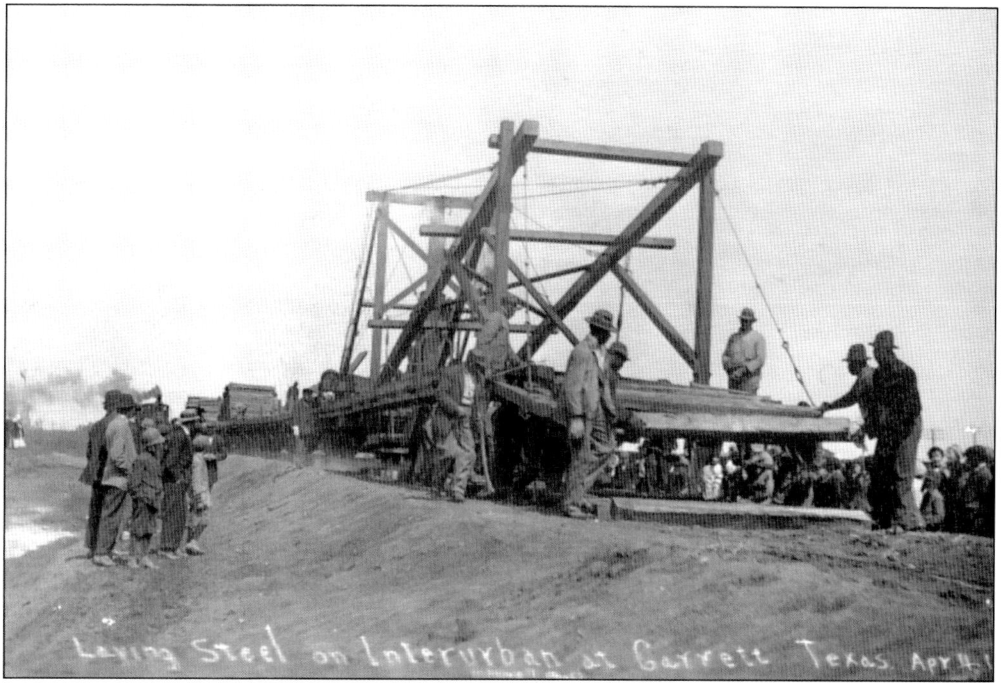

From Dallas, the Texas Electric Railway ran two lines south through Ellis County. One went through Waxahachie to Waco, the other through Ennis to Corsicana. Pictured above is the line being laid through Garrett in April 1913. Residents can be seen watching as the "track-laying machine" comes through, laying down the steel for the track. Pictured below is a Texas Electric Railway ticket illustrating the stops along the way from Dallas to Corsicana and the costs for traveling to each of those stops. The punch marks indicated the travel origination and destination of the purchaser, in this case between Ennis and Rice. (Above, courtesy of Jimmy and Ginger Boon; below, courtesy of Ennis Public Library.)

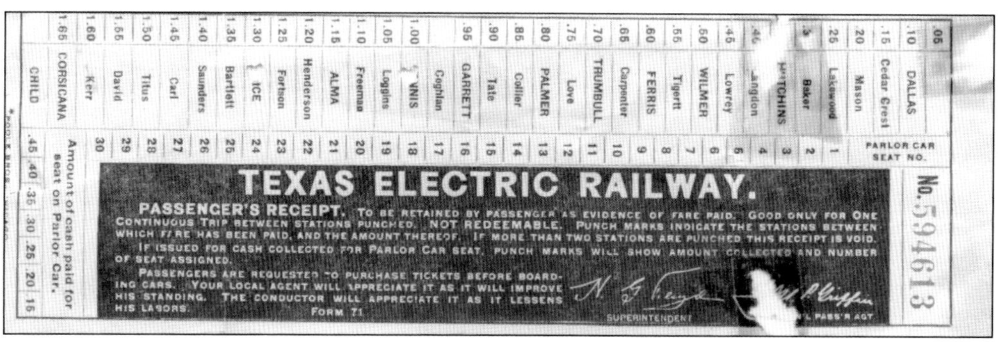

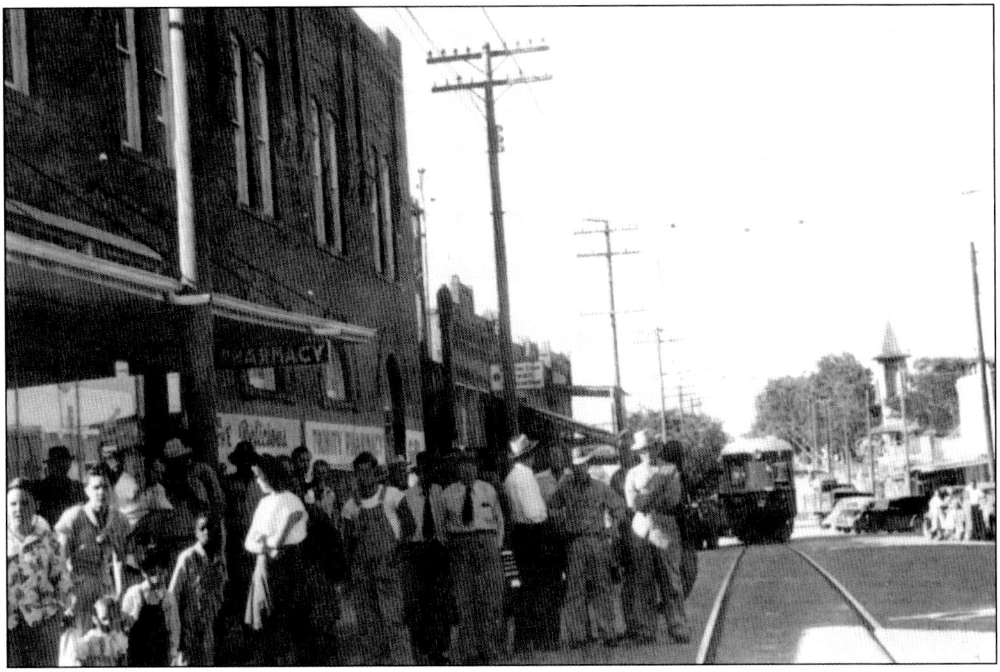

The Texas Electric Interurban was shut down in 1948 in Ellis County. On December 31 of that year, a crowd gathered on Main and College Streets in Waxahachie as the car arrived at its normal stop at the interurban station. This day, though, it was making its final run from Waxahachie to Waco, and many came to watch it pass by for the final time, as pictured above in a view looking north on College Street. One of the last interurbans to run out of Ennis to Corsicana is pictured below in 1948. (Above, courtesy of Ellis County Museum; below, courtesy of Ennis Public Library.)

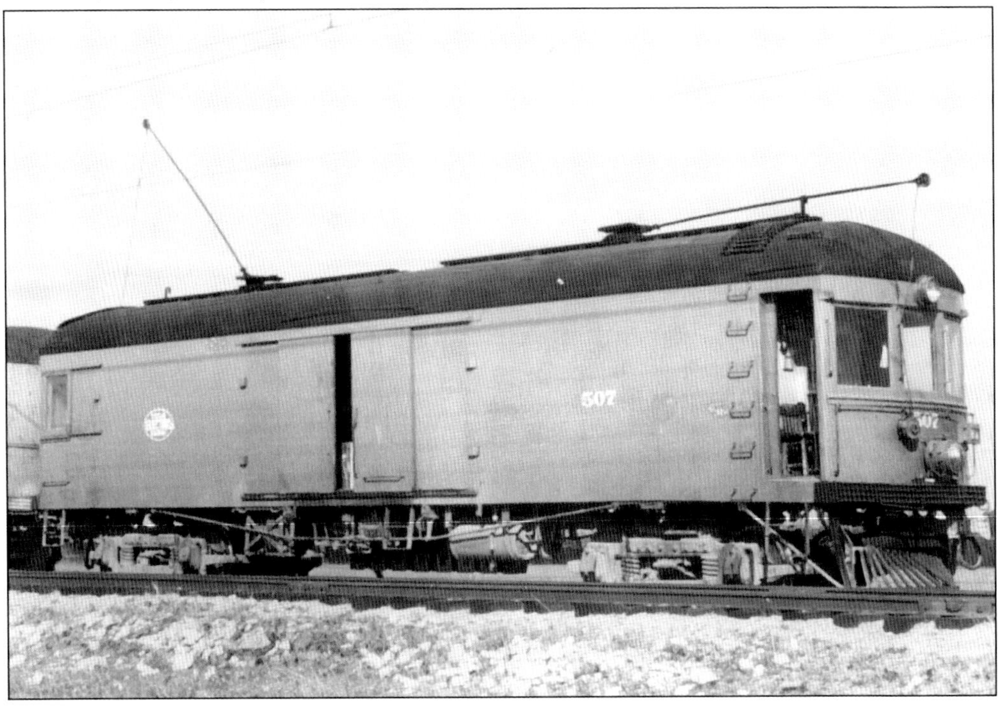

Six

Trains That Came Through

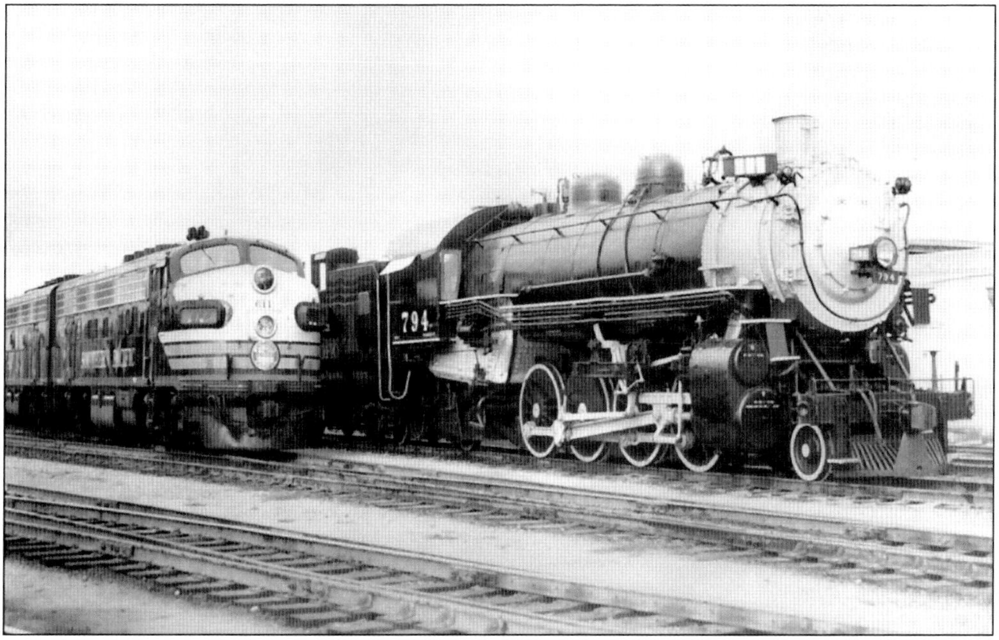

When the first diesel engine came through Ennis in the late 1940s, hundreds lined North Main Street near the depot to see it. The first freight diesel locomotive arrived in Ennis on May 13, 1949. On July 9, 1949, the first passenger diesel engine, Sunbeam No. 13, arrived in Ennis with division superintendant F. E. Hoefler among its first passengers. Yet with the diesels would come change to all Ellis County. Nowhere would it be felt as in Ennis, a city born on the rail. As the steam engines were phased out, more and more diesels were sent elsewhere for repairs. In the fall of 1953, three steam engines left the Ennis roundhouse. Those that gathered to watch their departure understood it was the end of an era. There would be no more. The time of the steam engine, the pride of the Ennis roundhouse, was over. Pictured side by side are diesel engine No. 611 to the left and steam engine No. 794 to the right. (Courtesy of the City of Ennis.)

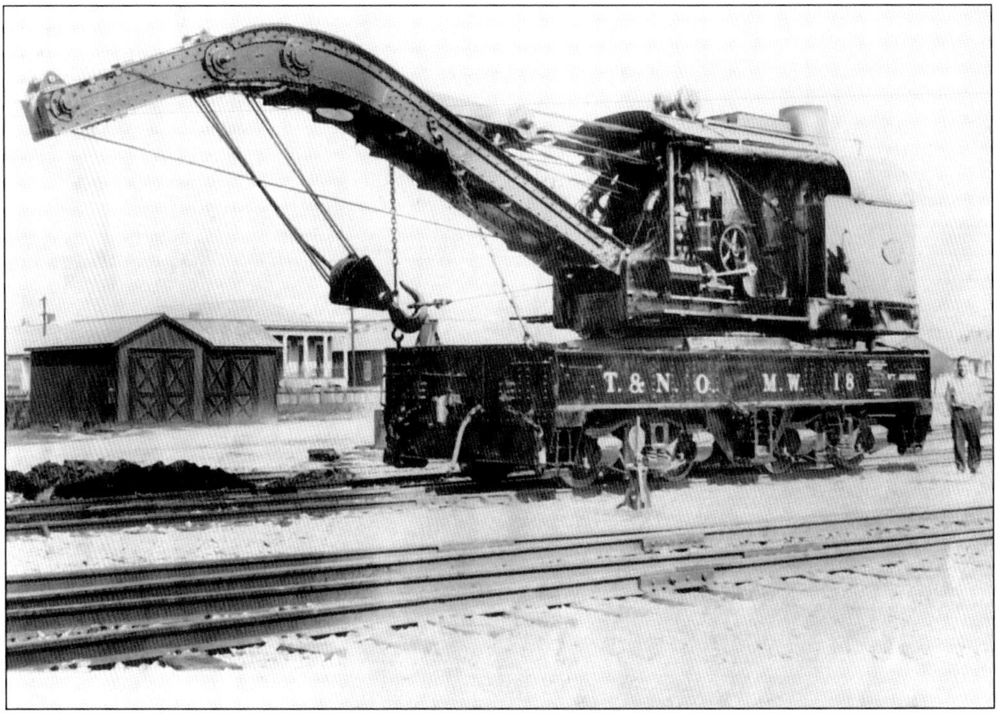

A Texas and New Orleans Railroad wrecker is pictured in April 1930 in Ennis. Transported to the site of an accident or derailment, tracks were built under it to allow it to clean up the site. (Courtesy of Ennis Public Library.)

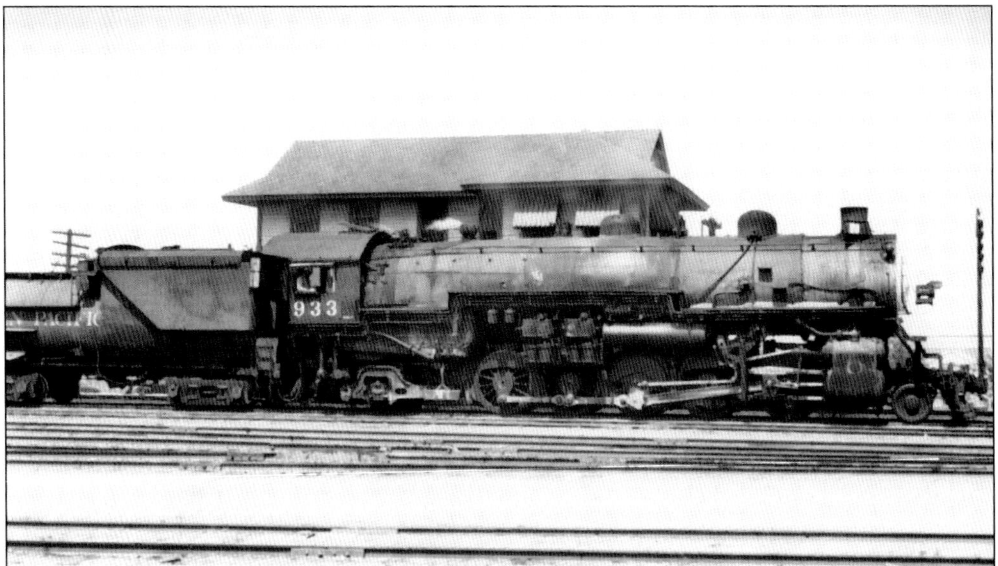

Southern Pacific engine No. 933, a steam engine, is pictured on the inbound track in front of the yard office at the Ennis roundhouse in the 1940s. (Courtesy of the Ennis Public Library.)

The Katie Flyer, pictured at right around 1940, is leaving Waxahachie for St. Louis and Chicago, and then Kansas City, as detailed by the Missouri, Kansas, and Texas Railroad advertisement, pictured below. Three trains ran the route each way on a daily basis. The advertisement also provides information on the Cannon Ball and Night Express of the Texas and Pacific Railway that ran between St. Louis, Memphis, and into the southeast United States. (Both, courtesy of the Ellis County Museum.)

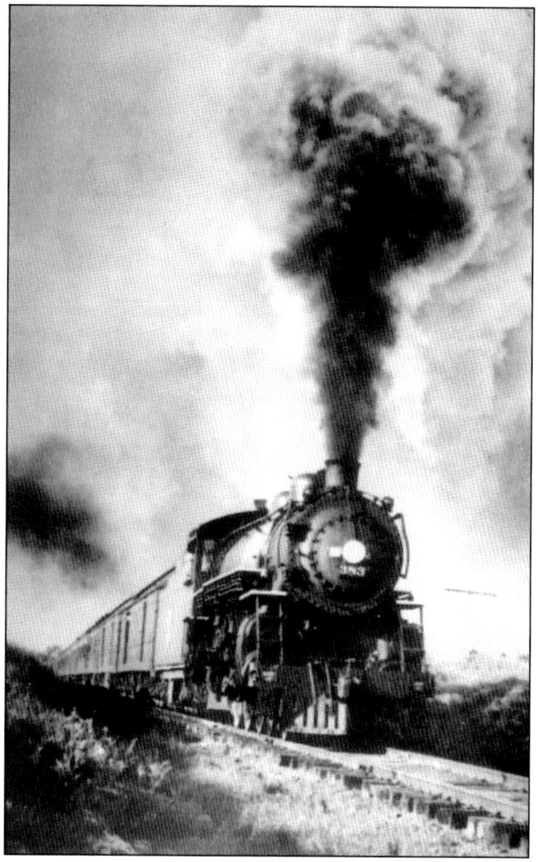

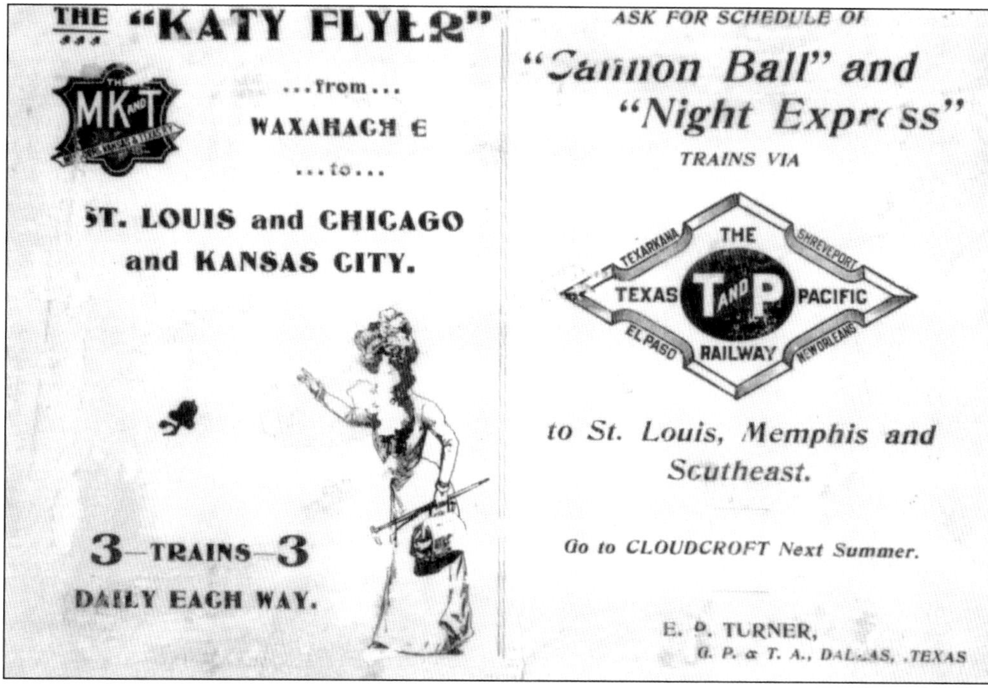

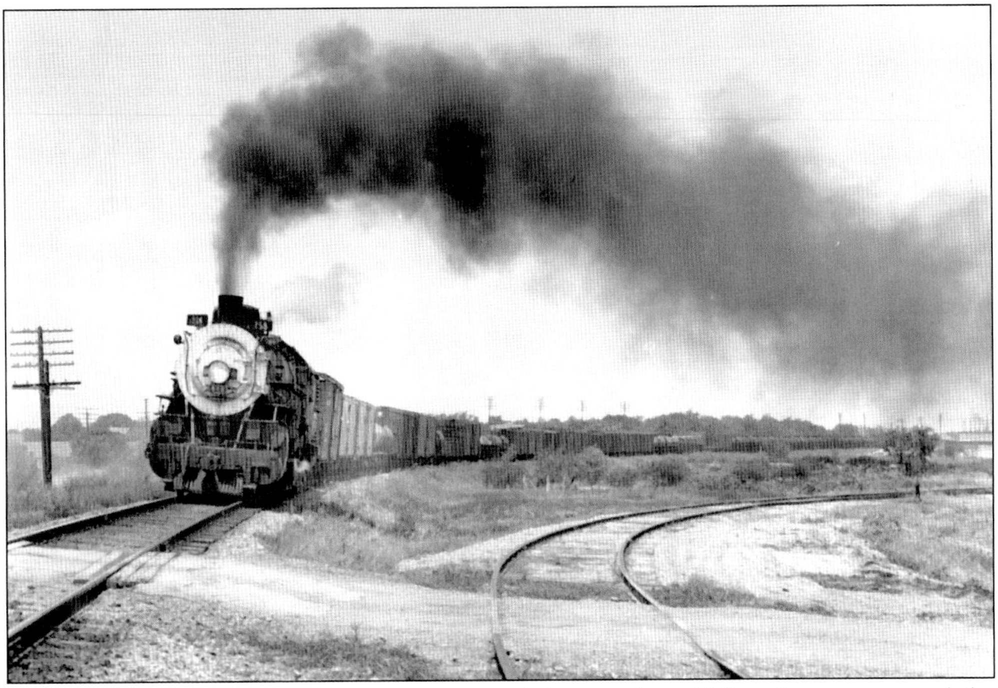

Train No. 258, on its way to Hearne, is pictured above in June 1951 as it comes around the "Compress Curve," located approximately 1 mile south of the downtown Ennis area. (Courtesy of Dane Williams, part of the Ford Curry Collection.)

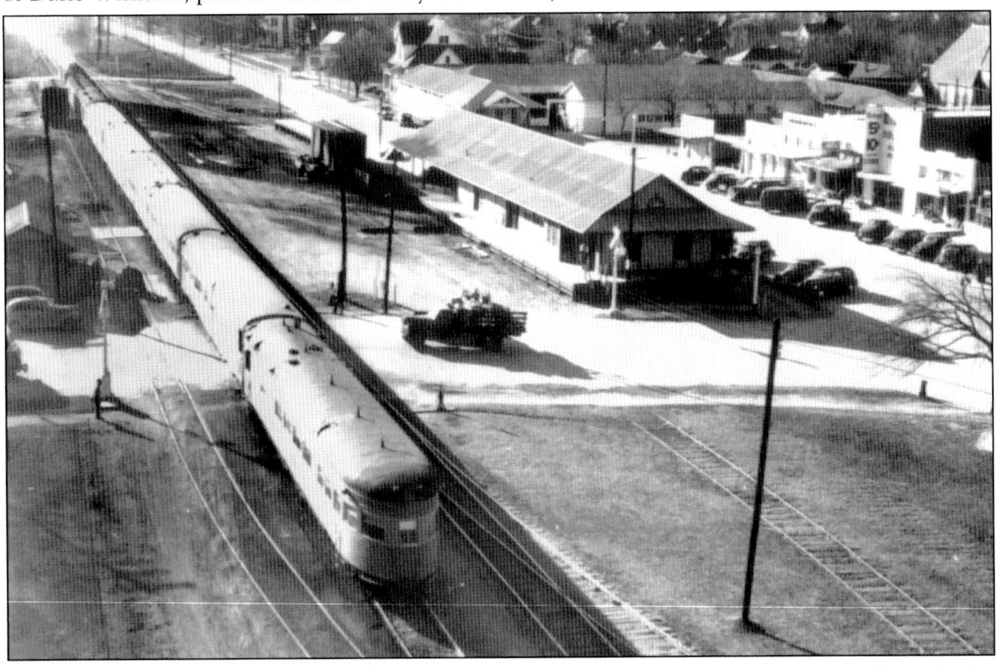

The Hustler train No. 16 is seen above as it passes across Ennis Avenue going south, with the freight depot visible to the right. The north end of the freight depot along Ennis Avenue was where paychecks were picked up by railroad employees. (Courtesy of Dane Williams, part of the Ford Curry Collection.)

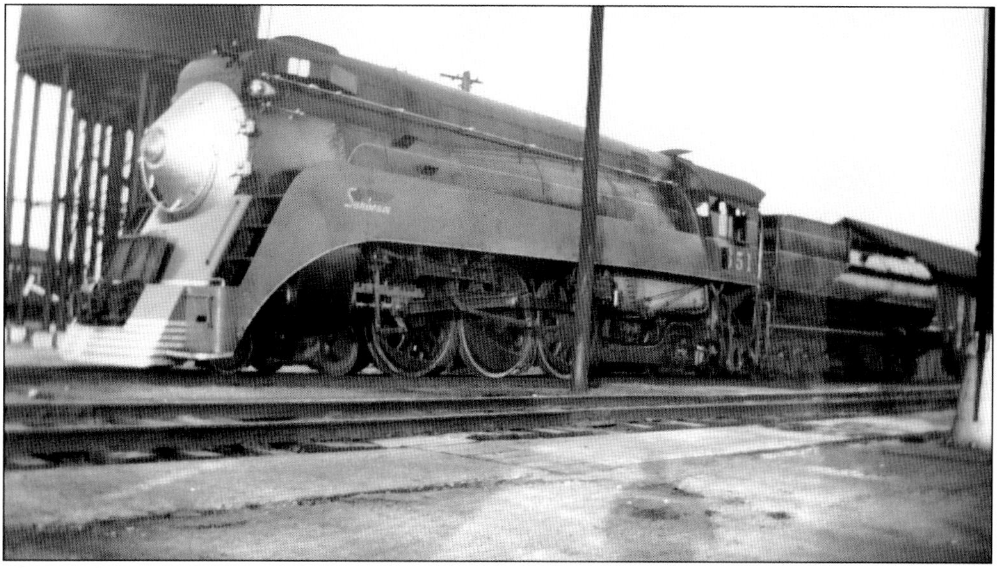

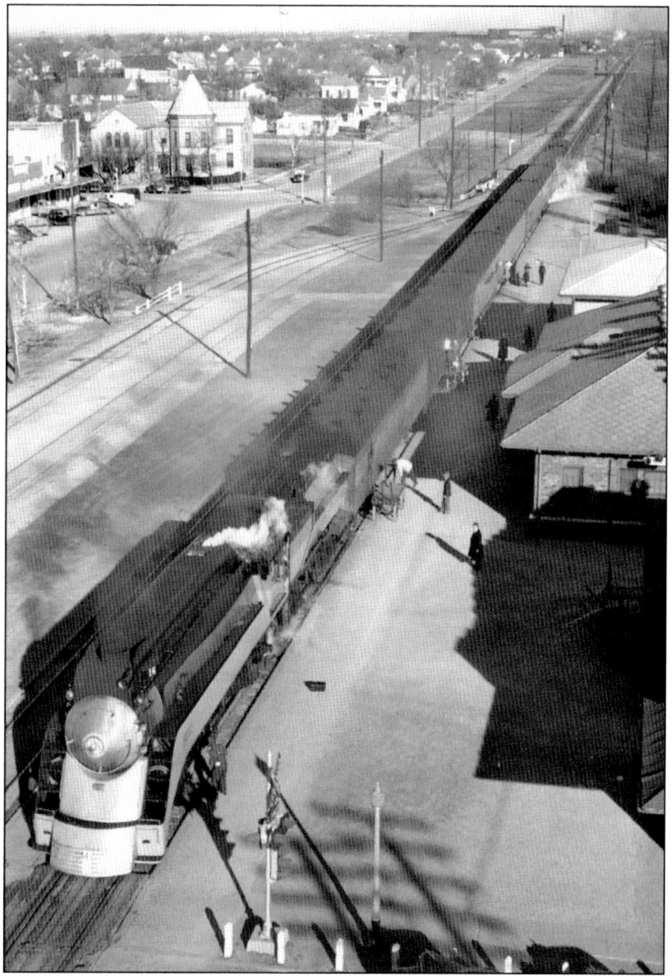

The Sunbeam, pictured above, is heading southbound on the main line out of Ennis. In 1937, Forrest Fountain remembered when B. H. Holliman, then assistant general manager, told engineer Norris I. Lipscomb, to test his Sunbeam, to "open her up." Lipscomb brought it five notches ahead of dead center and pulled the throttle bar slightly. The engine climbed to 118 miles per hour and still was not wide open. Holliman was said to have tapped engineer Lipscomb, saying that was fast enough. The schedule would be met. Pictured at right, the Ennis depot is to the right. To the upper left, with its prominent turret, is the Southern Pacific division headquarters, and in the distance, north of the city along the upper edge of the photograph, is the Ennis roundhouse. (Both, courtesy of Dane Williams, part of the Ford Curry Collection.)

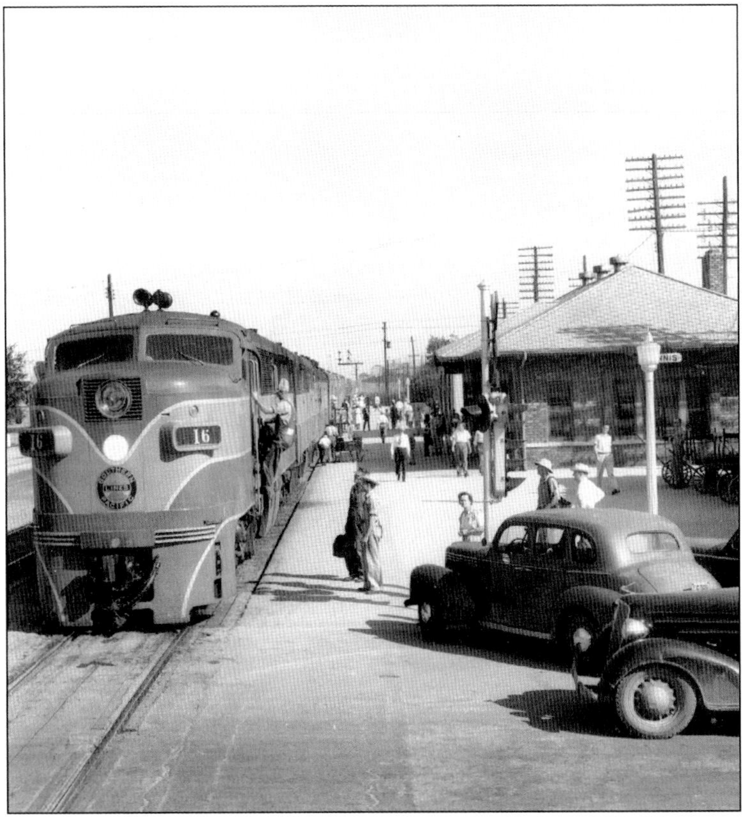

Fireman A. L. Mynatt is seen at left on the side of Southern Pacific Lines train No. 16, the Hustler. Stopped at the Ennis passenger depot in January 1953, passengers can be seen boarding, and mail is being loaded on to the train. The Ennis Express Office facing the rail and located on East Ennis Avenue can be seen below on the lower right edge of the photograph in the 1940s as a Sunbeam pulls into Ennis. (Above, courtesy of Dane Williams, part of the Ford Curry Collection; below, courtesy of Joe V. Pool.)

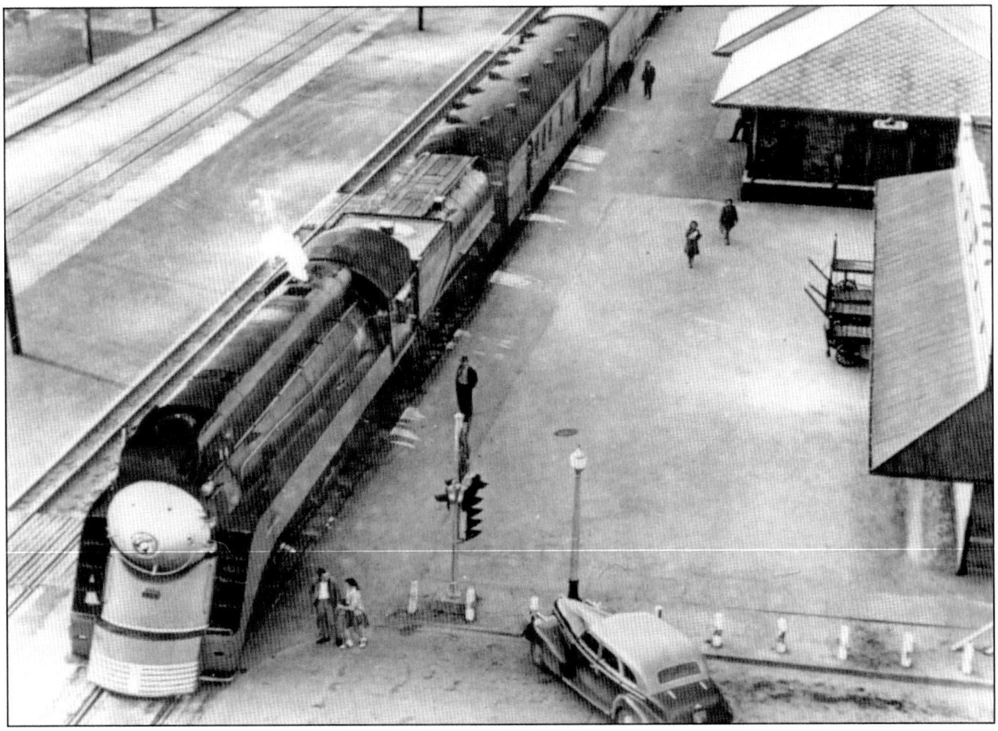

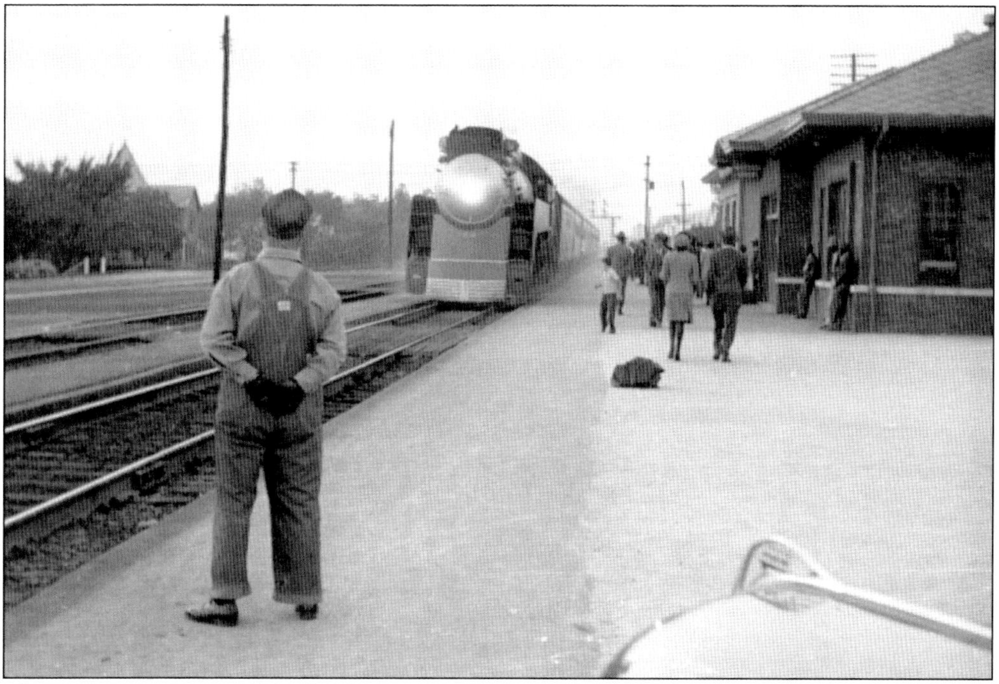

The Sunbeam was part of the landscape in Ennis, as in many other cities in Ellis County. Pictured above, a Sunbeam can be seen arriving at the Ennis depot in the late 1940s, with the passenger depot to the right and the Southern Pacific division headquarters visible to the left, with its prominent turret still a defining highlight of the city's skyline. Pictured below, Sunbeam engine No. 650 is at the Ennis depot. The sidewalk that once led to the stairs down to Northwest Main Street is seen in the left of the photograph. (Above, courtesy of Dane Williams, part of the Ford Curry Collection; below, courtesy of Eddie Luksa.)

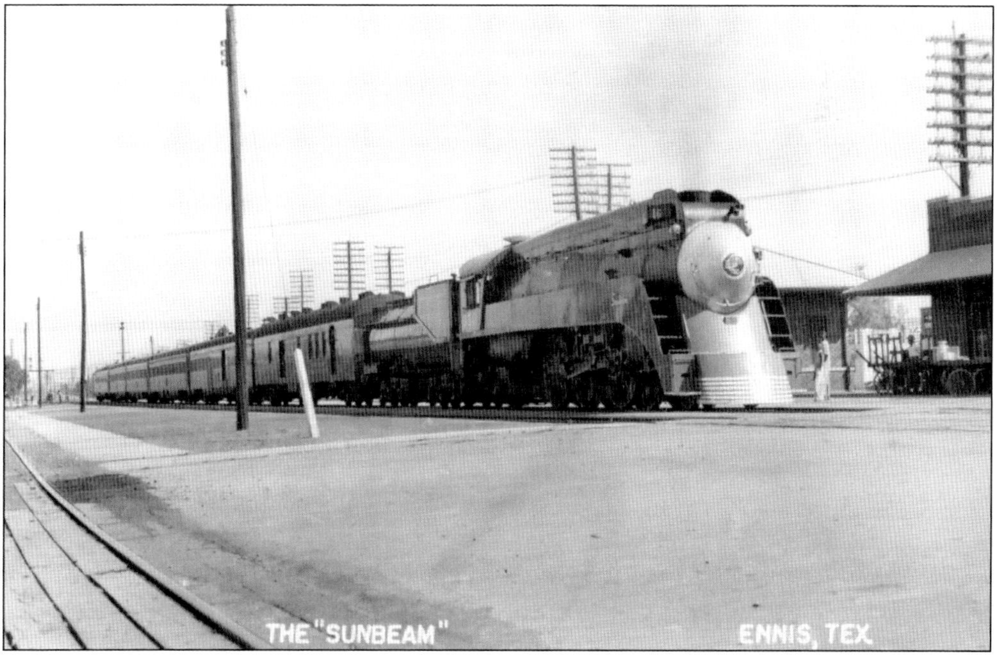

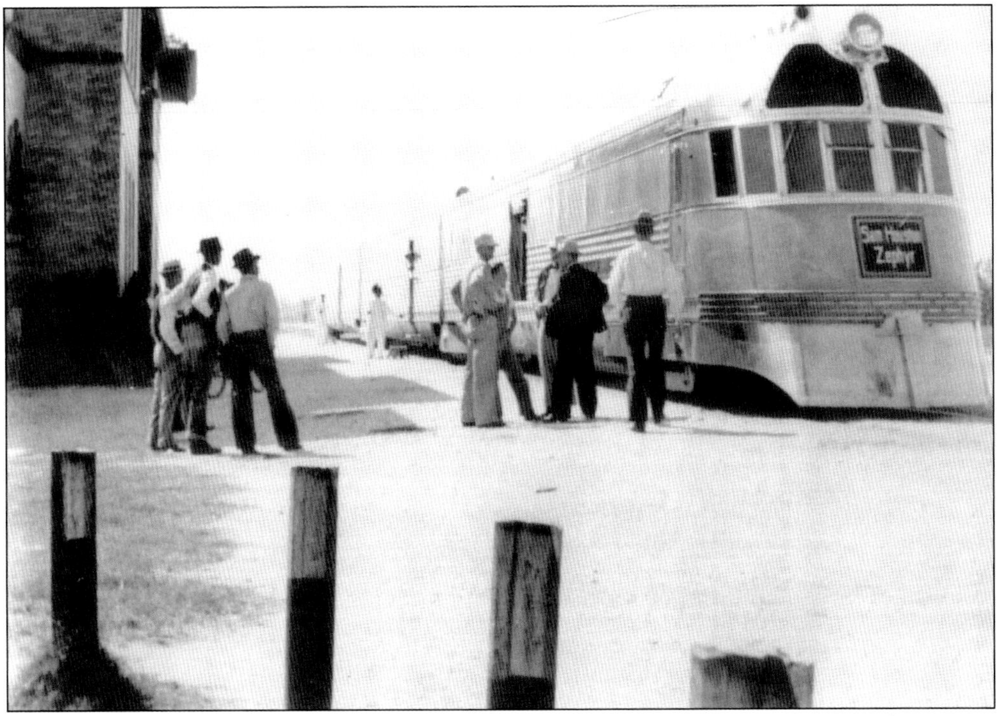

The diesel streamliners made the trip from Waxahachie to Houston in three hours, beginning around 1934. They had air-conditioning, dining cars, and art deco–style interiors. The Zephyr, pictured above, is one of many that made its way in the run through Waxahachie between Houston and Dallas and beyond. (Courtesy of Ellis County Museum.)

2

SOUTHWARD TRAINS — DALLAS SUBDIVISION — SOUTHWARD TRAINS

FOURTH CLASS	THIRD CLASS			Distance from St. Louis	TIME TABLE No. 26-A	Symbols and Capacity of Sidings	FIRST CLASS				
95 Way Freight	793 C. R. I. & P. Freight	181 Freight	775 C. R. I. & P. Freight		Effective 12:01 A. M. June 1, 1952		1 Passenger	7 Passenger	507 C. R. I. & P. Passenger	813 C. R. I. & P. Passenger	5 Passenger
Monday Wednesday Friday	Daily	Daily Except Sunday	Daily		STATIONS		Daily	Daily	Daily	Daily	Daily
AM 7.50		PM 5.30		767.0	N DALLAS YARD DY (0.2)	D F WPT YS					
				767.2	N DALLAS UT (2.1)	P	AM 7.45	AM 9.10	AM 9.25	PM 5.00	PM 10.45
AM 8.05	PM 9.00	PM **5.46**	PM 4.00	769.3	GC&SF Interlocking--CRI&P Jct. ENDOT (3.4)	P	AM 7.50	AM 9.15	AM 9.30	PM 5.05	PM 10.50
8.15	9.07	5.52	4.07	772.7	PEELER (9.0)	49 WP	7.54	9.19	9.34	**5.08**	10.54
8.39	9.25	6.10	**4.25**	781.7	N LANCASTER CA (5.3)	91 P	8.03	s 9.32	9.43	5.16	11.03
8.55	9.35	6.18	4.35	787.0	ELVA (4.2)	71 P	8.08	9.39	9.49	**5.27**	11.09
9.10	9.43	6.24	4.43	791.2	STERRETT (3.4)	84 P	8.12	9.47	9.53	5.32	11.13
9.20	9.50	6.30	4.50	794.6	TATE (2.0)	85 P	**8.15**	9.51	9.57	5.35	11.17
				796.6	N T&NO Interlocking HC (0.9)	P					
9.30	10.00 PM	6.40	5.00 PM	797.5	M-K-T JUNCTION (0.6)	NS	8.19	9.56	10.02 AM	5.40 PM	11.21
9.58		6.43		798.1	WAXAHACHIE (1.9)	57 WP	8.20	s **9.58**			s11.23
10.20		6.51		800.0	NELSON (4.3)	60 P	8.25	**10.08**			11.33
10.45		6.57		807.3	FORRESTON (5.8)	35 P	8.29	s10.15			11.38
11.15		**7.20**		813.1	D ITALY BG (5.2)	60 P	8.35	s10.25			11.44
11.45		7.28		818.3	D MILFORD M (7.5)	50 P	8.40	f10.34			11.49
PM 12.15		7.39		825.8	FRASER (7.4)	31 P	**8.48**	10.44			11.58
12.35		7.50		833.2	HILLSBORO (1.1)	Y P	8.57	s10.56			AM 12.07
12.40 PM		7.57 PM		834.3	N WINSLOW HB	Yard 64 P W	9.00 AM	11.00 AM			12.10 AM
95	793	181	775		(67.1)		1	7	507	813	5
13.9	28.2	27.5	28.2		Average speed per hour		53.7	36.6	49.1	45.5	47.4

Two Main Tracks — Auto Block Signals

No. 2 IS SUPERIOR TO ALL TRAINS

No. 1 IS SUPERIOR TO ALL TRAINS EXCEPT No. 2

Denison and Winslow will be initial and terminal stations for trains Nos. 1, 2, 5, 6, 7 and 8 on combined pages 1, 2 and 3 of the Dallas Subdivision.

The North Texas Division Employees Time Table for the Missouri-Kansas-Texas Railroad Company of Texas effective June 1, 1952, is pictured at left. Ellis County communities included on the schedule are Waxahachie, Nelson, Forreston, Italy, and Milford. Ellis County doctors listed in the time table as members of the employees hospital association included T. G. Estes, M. E. Hastings, and S. H. Watson of Waxahachie and A. O. Dykes of Italy. (Courtesy of Joe V. Pool.)

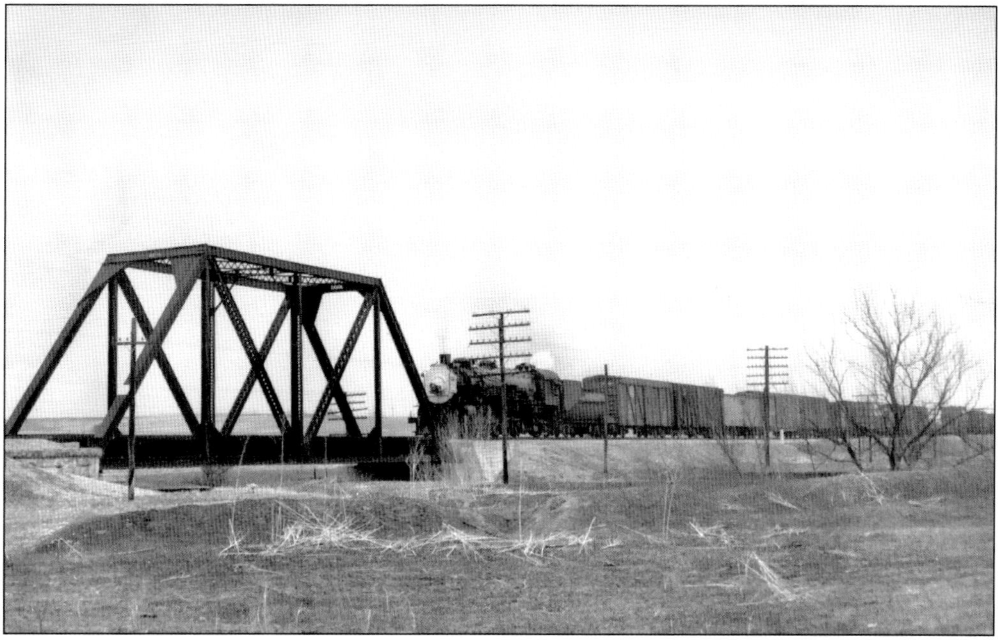

Engine No. 961, a Class F-1 engine, is coming up to 10-Mile Creek Bridge in Ferris as it hauls freight in February 1951. (Courtesy of Dane Williams, part of the Ford Curry Collection.)

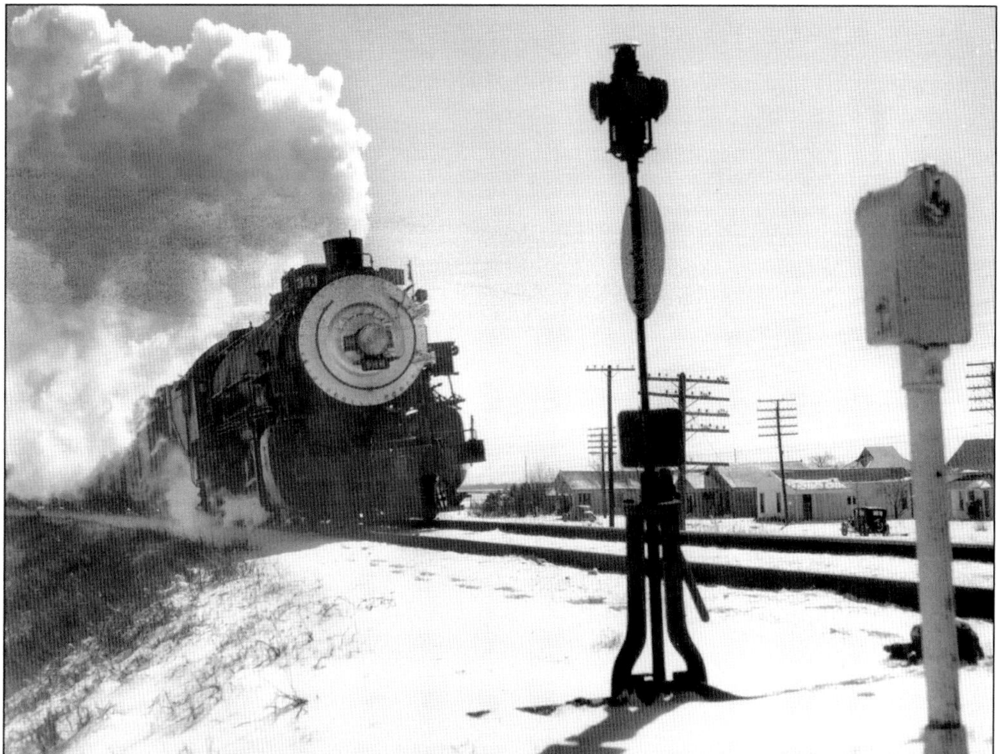

Engine No. 966 is heading south toward the Ennis Cotton Compress south of downtown Ennis in January 1953. (Courtesy of Joe V. Pool.)

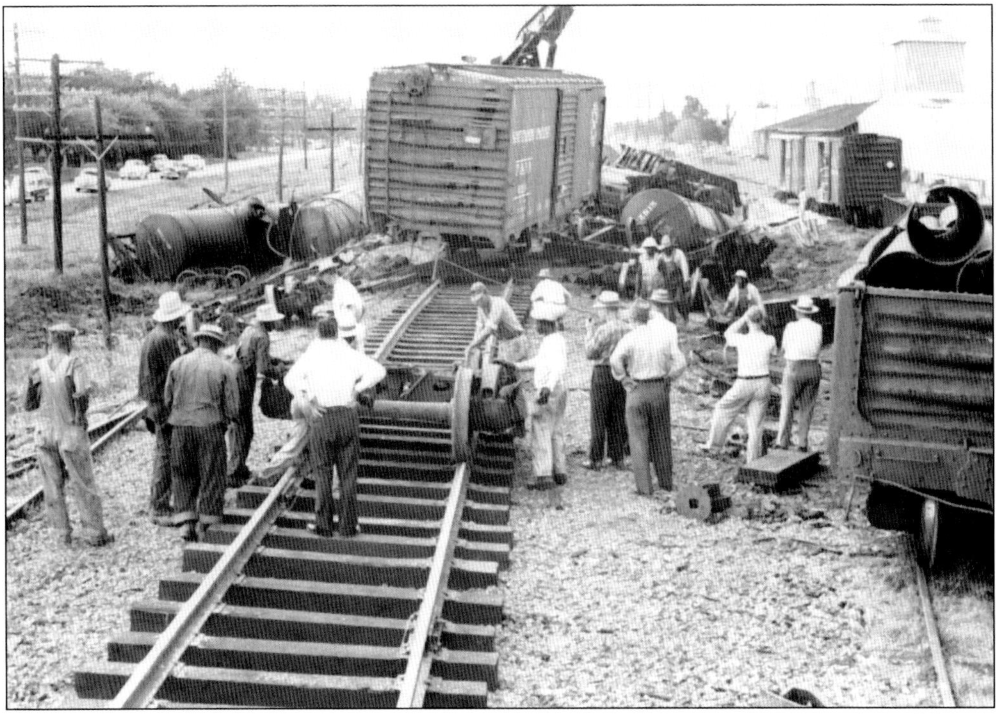

In late September 1955, a freight train accident closed the Dallas-Houston main line, delaying passenger trains overnight. An 85-car freight train wrecked at the switch near the Planters Cotton Oil Mill and Ennis Compress, both located to the south of the city. Seventeen cars of the northbound train piled up in the derailment. Scenes from the accident are pictured here. The Ennis Compress can be seen to the upper right of each photograph. (Both, courtesy of Dane Williams, part of the Ford Curry Collection.)

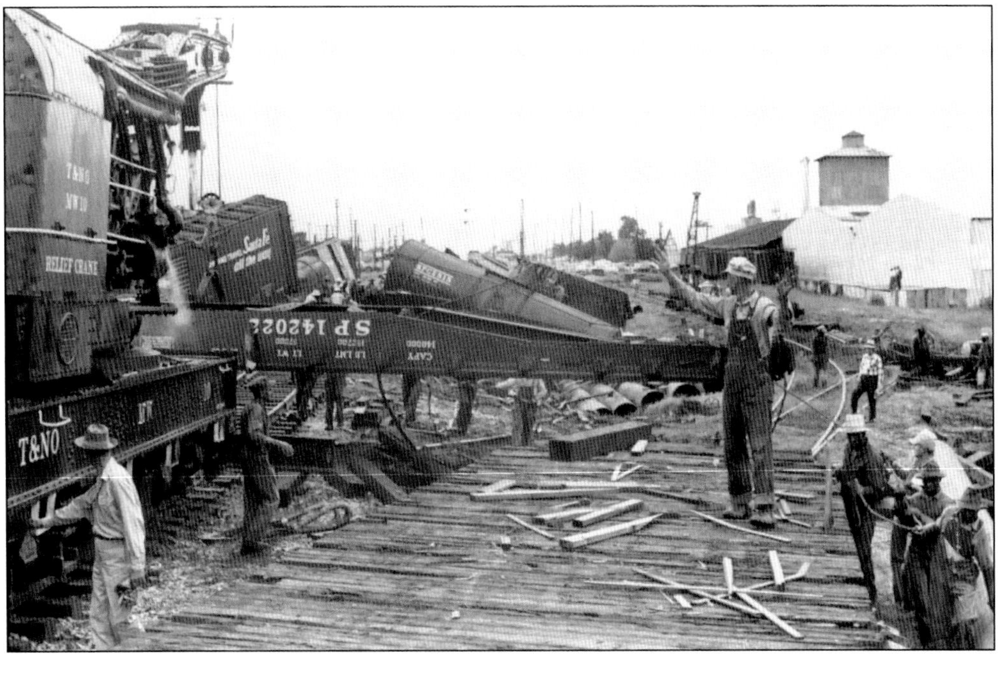

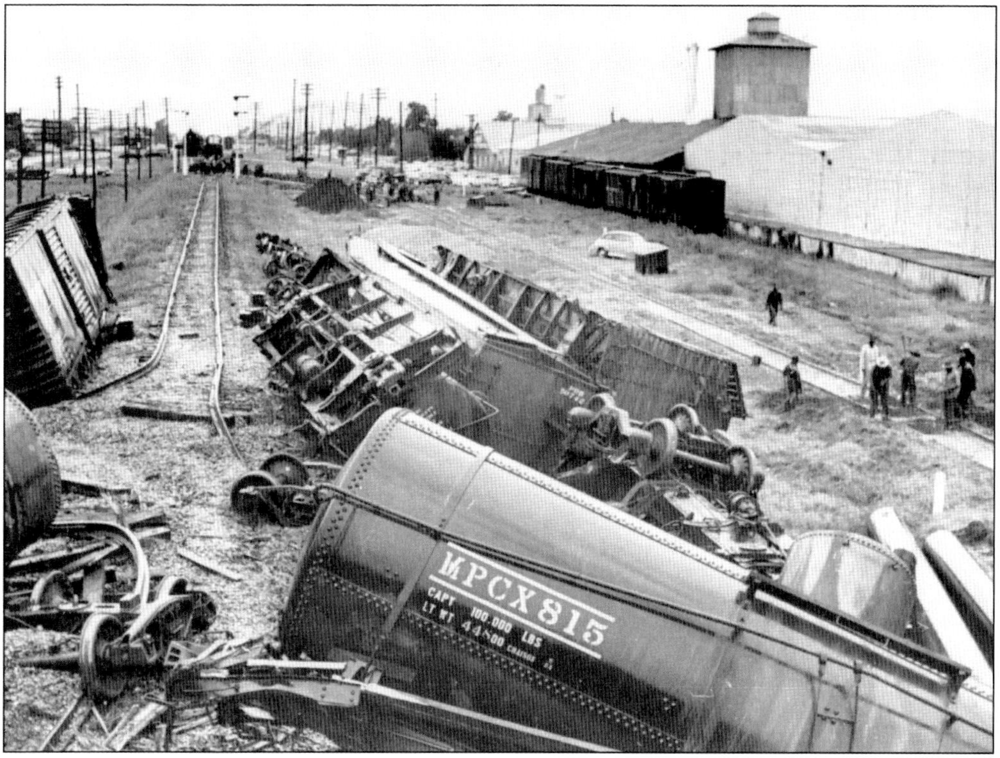

The division superintendant of the Southern Pacific Railroad, F. E. Hoefer, stated at the time that a faulty journal was the cause of the freight train accident near the Ennis Compress in September 1955 that shut down the main line. Both the engineer and conductor of the train, E. E. Whitacre and L. C. Vandaveer, were residents of Ennis. Despite the gravity of the accident, as pictured, there were no injuries. Above, in a north-looking view, the Ennis Compress is to the upper right of the photograph. Pictured below is the continuing clean up and repairs to the "Compress Curve" after the accident. (Both, courtesy of Dane Williams, part of the Ford Curry Collection.)

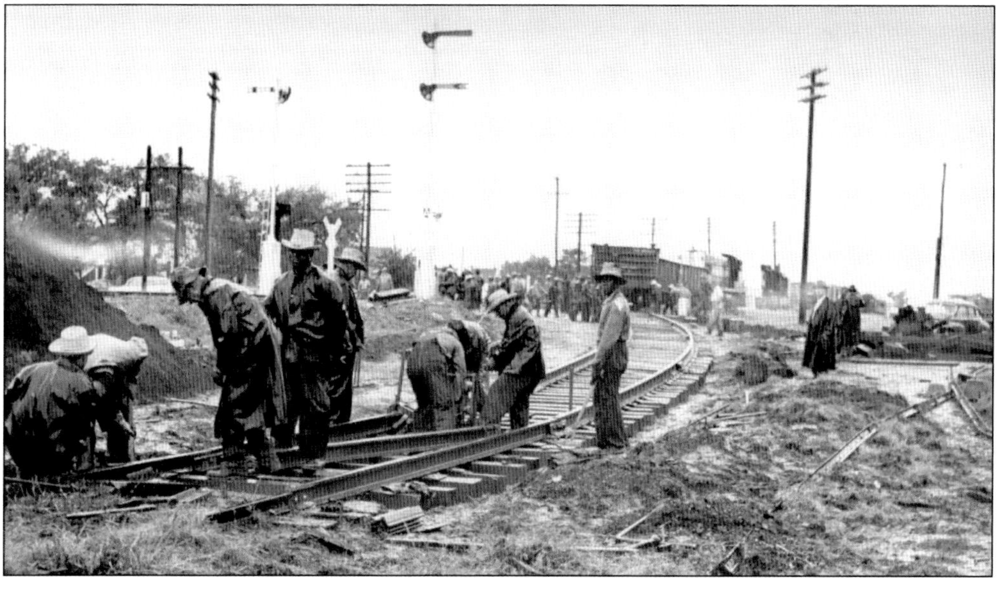

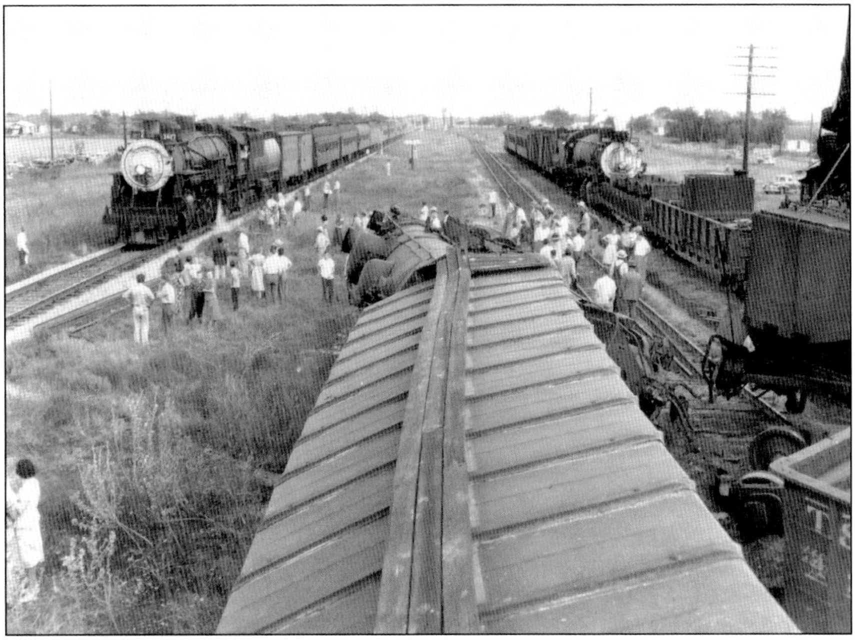

On September 16, 1949, the Fort Worth Local, with engine No. 974 pulling 75 cars, approached Garrett. Just over 2 miles north of Ennis, gravel inadvertently left on the outside rail by a grader caused the leading left front wheel of the locomotive engine to lift off the track, derailing several of the driving wheels, causing the engine to turn over. Engineer Archie Crane, filling in for O. K. Moreland, was scalded by escaping steam from the broken fountain valve of the boiler. He died later that night from his injuries. Fireman John R. Percival and two brakemen escaped without major injuries. Pictured above, Pacific No. 627 is passing the accident scene. Pictured below, officials and local residents are seen watching the efforts of the wrecker that has arrived from Ennis. (Both, courtesy of Dane Williams, part of the Ford Curry Collection.)

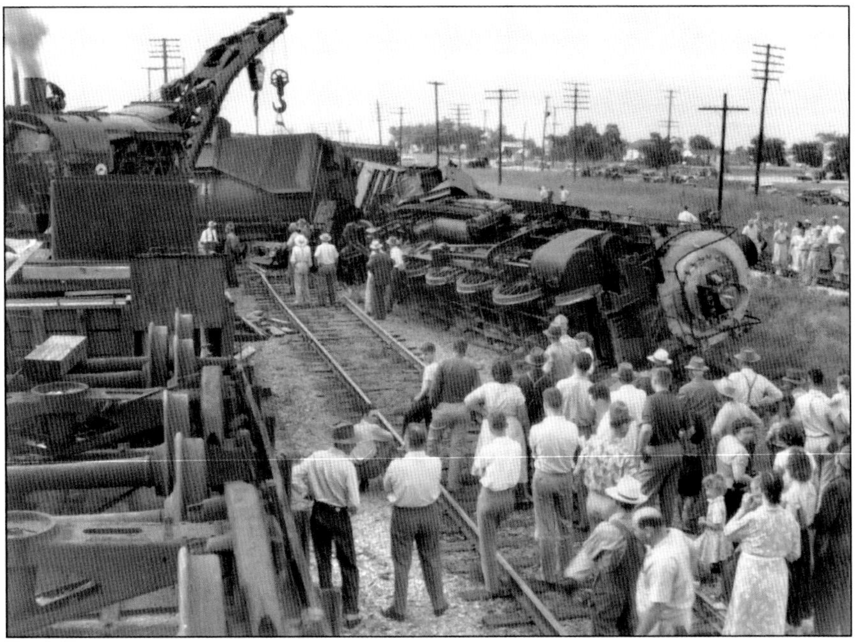

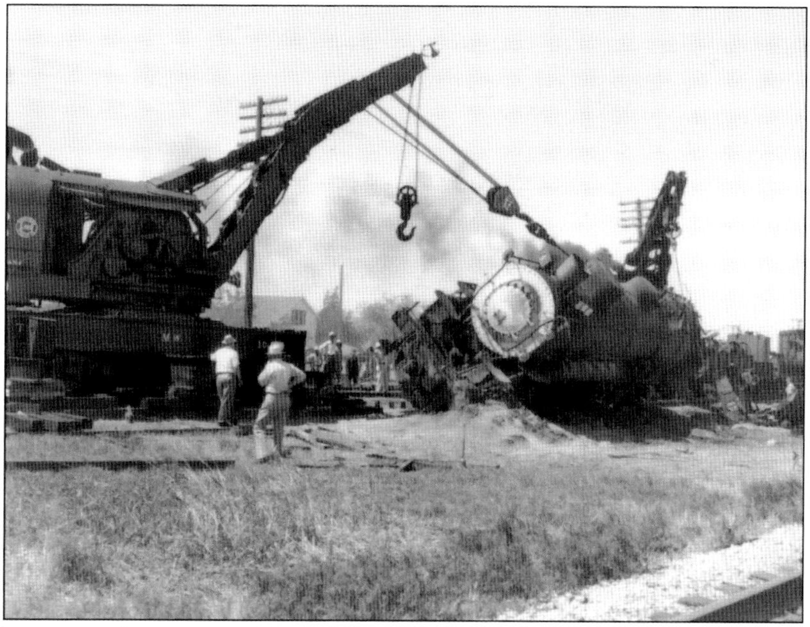

The 1949 train accident was not Garrett's first. On December 30, 1886, a northbound Houston and Texas Central passenger train collided with a freight train in Garrett. The freight train's caboose and three other cars were significantly damaged, as was the passenger trains engine. Passengers on the train were thrown from their seats by the impact and suffered slight bruises though some, including W. H. McGrain and the five-year-old son of a Mr. Darby, suffered more serious injuries. Also known to be on the train at the time of the accident were Col. W. H. Slemmins, a Mr. Ellison, and a Miss Stokes. Pictured are additional photographs of the 1949 Garrett accident as the wrecker continues to clear the track. (Both, courtesy of Dane Williams, part of the Ford Curry Collection.)

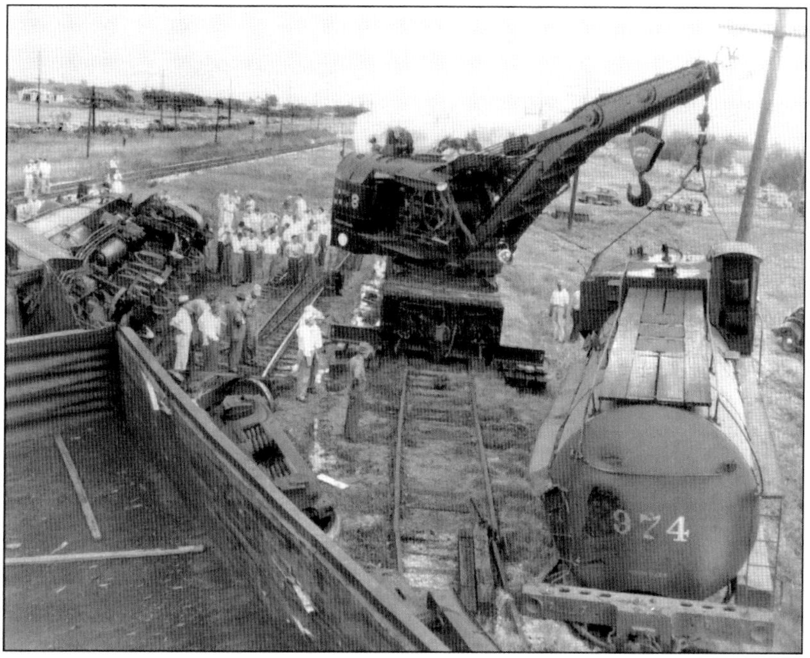

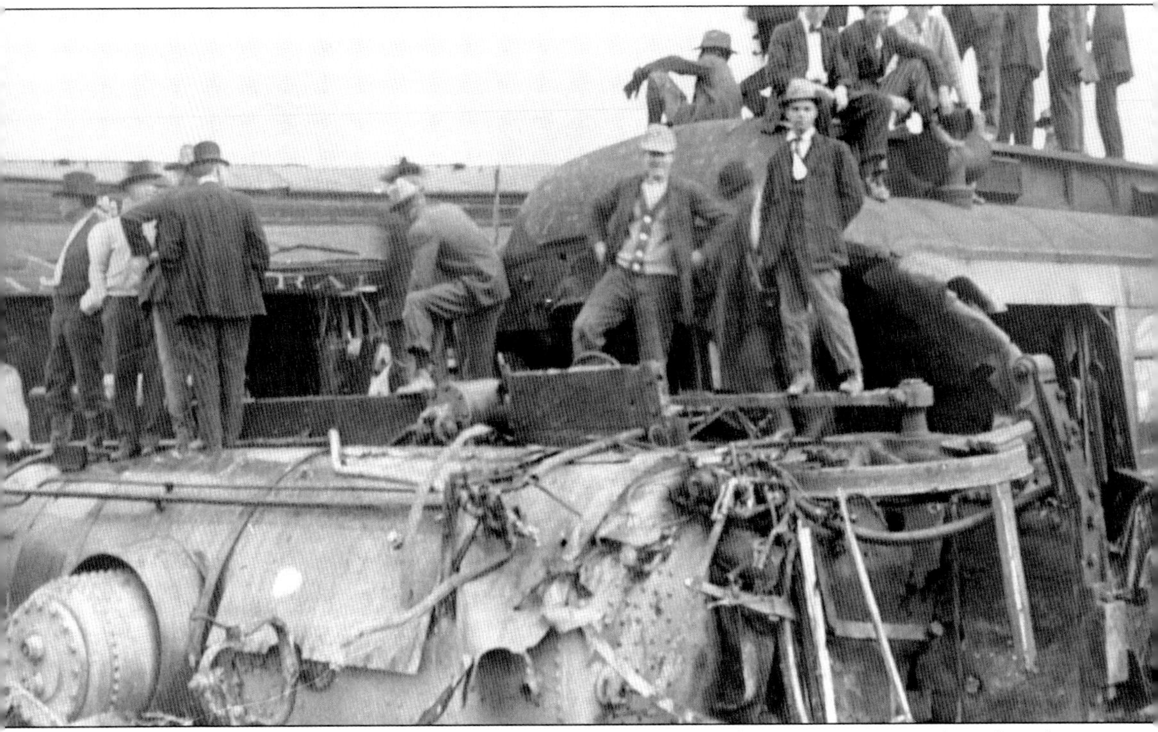

Railroad work was not without risks. Numerous men suffered serious injuries or lost their lives over the years. In 1888, J. L. Quinn, a Central and Northwestern Railroad employee, was killed after being dragged past Moffett's Mill in Waxahachie then falling across the track. John Bayle of Waxahachie and a section hand for the railroad, died in 1893 when he fell on the track while attempting to board a moving freight train. In 1905, just a few miles south of Ennis, a Houston and Texas Central engine blew up without warning, killing brakeman Monroe Glenn and engineer Jim Davenport. Fireman H. C. Traylor was seriously injured. All were from Ennis. In January 1907, fireman A. Garlinghouse was killed and engineer G. W. Haberlin seriously injured when the boiler exploded about 40 miles south of Ennis, where both were from. J. C. Hand, also from Ennis, was a fireman for the Houston and Texas Central Railroad. In 1911, he fell on the track when an engine came loose from the tank; the second engine and several cars ran over him, killing him instantly. (Courtesy of Ennis Fire Department.)

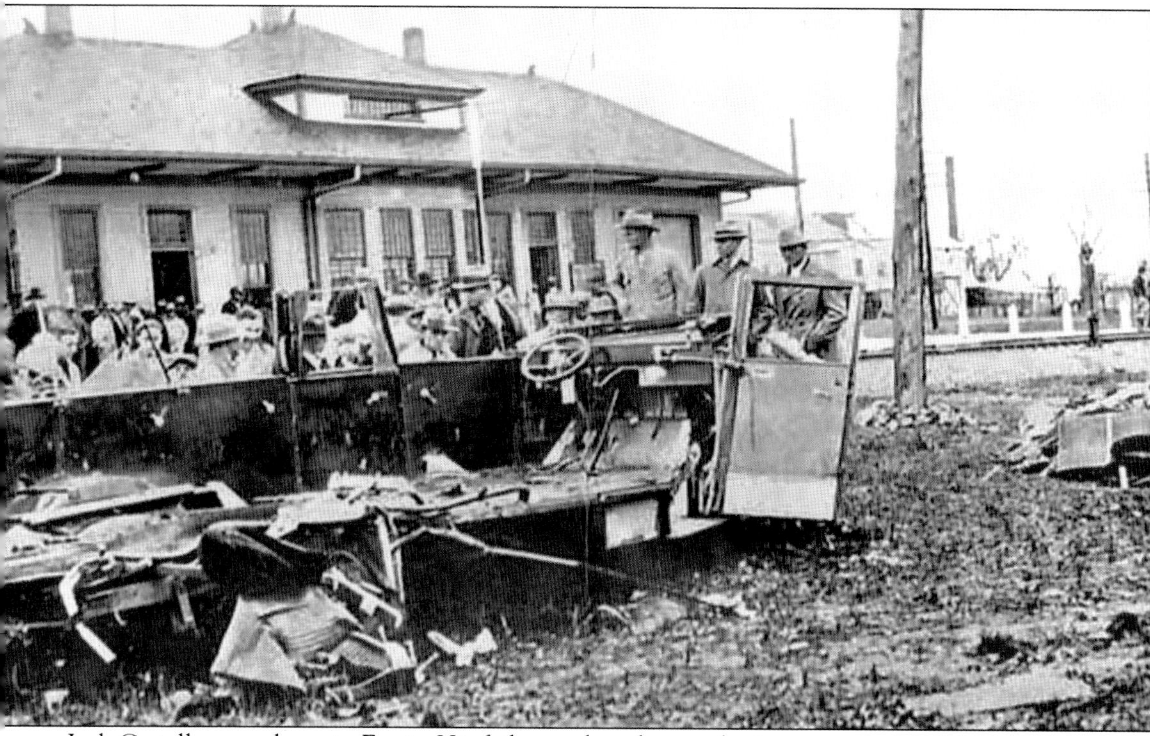

Jack Castellaw was born in Ennis. His father and uncle were business owners in the city, and both were active in civic affairs. His death in January 1927, along with nine others on the Baylor University basketball team, when the bus they were traveling on was hit by a train in Round Rock, Texas, had an impact in Ennis and beyond. Laws were changed as a result of the tragic accident, requiring overpasses and signal lights at railroad crossings, the first built in Texas where the accident took place in Round Rock. Decades later, his mother, Janie Pender Castellaw, donated more than $700,000 to Baylor University for the Castellaw School of Communications. To this day, the "Immortal 10" are honored yearly at Baylor University at a candle-light ceremony. (Courtesy of City of Ennis.)

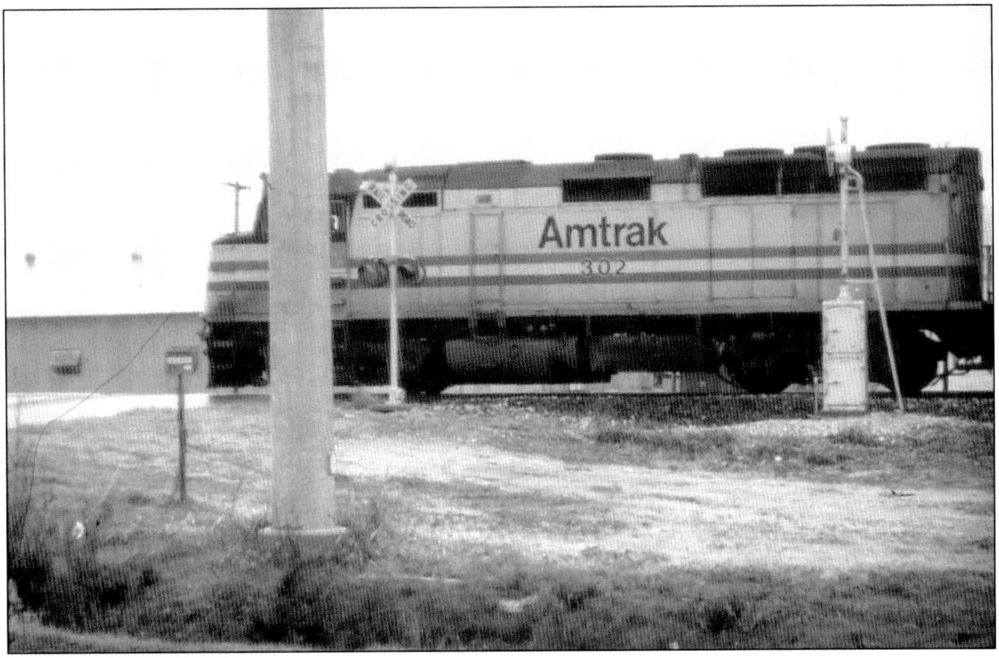

Amtrak passenger trains served Ellis County as well. Amtrak engine No. 302 is seen above as it travels north, coming up to the Lampasas Street crossing in Ennis, with conductor Joe V. Pool and engineer Gary K. Head on board. Pictured below, the same Amtrak train can be seen from a distance as it approaches the crossing in December 1988. (Both, courtesy of Sugar Glaspy.)

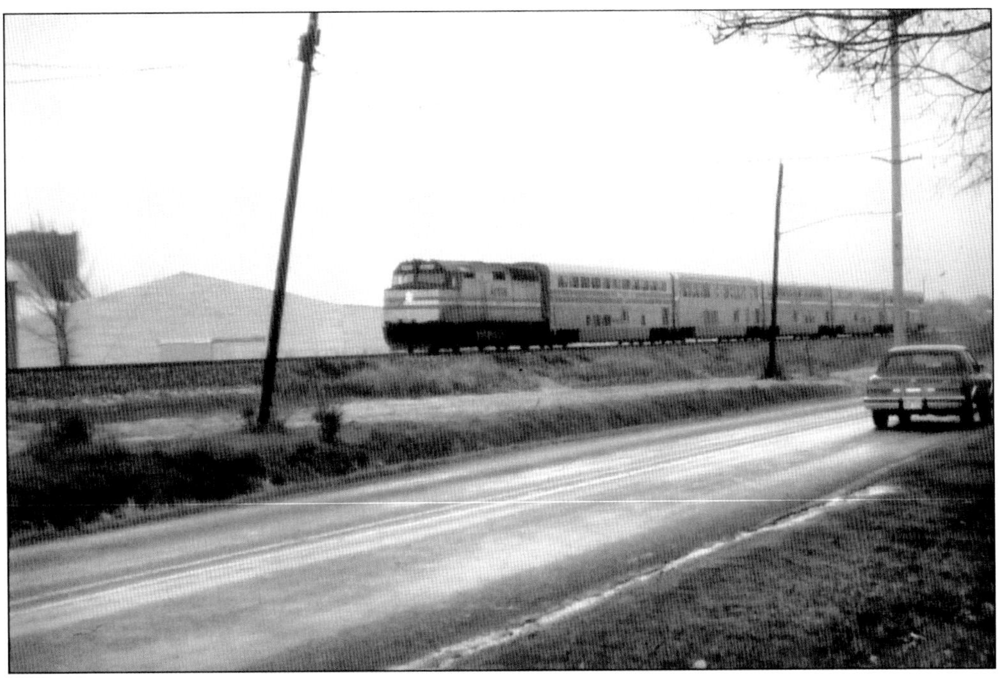

Seven

The People of the Rail

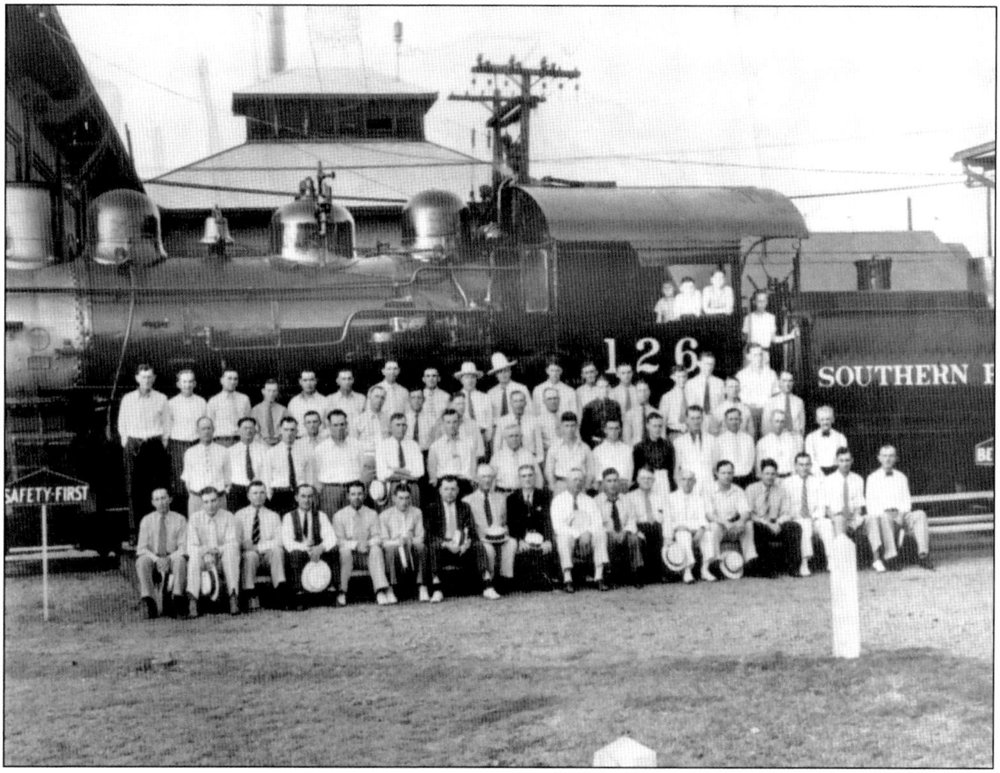

It is the 1930s. There are changes to come. With a Southern Pacific Railroad steam engine at their back, the Ennis roundhouse to their left, and the shop yard office in the background, they have gathered for a photograph. Pictured from left to right are (first row) A. E. Mahan, S. A. Turbeville, Joe Hubacek, Joe Rogala, Lewis Baldridge, E. J. Jilek, Gordon Lyon, John Simpson, W. M. Donahue, T. M. Spence, T. H. Leatham, Alfred Rawlins, D. R. Prince, George Hedrick, James Taylor, Alan McEver, unidentified, and Joe Schramek; (second row) Tom Phifer, Fred Calhoun, Charlie Zaludek, Theodore Farrar, William Harris, Fred Norman, Paddy Schramek, George Bolen, Lloyd Smith, Clois Bennight, Billy Percival, John Ensor, T. Williams, Jim Walker, and Frank Schwab; (third row starting behind W. E. Harris and Fred Norman) Walter Owens, R. Parkins, B. O. Brown, unidentified, Tom Riss, Buster Norman, Emmitt Alexander, T. F. Lindle (behind Togy Williams), and Henry Hough; (fourth row) unidentified, J. L. Nelson, Tom Collier, Dick Powers, Gus Hernandez, W. P. Petermann, Bill Martin, Philip Martinez, Ronald Percival, Martin Rogala, Charles Toal, Will Mathews, John Kouba, Carl Holder, unidentified, Yancy Sweatman, (in cab) Skip Taylor, Bryant Leatham, and two unidentified. (Courtesy of Eddie Luksa.)

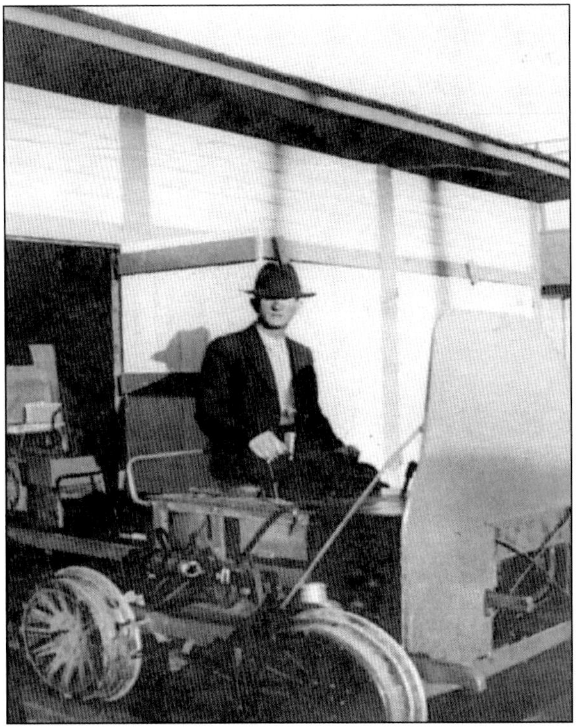

Motorcars were used by the Southern Pacific Railroad as a means of transportation for the section crews. It provided the means to reaching tracks in need of repair. They were capable of pulling a flatbed car if necessary. Pictured is motorcar repairman W. T. Pierce of the Southern Pacific Railroad, Dallas division. His territory extended from Houston to Denison and from Fort Worth to Paris. (Courtesy of City of Ennis.)

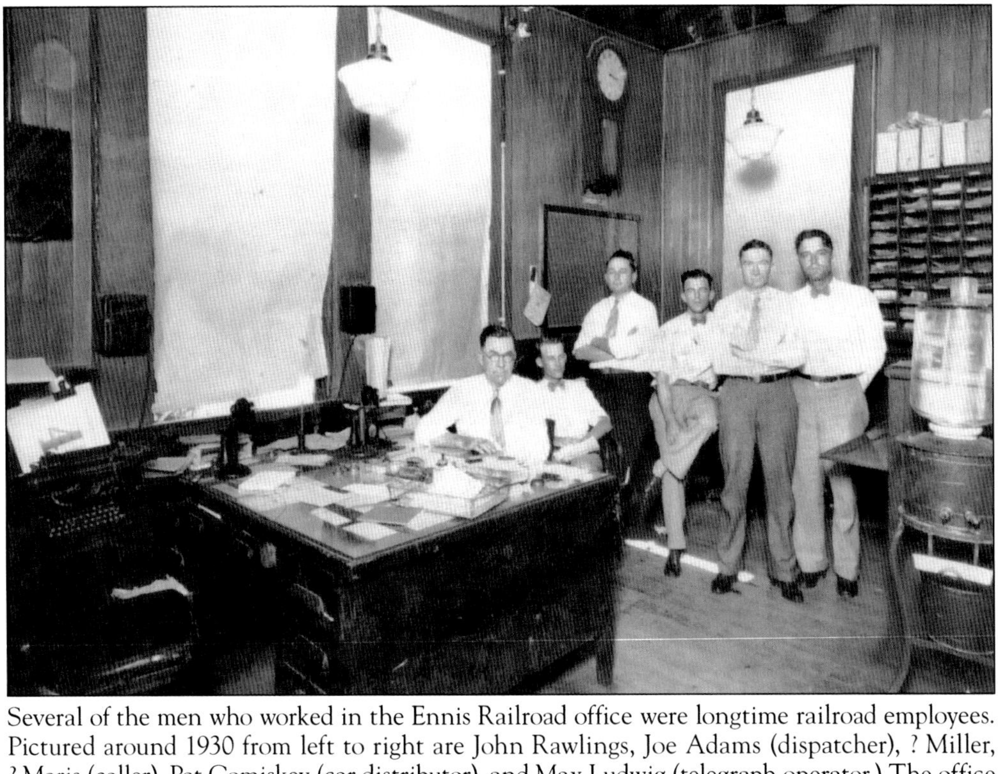

Several of the men who worked in the Ennis Railroad office were longtime railroad employees. Pictured around 1930 from left to right are John Rawlings, Joe Adams (dispatcher), ? Miller, ? Maris (caller), Pat Comiskey (car distributor), and Max Ludwig (telegraph operator.) The office was located at the north end of the platform. (Courtesy of City of Ennis.)

A. Q. Williams, pictured at right around 1940, began with the Texas and New Orleans Railroad in 1937 as a brakeman on passenger trains. Some of the earlier brakemen with the Houston and Texas Central Railroad in Ennis from the 1870s and 1880s included J. I. Bennett, Joe Brenham, and Owen Johnson. Ed Vaughn of Waxahachie was also an early railroad brakeman. (Courtesy of Dane Williams, part of the Ford Curry Collection.)

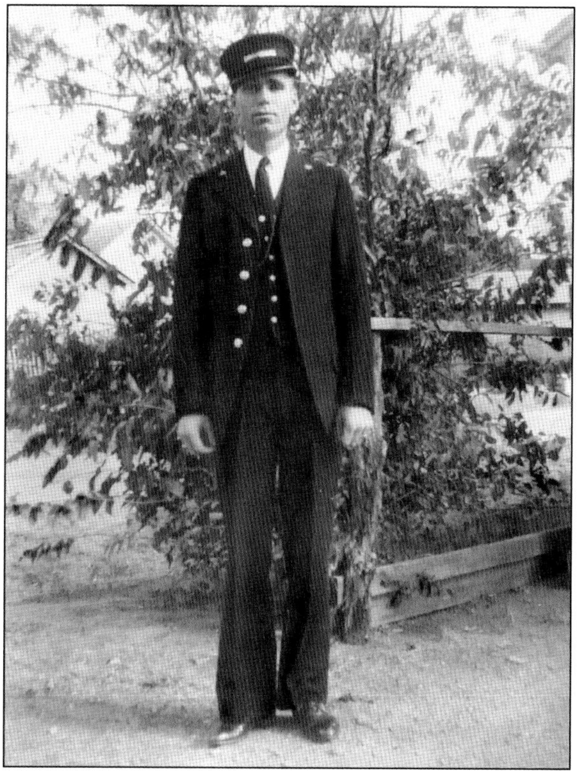

AGREEMENT

Between

Southern Pacific Lines In Texas and Louisiana

(Texas and New Orleans Railroad Company)

(Lines of: The Houston & Texas Central Railroad Company

Texas Midland Railroad

The Galveston, Harrisburg & San Antonio Railway Company (Austin Division))

and the

Brotherhood of Railroad Trainmen

Effective February 1, 1953

(Wage Rates in Effect March 1, 1951)

ARTICLE 1.

PASSENGER SERVICE–BRAKEMEN

SECTION 1. Passenger districts for regular or irregular service, according to assignment or operation of service, to be as follows:

Between	Monthly Rate	Mileage Rate (Cents)	Daily Rate	Month's Work
Houston and Ennis	$343.50	7.634	$11.45	4500 Miles or less
Ennis and Denison	343.50	7.634	11.45	4500 Miles or less
Ennis and Ft. Worth via Dallas	343.50	7.634	11.45	4500 Miles or less
Mexia and Dallas	343.50	7.634	11.45	4500 Miles or less
San Antonio and Hearne	343.50	7.634	11.45	4500 Miles or less
San Antonio and Dallas	343.50	7.634	11.45	4500 Miles or less

1

Pictured is the cover page of the 1953 edition of the published "Agreement Between Southern Pacific Lines in Texas and Louisiana and the Brotherhood of Railroad Trainmen." The agreement covers topics including pay, seniority, responsibilities, crew runs, freight, switching, and other topics such as a troop train agreement. (Courtesy of Jim and Helen Templin.)

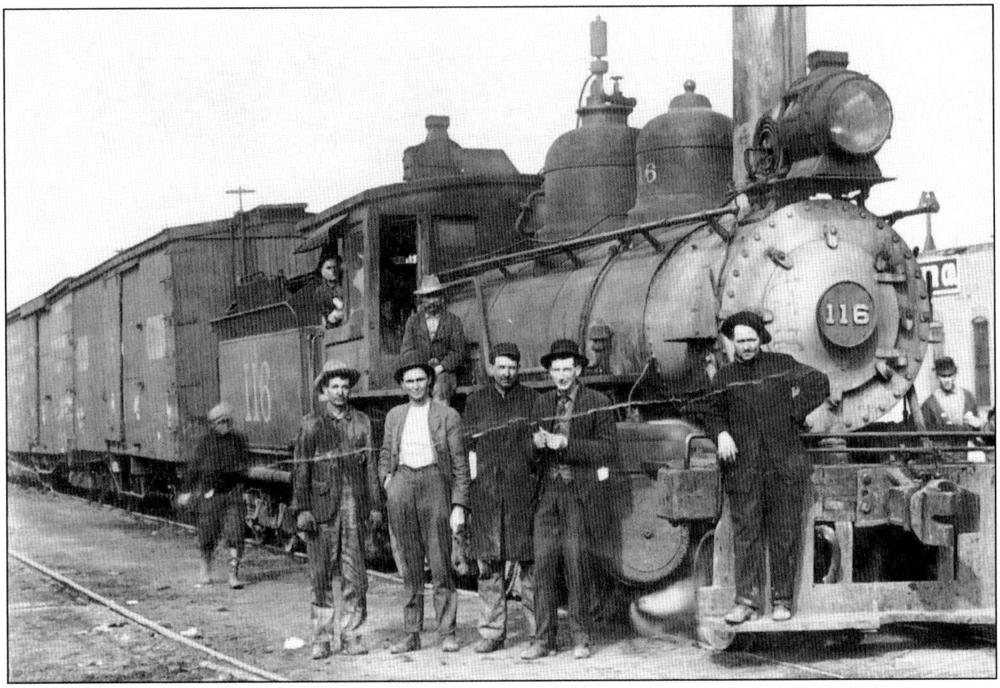

Pat Connolly stands on the cowcatcher of Engine No. 116 in Ennis, pictured above around 1920. He was a brakeman for the Houston and Texas Central Railroad. Cowcatchers served a vital purpose. Should any object, including cows, present a danger of impeding the forward movement of the train, the cowcatcher deflected and moved the object out of the path of the train, preventing potentially dangerous collisions. Pictured below are a number of early employees of the roundhouse and machine shops in Ennis standing outside the facility next to engine No. 968. (Above, courtesy of City of Ennis; below, courtesy of Ennis Public Library.).

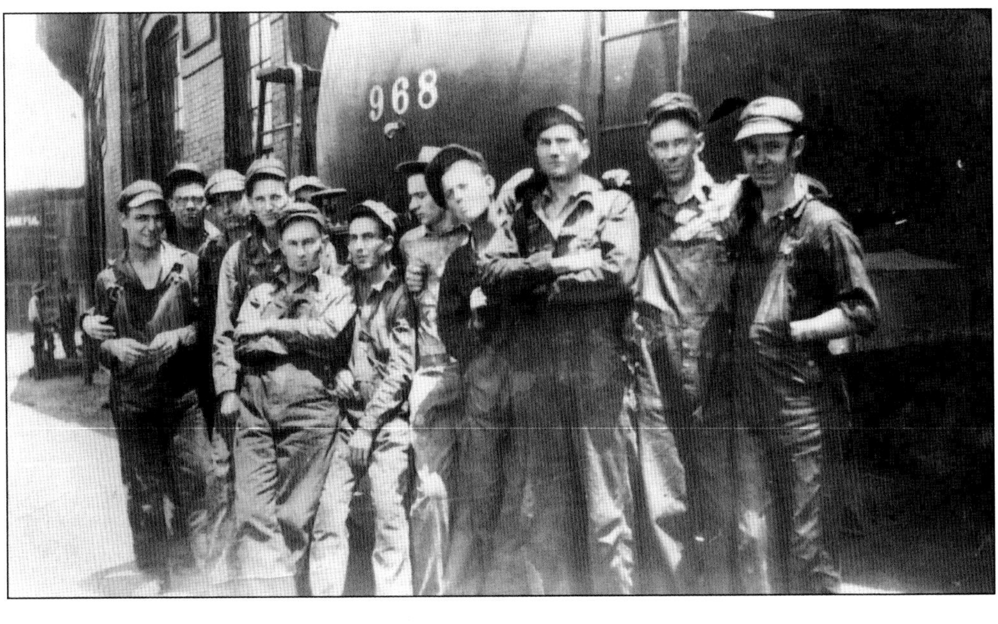

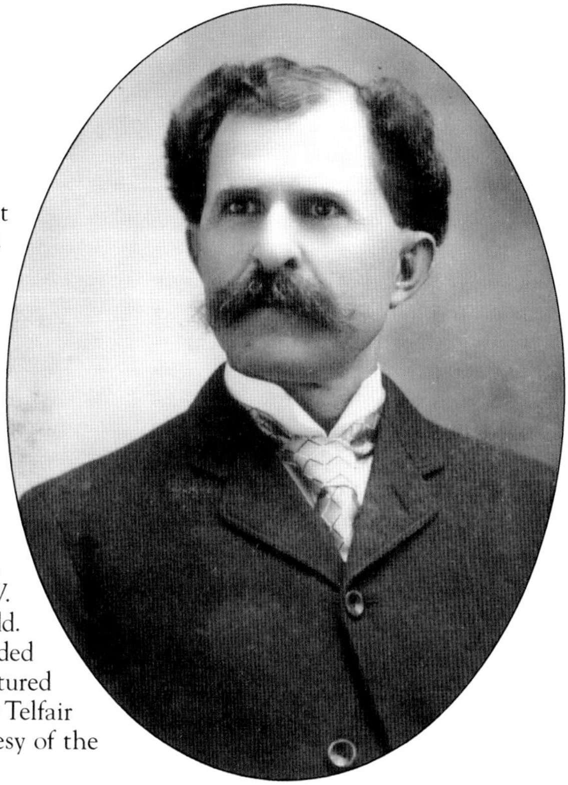

John Spier Telfair, pictured at right around 1900, came to Ennis in the 1890s as a conductor with the Houston and Texas Central Railroad. He worked for the railroad his entire career. In May 1895, Telfair and other area conductors, including H. P. Barkley, S. H. Clanton, W. G. Griffith, and C. E. McDuffie, represented the Ennis division at the Conductors' Convention in Atlanta, Georgia. Other early conductors from Ennis included C. L. Backloup, C. Farriss, John Lockhart, D. McKnight, Fred Neal, W. L. Spann, W. E. Shipp, W. Snodgrass, W. E. Spellman, George Todd, and Sam Todd. Early conductors from Waxahachie included Charles R. West and Clint Winkler. Pictured below are the lanterns and gun carried by Telfair during his railroad career. (Both, courtesy of the Telfair family.)

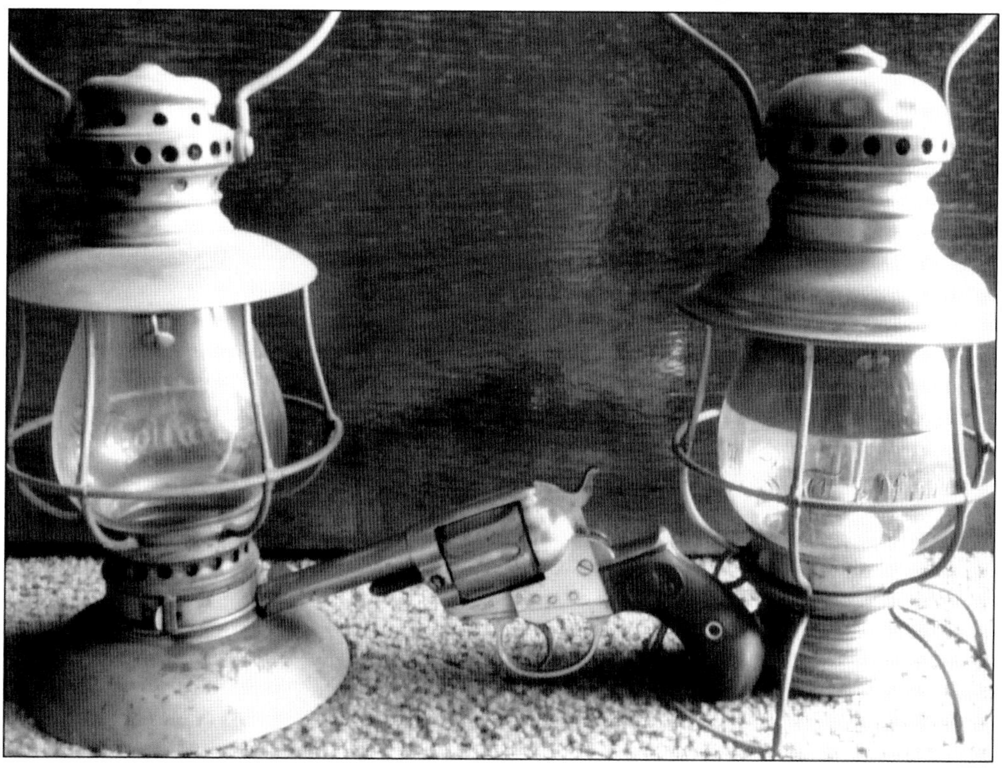

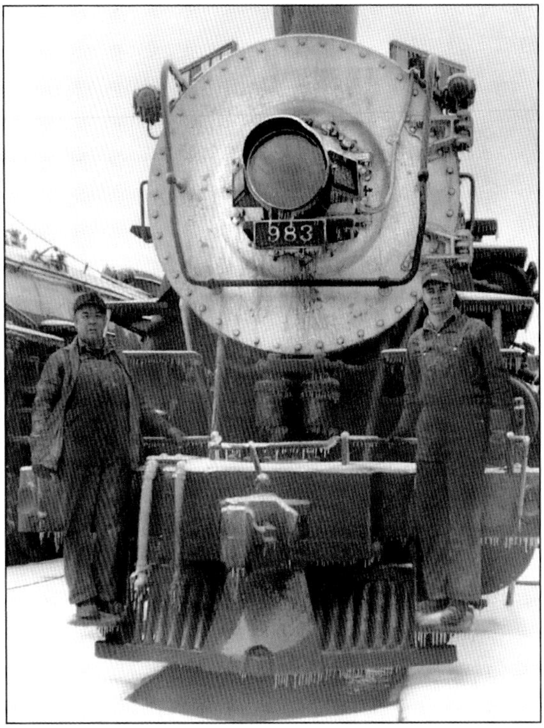

Pictured on engine No. 983 are Gus Hernandez (left) and Rookie Farrar. Farrar was an apprentice with the railroad; Hernandez was a machinist and retired after a long career with the railroad. (Courtesy of Dane Williams, part of the Ford Curry Collection.)

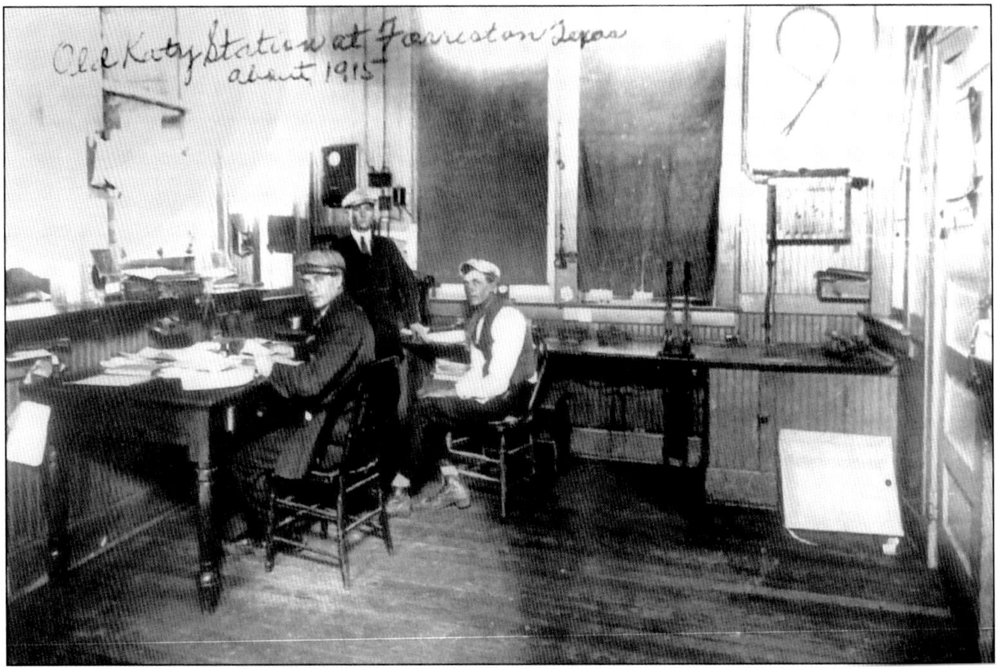

Forreston was first known as Howe's Settlement, named for its first settler, William R. Howe, who arrived in 1843. The Missouri-Kansas-Texas Railroad, arrived in Forreston 50 years later in the early 1890s. Capt. Carr Forest, the first postmaster of the community donated the land for the depot. Pictured inside the depot around 1915 are, from left to right, a Mr. Lowe (agent), Clarence Bohanon (assistant agent), and Bill Worley. (Courtesy of Ellis County Museum.)

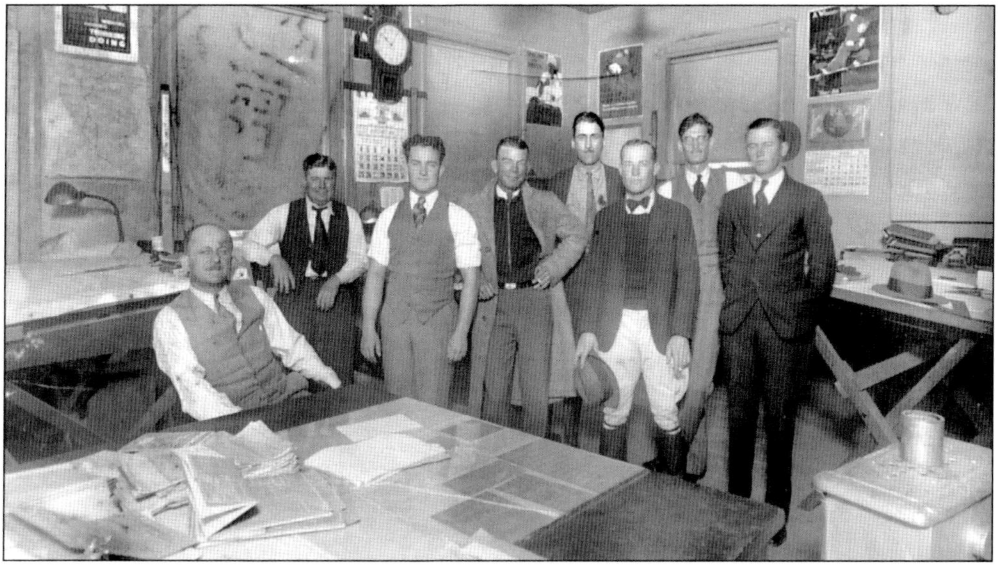

On December 31, 1930, several members of the Ennis engineering force gathered at the division headquarters in Ennis. Pictured from left to right are Herbert Fisher (assistant division engineer,) Lee Loggins (instrument man), ? Barney, Joe Rosson (rodman), A. C. Wright (instrument man), Murry Doyle (rodman), Marvin Stephens (office engineer), and Robert McDowal (rodman). (Courtesy of Ennis Public Library.)

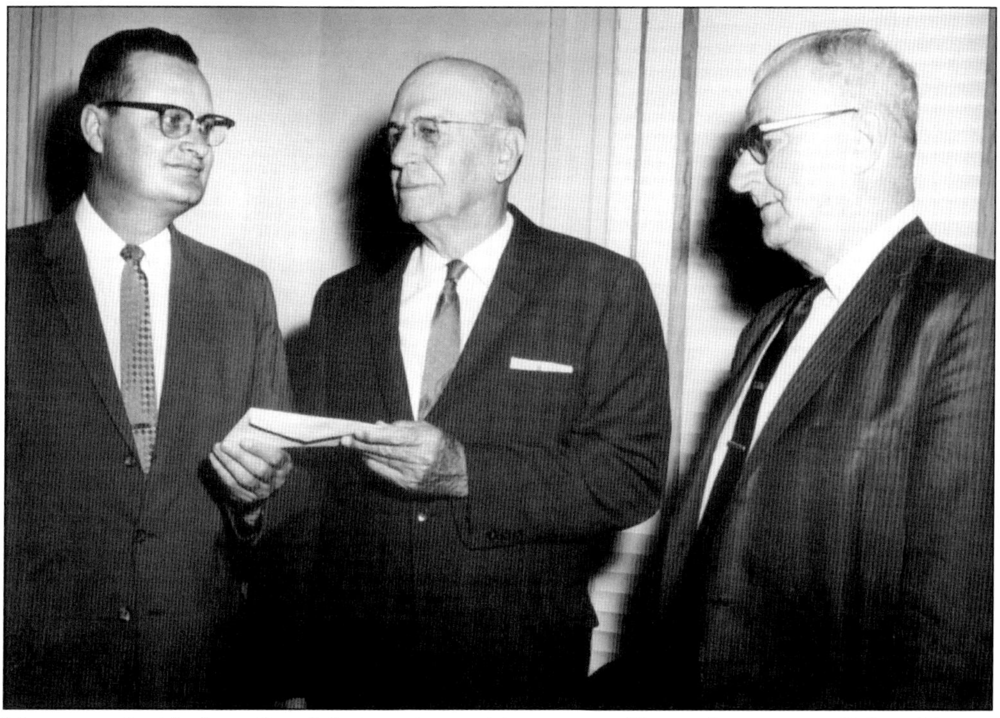

Many stayed with the railroad their entire working careers. Pictured is engineer Robert Hinton Ridley at his retirement after 43 years with the railroad, from 1920 to 1963. From left to right are superintendant L. A. Patterson, Robert Hinton "Bob" Ridley, and O. D. Beckman. (Courtesy of Ennis Public Library.)

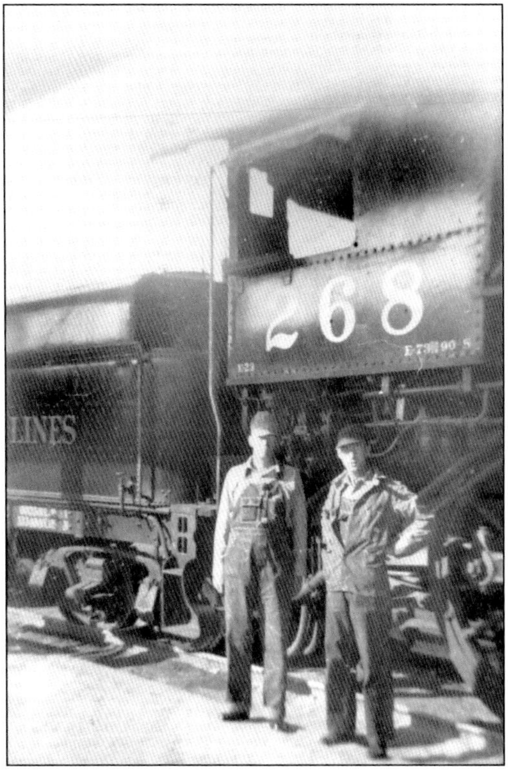

Standing in front of steam engine No. 268 is railroad engineer Robert Hinton Ridley (left) and an unidentified coworker. Some of the earliest engineers from Ennis included R. A. Booth and Eusebe Lalumiere, both of whom were with the Houston and Texas Central Railroad in the mid-1870s. Richard Gwalkney began with the rail in the 1880s. Edward Spaulding was a locomotive engineer in the late 1800s from Waxahachie. (Courtesy of the Ennis Public Library.)

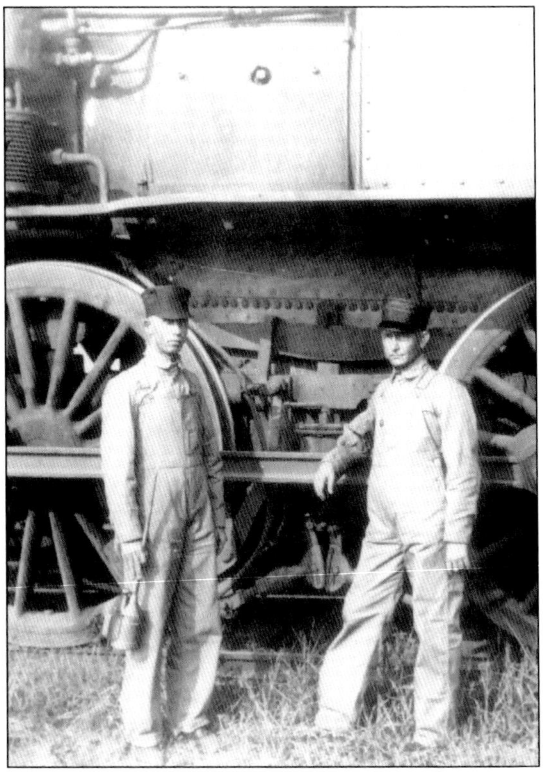

Waxahachie railroad engineer, J. M. Stevens (left) holds an oil can used to oil his locomotive. The drive wheels of the locomotive, as tall as Stevens himself, were necessary to achieve the high speeds on crack passenger runs. (Courtesy of Ellis County Museum.)

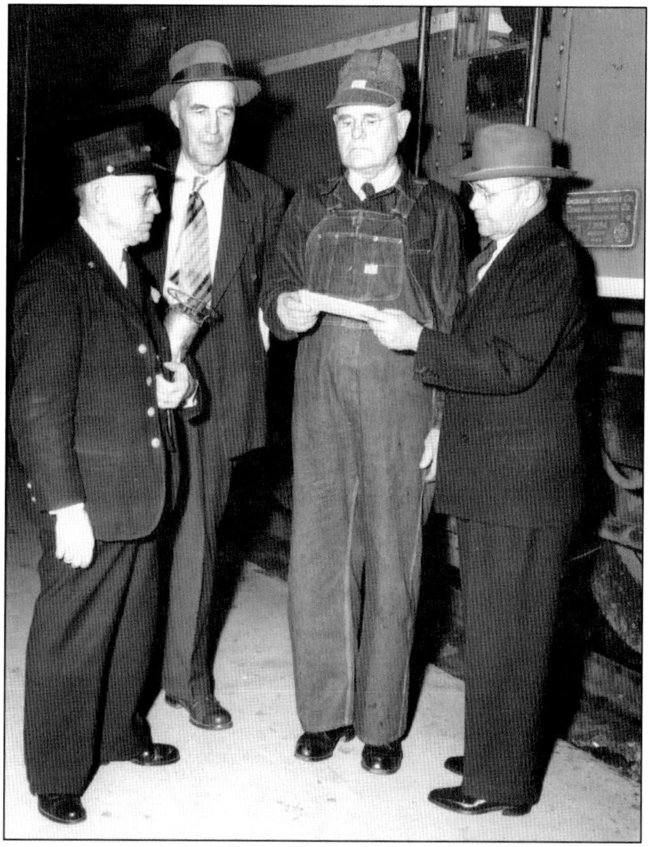

On March 31, 1950, engineer P. E. Duncan of Ennis made his last run on train No. 13, a Sunbeam, before retiring upon his return to Ennis. With him after his final trip are, from left to right, conductor Sam Curry, Carlisle Parish, P. E. Duncan, and F. E. Hoefer, the division superintendant. Below is engineer W. Henson on another Sunbeam, train No. 652. (Right, courtesy of Dane Williams; part of the Ford Curry Collection; below, courtesy of Ennis Public Library.)

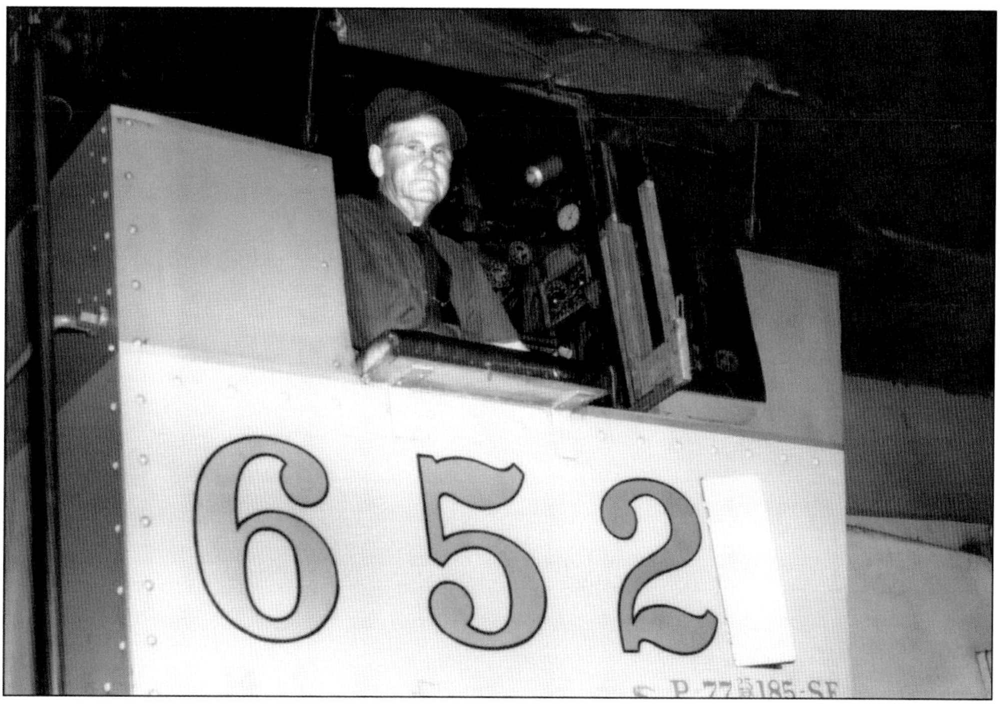

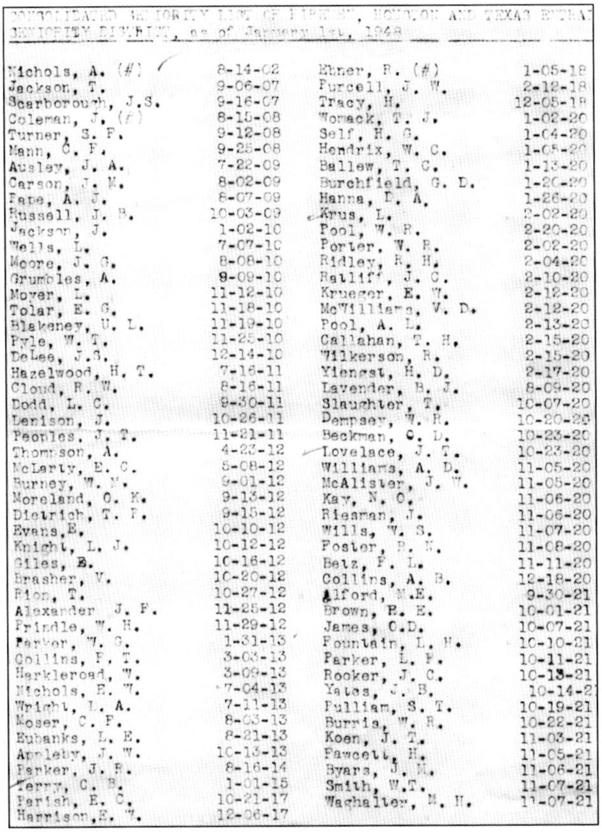

CONSOLIDATED SENIORITY LIST OF FIREMEN, HOUSTON AND TEXAS CENTRAL SENIORITY DISTRICT, as of January 1st, 1948

Nichols, A. (#)	8-14-02	Ebner, R. (#)	1-05-18
Jackson, T.	9-06-07	Purcell, J. W.	2-12-18
Scarborough, J.S.	9-16-07	Tracy, H.	12-05-18
Coleman, J. (#)	8-15-08	Womack, T. J.	1-02-20
Turner, S. F.	9-12-08	Self, H. G.	1-04-20
Mann, C. F.	9-25-08	Hendrix, W. C.	1-05-20
Ausley, J. A.	7-22-09	Ballew, T. C.	1-13-20
Carson, J. M.	8-02-09	Burchfield, G. D.	1-20-20
Pape, A. J.	8-07-09	Hanna, D. A.	1-26-20
Russell, J. B.	10-03-09	Krus, L.	2-02-20
Jackson, J.	1-02-10	Pool, W. R.	2-20-20
Wells, L.	7-07-10	Porter, W. R.	2-02-20
Moore, J. G.	8-08-10	Ridley, R. H.	2-04-20
Grumbles, A.	8-09-10	Ratliff, J. C.	2-10-20
Moyer, L.	11-12-10	Krueger, E. W.	2-12-20
Tolar, E. G.	11-18-10	McWilliams, V. D.	2-12-20
Blakeney, U. L.	11-19-10	Pool, A. L.	2-13-20
Pyle, W. T.	11-25-10	Callahan, T. H.	2-15-20
DeLee, J.S.	12-14-10	Wilkerson, R.	2-15-20
Hazelwood, H. T.	7-16-11	Yiengst, H. D.	2-17-20
Cloud, R. W.	8-16-11	Lavender, B. J.	8-09-20
Dodd, L. C.	9-30-11	Slaughter, T.	10-07-20
Denison, J.	10-26-11	Dempsey, W. R.	10-20-20
Peoples, J. T.	11-21-11	Beckman, C. D.	10-23-20
Thompson, A.	4-23-12	Lovelace, J. T.	10-23-20
McLarty, E. C.	5-08-12	Williams, A. D.	11-05-20
Burney, W. M.	9-01-12	McAlister, J. W.	11-05-20
Moreland, O. K.	9-13-12	Kay, N. O.	11-06-20
Dietrich, T. F.	9-15-12	Riesman, J.	11-06-20
Evans, E.	10-10-12	Wills, W. S.	11-07-20
Knight, L. J.	10-12-12	Foster, R. N.	11-08-20
Giles, B.	10-16-12	Betz, F. L.	11-11-20
Brasher, V.	10-20-12	Collins, A. B.	12-18-20
Rion, T.	10-27-12	Alford, M.E.	9-30-21
Alexander J. F.	11-25-12	Brown, R. E.	10-01-21
Prindle, W. H.	11-29-12	James, C.D.	10-07-21
Parker, W. G.	1-31-13	Fountain, L. H.	10-10-21
Collins, F. T.	3-03-13	Parker, L. F.	10-11-21
Harkleroad, W.	3-09-13	Rooker, J. C.	10-13-21
Nichols, E. W.	7-04-13	Yates, J. B.	10-14-21
Wright, L. A.	7-11-13	Pulliam, S. T.	10-19-21
Moser, C. F.	8-03-13	Burris, W. R.	10-22-21
Eubanks, L. E.	8-21-13	Koen, J. T.	11-03-21
Appleby, J. W.	10-13-13	Fawcett, H.	11-05-21
Parker, J. R.	8-16-14	Byars, J. M.	11-06-21
Terry, C. B.	1-01-15	Smith, W.T.	11-07-21
Parish, E. C.	10-21-17	Waghalter, M. H.	11-07-21
Harrison, E. W.	12-06-17		

The earliest seniority date on the "Consolidated Seniority List of Firemen on the Houston and Texas Central District" (shown at left) was A. Nichols on August 14, 1902. The list, comprised of several pages, is filled with names of Ellis County residents whose careers with the railroad often spanned a lifetime, including Henry Baskin, T. C. Ballew, V. Blakley, L. H. Fountain, T. Gerron, J. Harrison, R. Hutchison, J. Kudrna, S. Molina, Herman Mounts, A. L. Mynatt, John Percival, M. Pierce, J. V. Pool, W. Ranton, V. Spann, Joe Sramek, G. Stokes, J. Svehlak, R. Ventrca, W. Weathers, R. Wells, L. Whitacre, and R. Wilderson. Pictured below are a few of the many railroad employees of the Ennis roundhouse over the decades. (Left, courtesy of Regina Adams and John Mounts, part of the Herman Mounts Collection; below, courtesy of City of Ennis.)

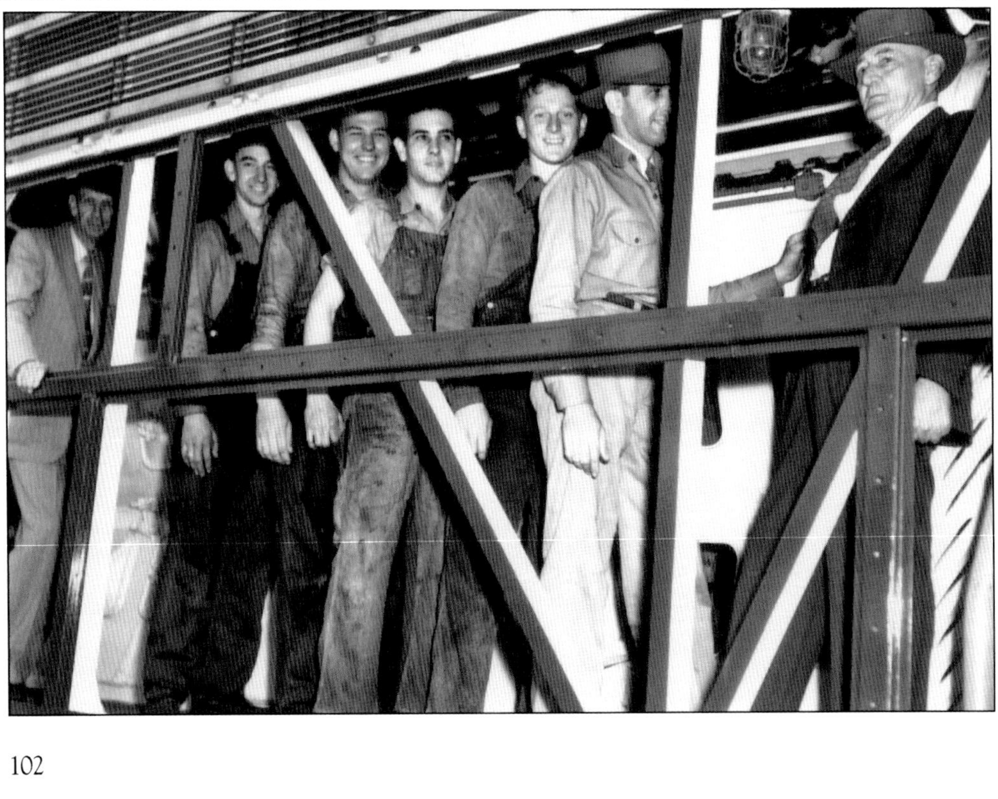

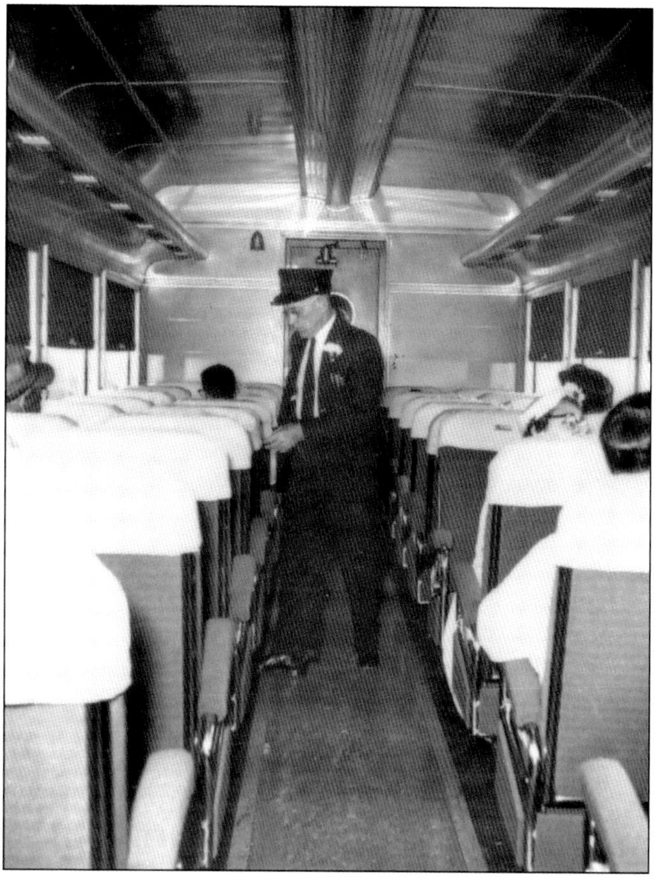

Conductor Sam R. Curry of Ennis is seen at right making his way down the aisle on Sunbeam train No. 13 on its way to Houston in June 1954. This trip was his last before retiring. Thomas O. and Alma Moore are pictured below in a caboose in Ennis during the early 1920s. Moore was involved in the design and construction of the Ennis roundhouse. (Right, courtesy of Dane Williams, part of the Ford Curry Collection; below, courtesy of Lyn Moore.)

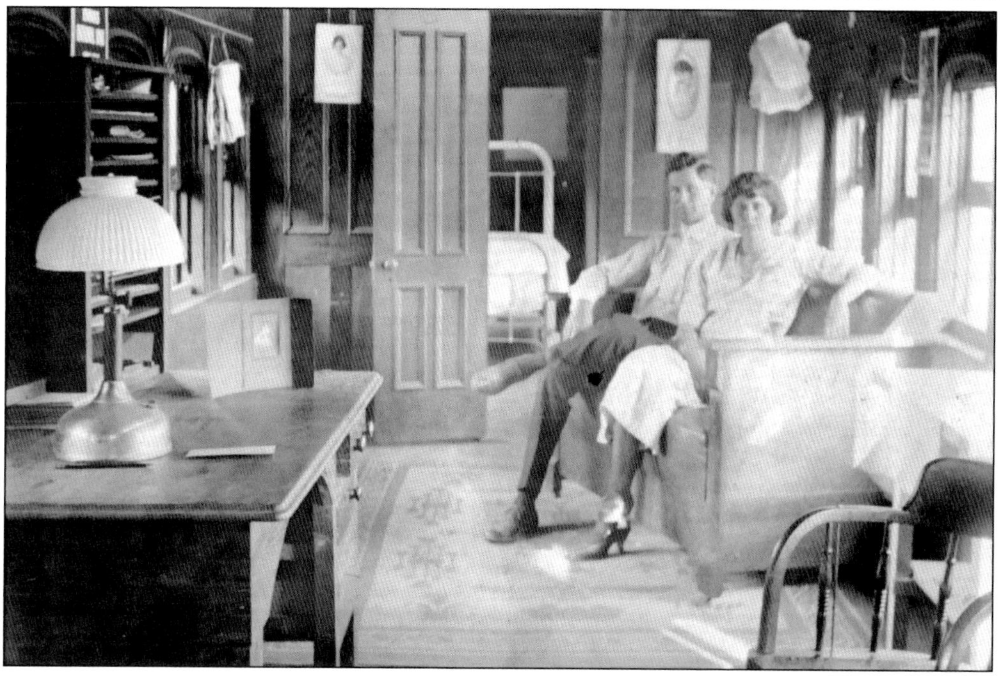

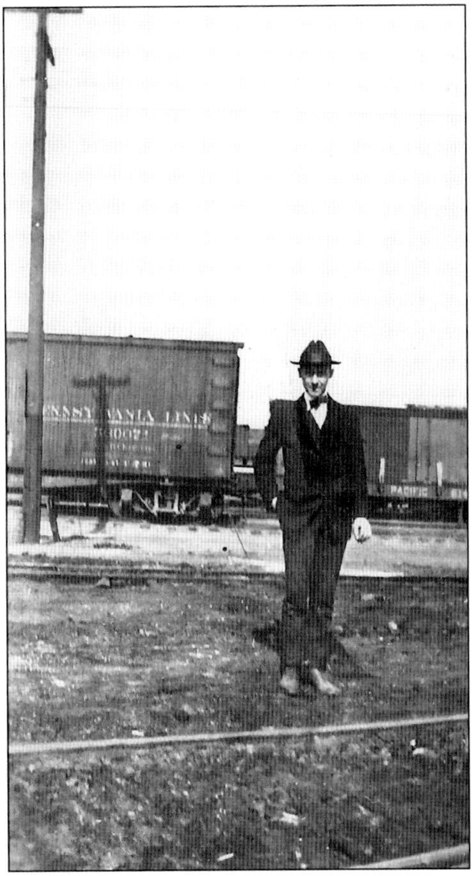

Artie Lee Bohanon Sr. came to Ennis around 1916. Like many, he came looking for a job with the railroad. He worked for the Texas and New Orleans Railroad and then the Southern Pacific Railroad shortly after his arrival in Ennis. He later owned and operated the Bohanon Motor Company on Southwest Main Street, directly across from the freight depot. (Courtesy of the A. L. Bohanon Jr. family.)

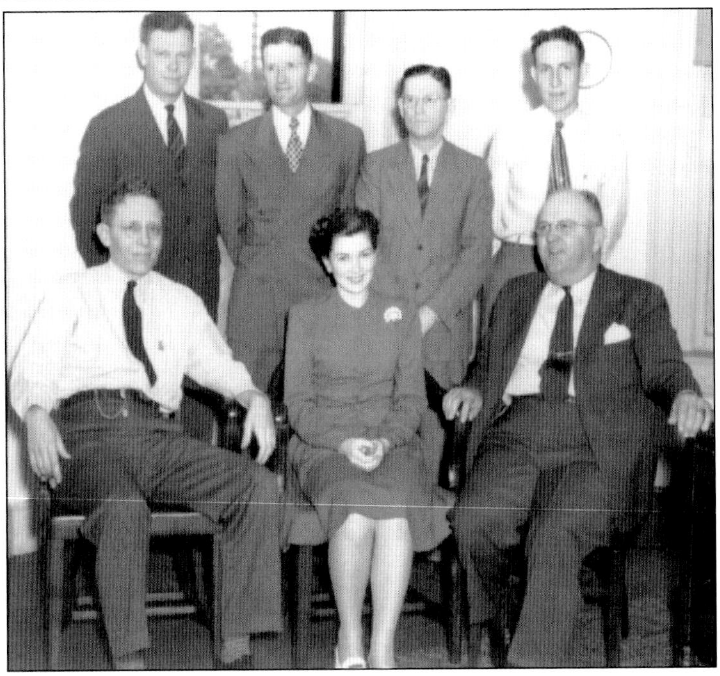

During World War II, employees of the Texas and New Orleans Railroad in Ennis served on a committee that worked to promote government bonds for the war effort. Members from the various departments included, from left to right, (first row) H. M. Pruitt (train dispatcher), Dorothy Comiskey (timekeeping department), and E. C. McClarty; (second row) Byrne Cooke (machine shops), unidentified, B. O. Brown, and unidentified. (Courtesy of the Comiskey family.)

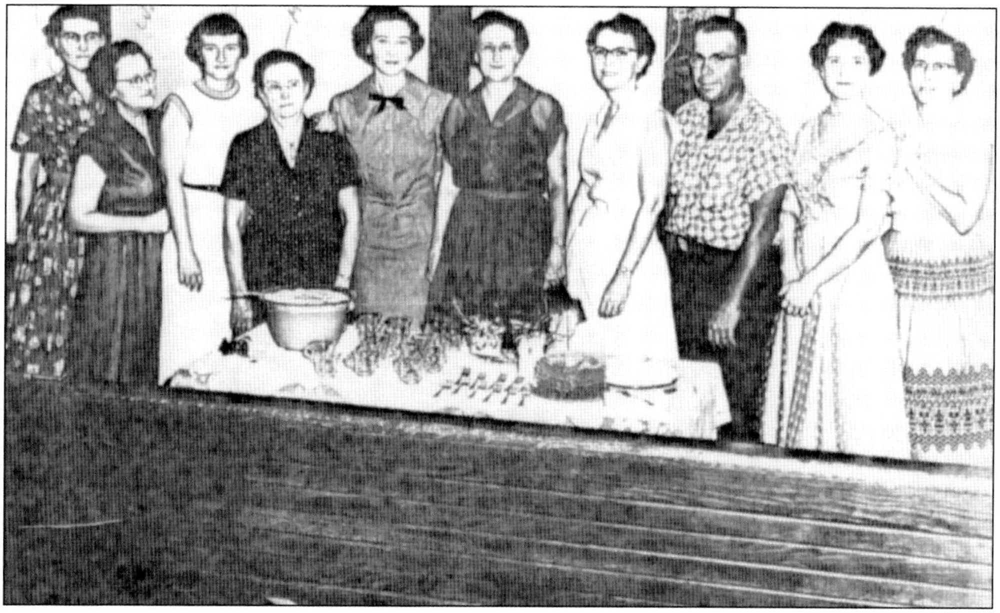

Many of the private branch exchange (PBX) operators for the Southern Pacific Division Headquarters in Ennis gathered around 1955. Pictured from left to right are unidentified, Willie Mae Davenel, Peggy Beckman, Myrtle Butler, Gladys McNeil, Clara Kelley, Jewel McCoy, C. E. McCaig, Frances Brown, and Ollie Dean Jackson. Long before children visited the Ennis Railroad Museum, they visited the depot and rode the train. Pictured below, as they wait for their train to Corsicana, are Mrs. W. A. Lyon's kindergarten class in 1952. From left to right are (first row) Karen Littleton Jones, Betty Rider Gordon, Margaret Barrington, Jimmy Allen, Joe McCall, Jimmy Percival, John Tolleson, Pam Dittberner Shelton, Paula Skrivanek Morgan, and Steve Fallen; (second row) Mike Reel, Greg Skrivanek, Betty Lou Bennett Shuffler, Judy Schoeps Werner, Pat Barkley Reel, Randy Pinsen, Bill Odom, Gary Scott, Lee Keever, and Jane Grant Hoffman. (Both, courtesy of City of Ennis.)

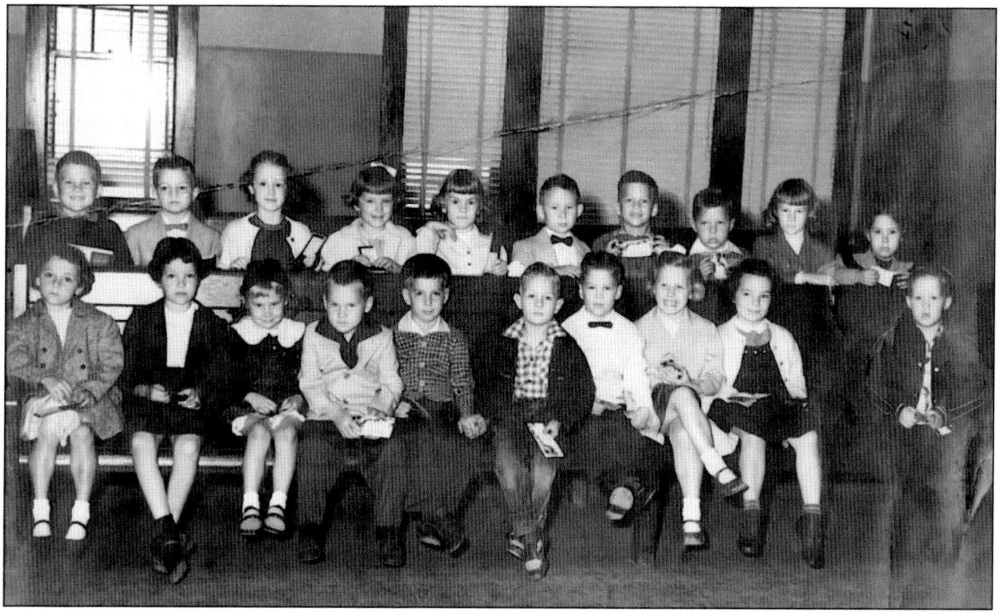

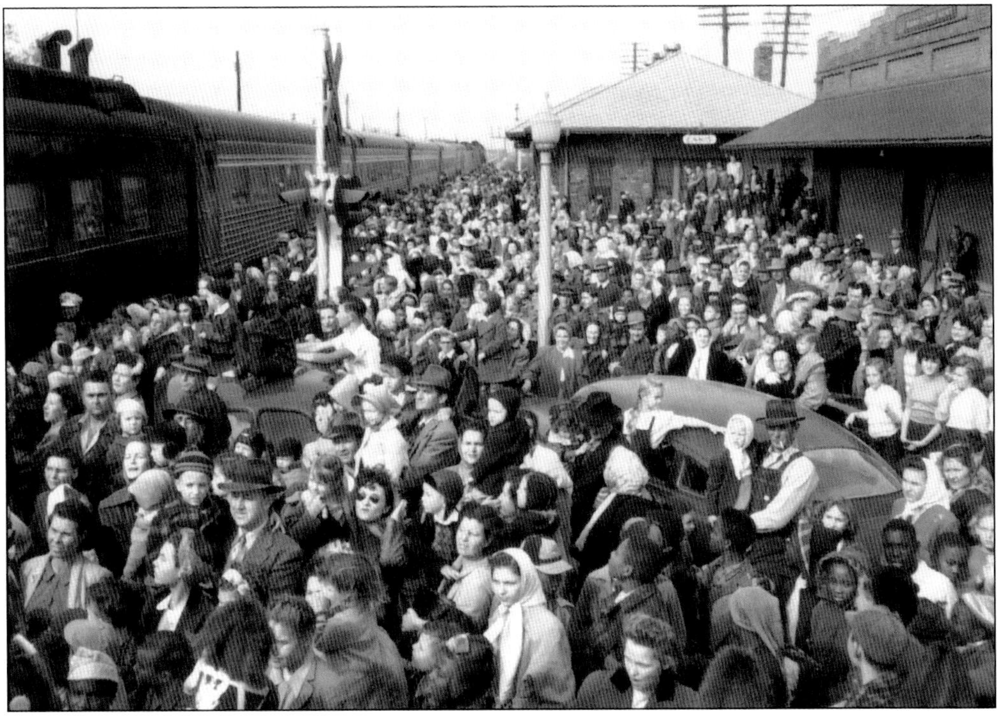

The rail brought good news and bad to Ellis County communities. In Ennis, hundreds gather in December 1948 at the passenger depot on Northeast Main Street, as pictured above, for the arrival of the train carrying Santa Claus. Over the years, the train also brought loved ones home, sometimes on their final journey. Among those gathered around the freight depot of Ennis at Southwest Main Street near Brown Street, pictured below in the early 1930s, are funeral home attendants with their hearse. (Both, courtesy of Ennis Public Library.)

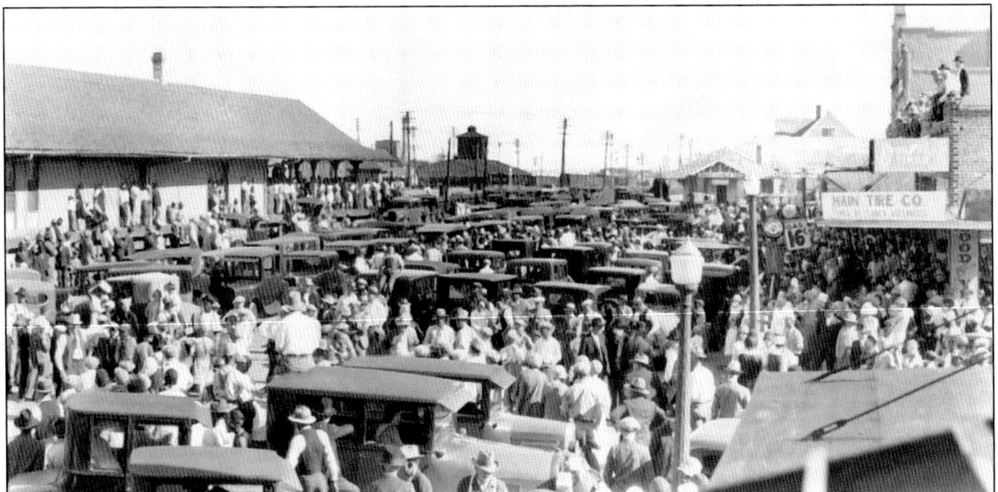

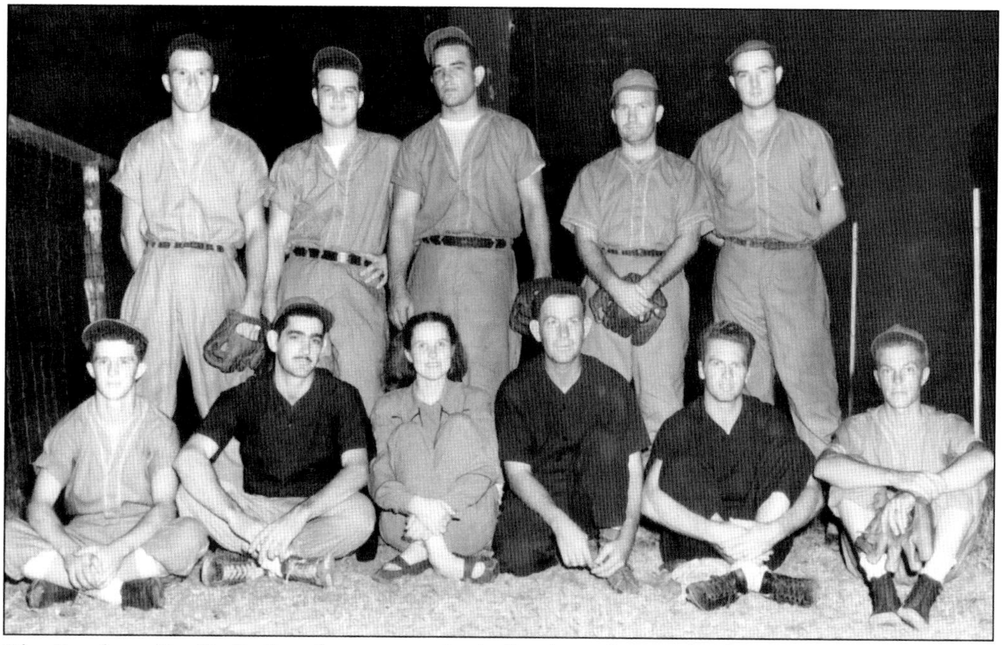

The Southern Pacific Railroad maintained a ballpark to the north of Ennis. Many games were played there, and teams were sponsored by local Ennis businesses. Pictured above from left to right are (first row) Sonny Tolar, Joe Cervantes, Sue Wilson, E. McCaig, Calvin Emmert, and Jack Burkhead; (second row) Tom Ridley, Beano Houdek, J. C. Seatman, Allen McEver, and John Overall. Pictured below is the 1949 Southern Pacific softball team. They won the city championship that year with W. B. Farrar pitching all four games. Pictured from left to right are (first row) M. Lamarque, C. F. Crews, T. W. Crowe, D. Claxton, T. Golden, and R. Hernandez; (second row) S. Ludlow, W. B. Farrar, A. S. McLelland, E. Newberry, L. C. Parks, and L. R. Hobbs. (Above, courtesy of City of Ennis; below, courtesy of Joe V. Pool.)

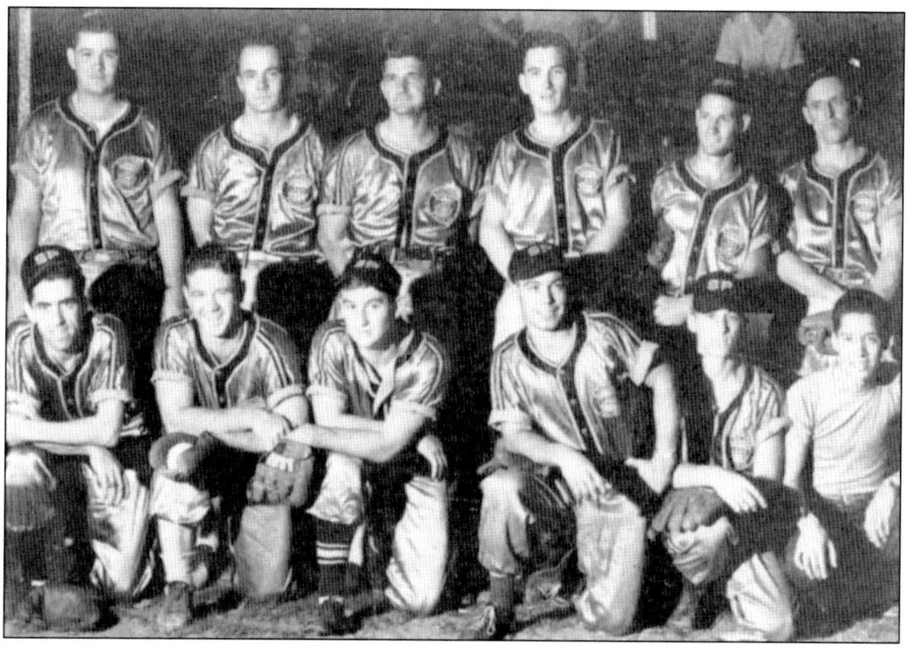

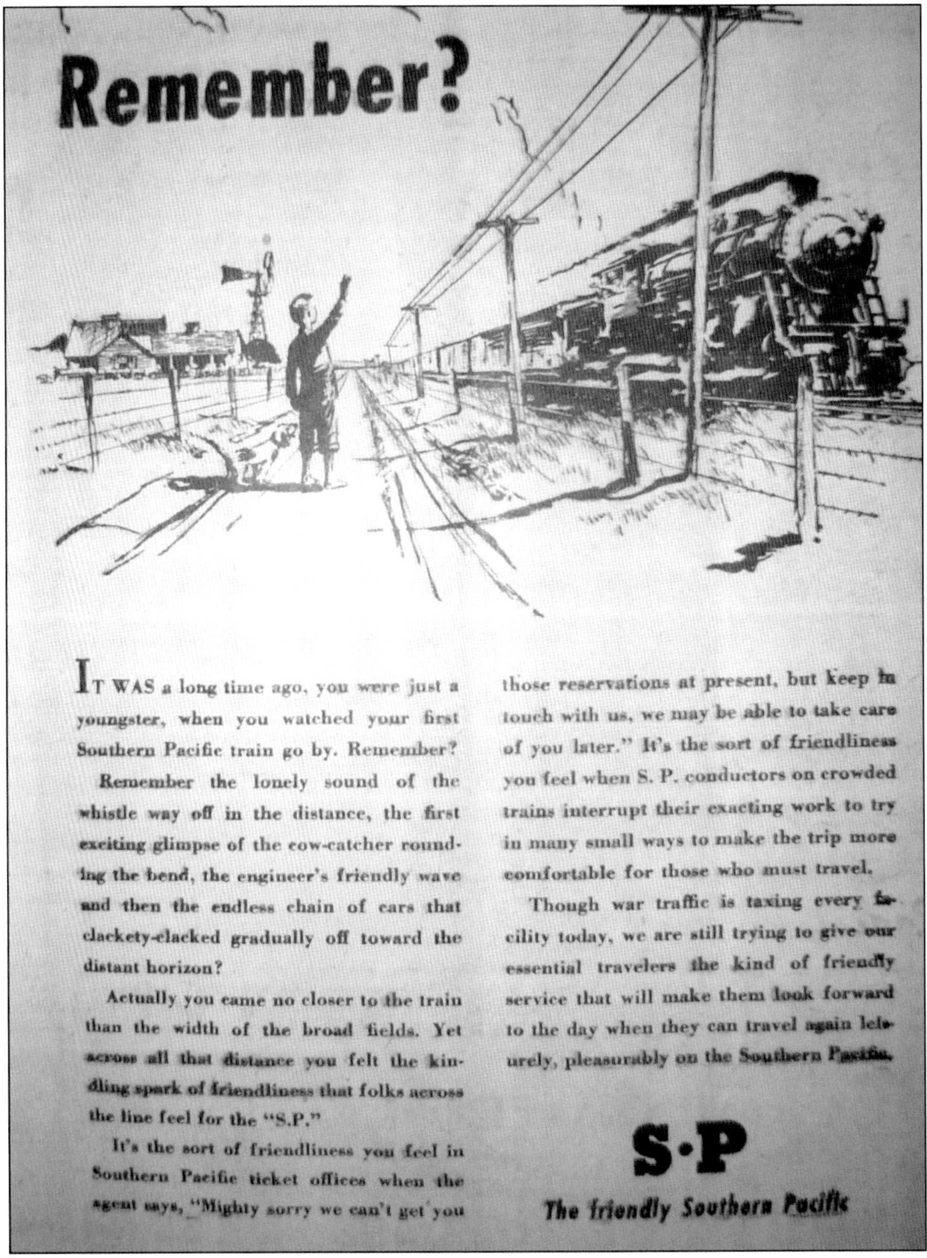

This Southern Pacific Railroad advertisement ran in the *Ennis Daily News* on Wednesday, July 25, 1945. Troop trains were an all too common sight during these years. Mary Ludwig of Ennis remembers as a young teenager, she and her friends would throw folded pieces of paper with their names and addresses at the troops as they went by. As once written by Ralph Essary, young Virginia Skroh of Ennis did the same, and years later after the war and much correspondence, Charles Chandler of Arkansas came to Ennis, where they eventually married. Chandler then began his career with the railroad as an apprentice carman. He later retired as an assistant division superintendant. The war years were busy ones for the rail in all communities. It is proudly told that in one 24-hour period during those years, 100 trains moved through the city smoothly, a testament to the skills and dedication of Ennis dispatchers. (Courtesy of *Ennis Daily News*.)

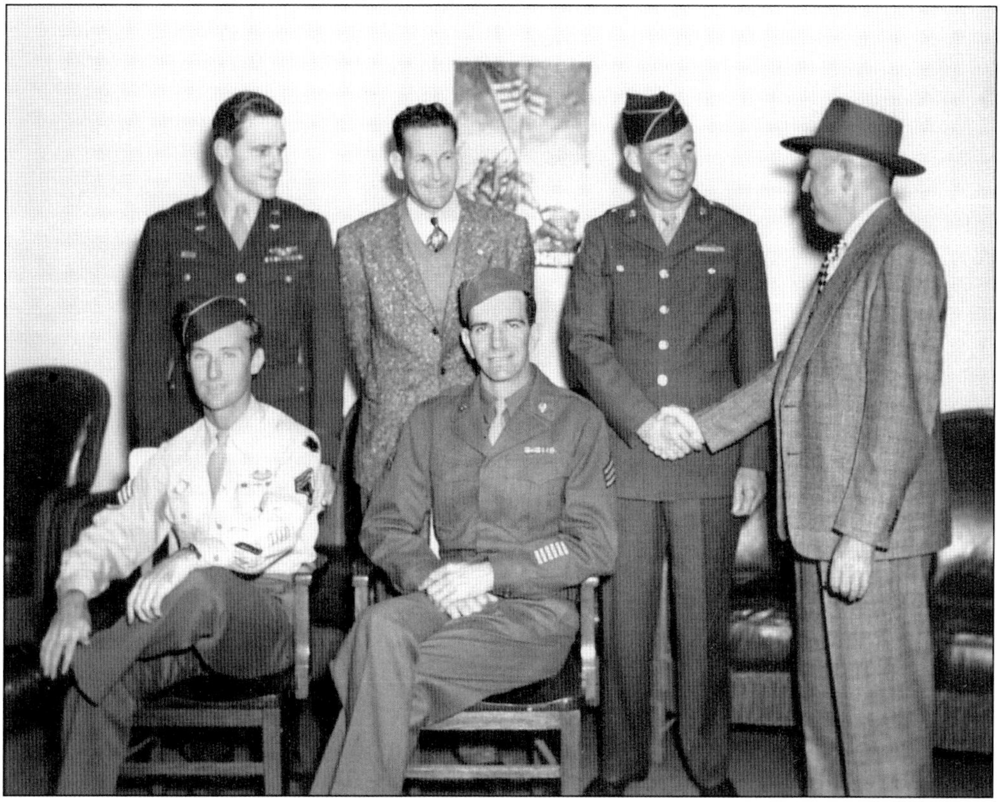

In late 1945, many Southern Pacific Railroad employees were returning home from military service. Pictured is assistant superintendant Bob Williams, who served in a wartime railroad battalion, welcoming them home. From left to right are (first row) George Graves and William A. Carrifee; (second row) Pete Germany, L. C. Cook, A. W. Hagler, and Bob Williams. (Courtesy of George Graves.)

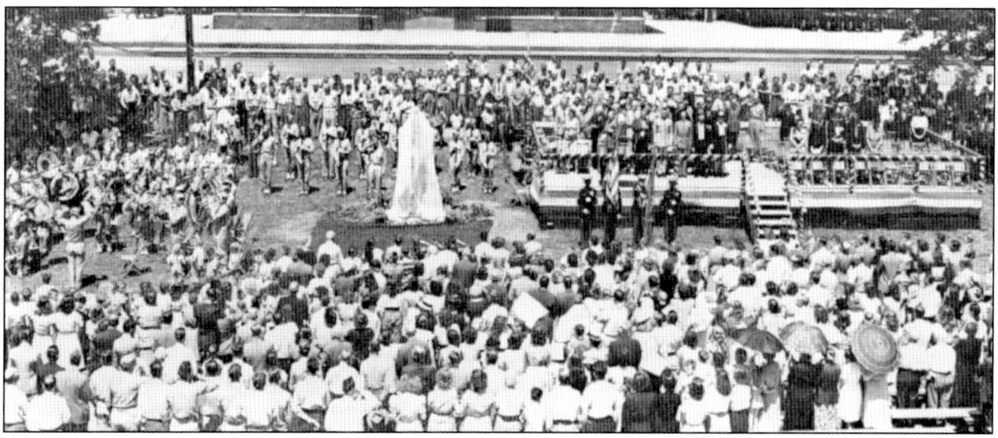

On Memorial Day, May 30, 1947, thousands attended the dedication of Pierce Park, pictured above with the Ennis passenger depot in the background. Funds were raised by Southern Pacific Dallas division employees for the monument that honored their fellow Dallas division employees who gave their lives in service in World War II, and it was named for the first of those to die in battle, William Thomas Pierce Jr. (Courtesy of Doris Pierce Gerron.)

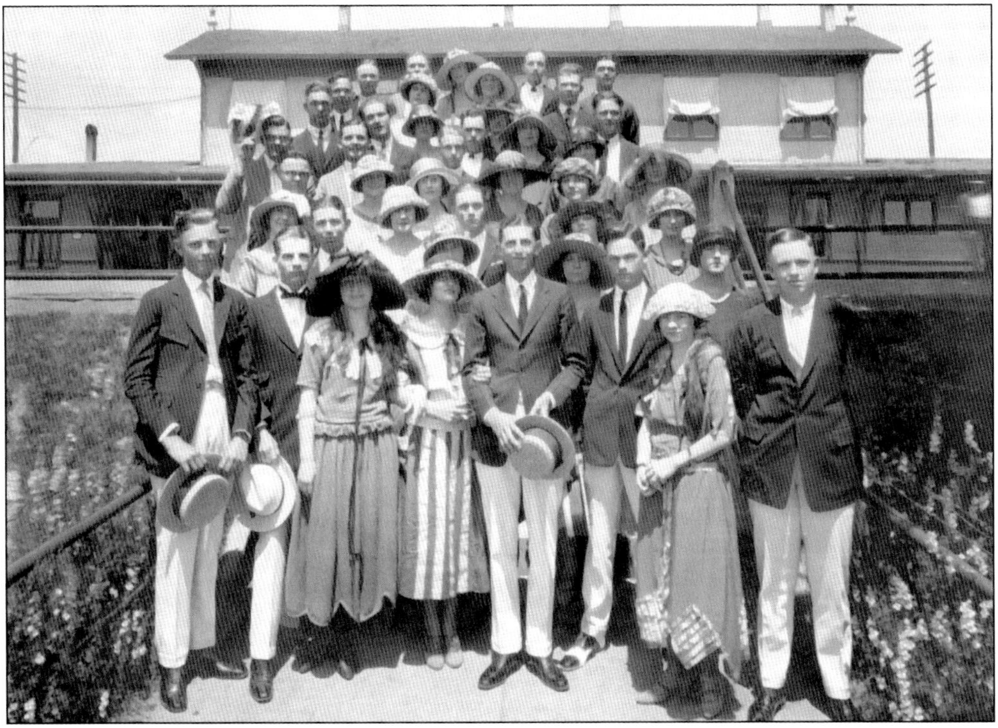

The depots of all Ellis County have traditionally been places of community gatherings. These were the places where family and friends were welcomed. Long before the instant communications of e-mail, the trains carried the mail, a crucial connection for all residents of the county. For many, it was the only form of transportation outside of their community, within Ellis County, and beyond. Soon to go their separate ways, members of the Ennis High School graduating class of 1923, pictured above, gather together in front of the Ennis depot. Pictured below in the late 1940s, Maureen Gallegher (left) and Elnora Bohanon are seen in the park area west of the Ennis passenger depot. (Above, courtesy of the Telfair family; below, courtesy of the A. L Bohanon Jr. family.)

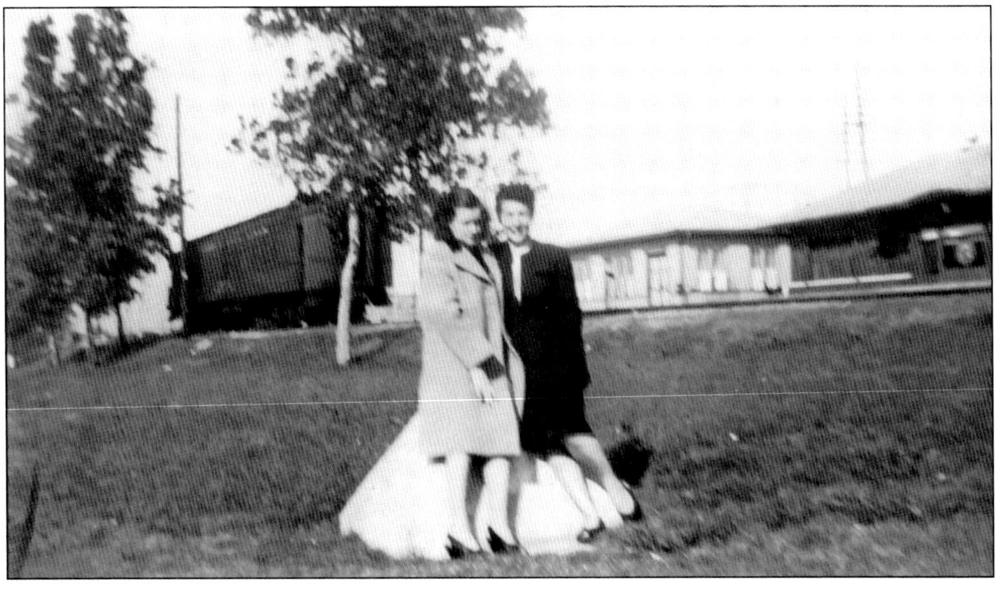

Eight

PRESERVING THE PAST

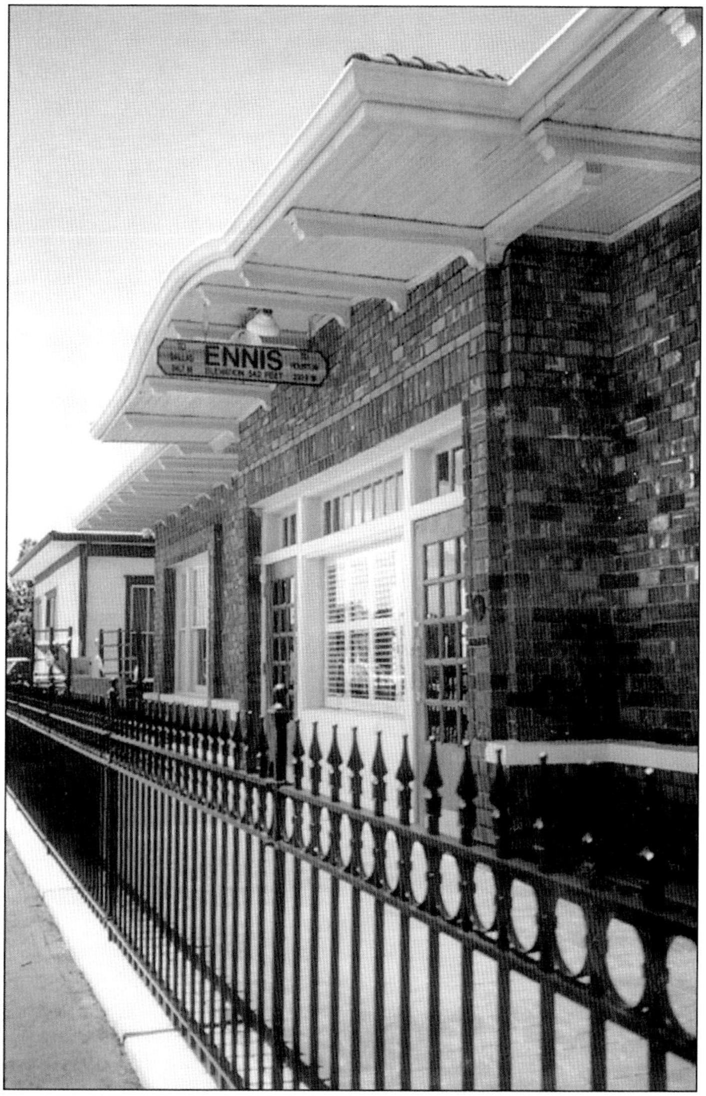

When Ennis was established in 1872, the Houston and Texas Central Railroad used small, wood-burning locomotives that required firewood and water every 10 miles. Stops and depots, including Ennis, were established to meet those needs. Locomotives for the line were purchased for $25,000 each, shipped by steamer from New York to Galveston, then from Galveston to Houston by barge. Almost 140 years later, the Ennis Railroad and Cultural Heritage Museum, pictured at right, is a legacy to those early days of railroad history. Located to the east of the track with the surviving southern end of the passenger depot built in 1895 beside it, the third passenger depot of Ennis still stands witness to the sounds of the trains, even today making their way through a community founded at the dawn of their reign. (Courtesy of Steve Howerton.)

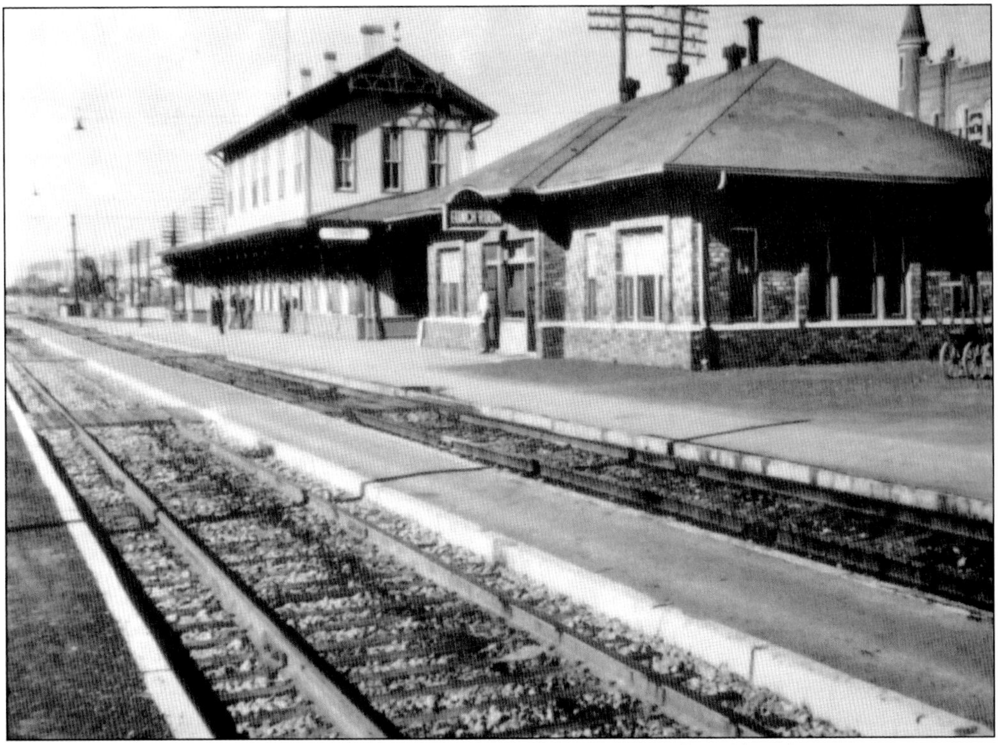

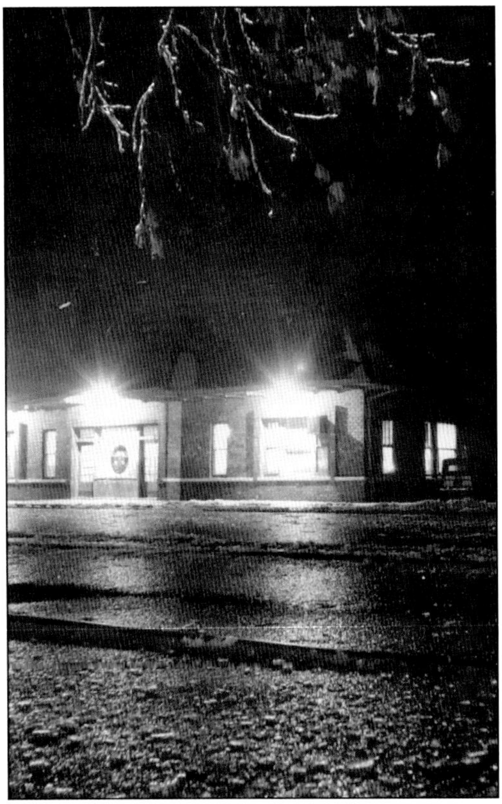

The Ennis Railroad lunchroom, as seen on the building's sign pictured above to the right, served the community in that capacity until the 1930s. Stories are that during the Depression, the family that ran the restaurant lived in the building's sparse basement. With the loss of the wooden passenger depot in the early 1930s, pictured above to the left, the restaurant was converted into a passenger depot, as can be seen at left in the late 1940s. Also pictured above, behind the lunchroom in the upper right hand corner, is the King Hotel. Built around 1900, the hotel was destroyed by fire in 1928. Victims of the fire, W. W. Osborne and G. P. Gage, were both Southern Pacific Railroad employees. (Above, courtesy of City of Ennis; left, courtesy of Dane Williams, part of the Ford Curry Collection.)

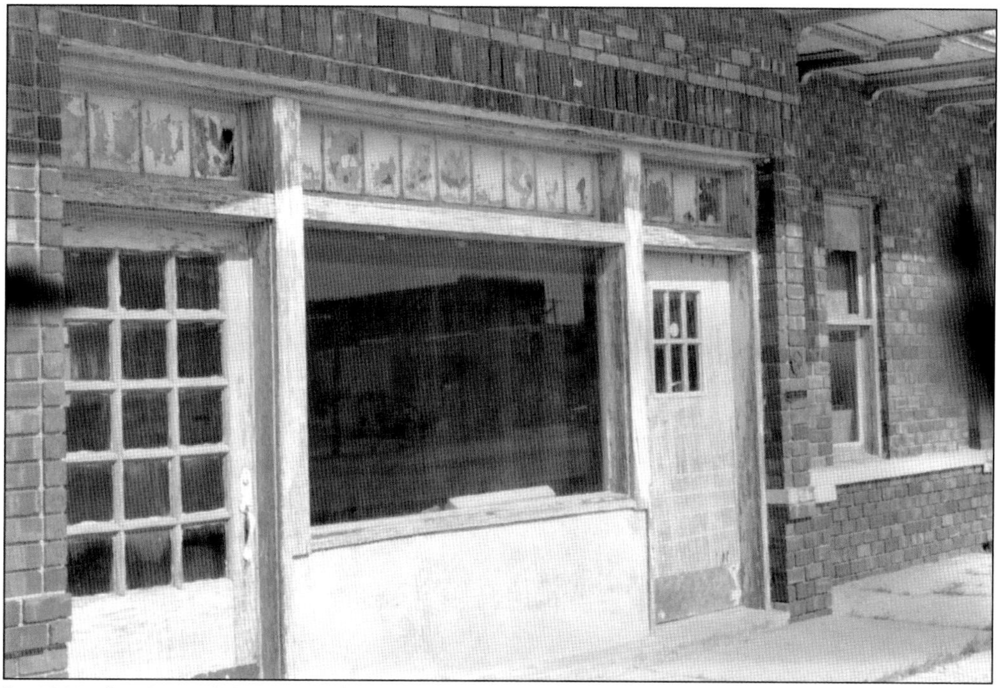

In 1991, the City of Ennis purchased the former passenger depot from the Southern Pacific Railroad. Extensive restorations were required, as seen in the above photograph of the western side of the building facing the track. City of Ennis employees were involved in the restoration efforts from start to finish, and the museum continues to be a great source of pride for the community. Pictured below during the restoration are, from left to right, Roger Peden, Tim Gump, unidentified (back to camera), and Roy Callahan. (Above, courtesy of City of Ennis; below, courtesy of Steve Howerton.)

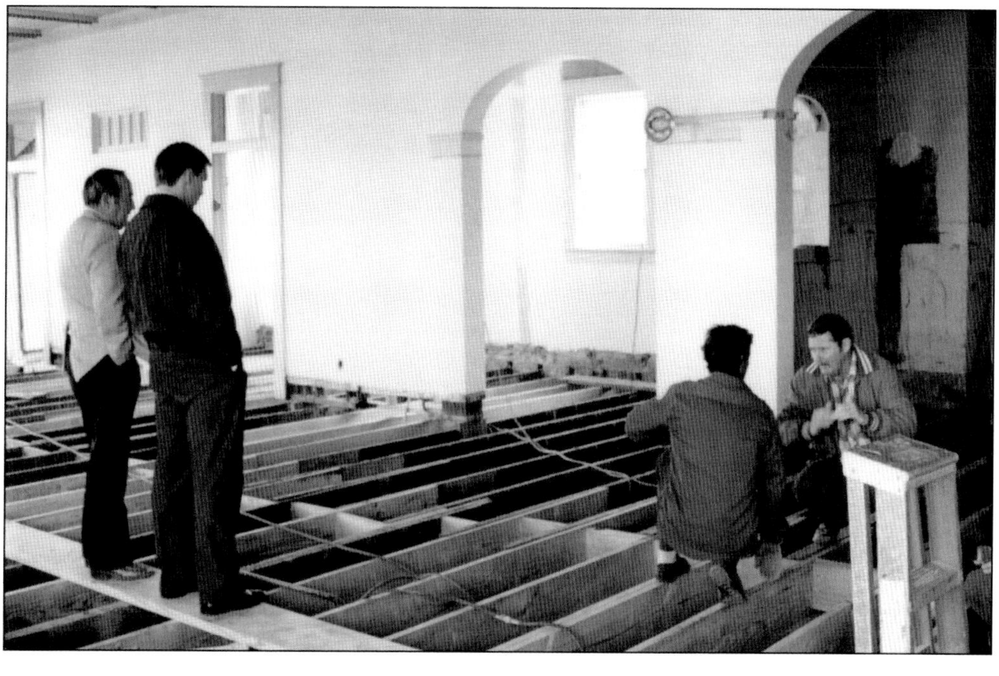

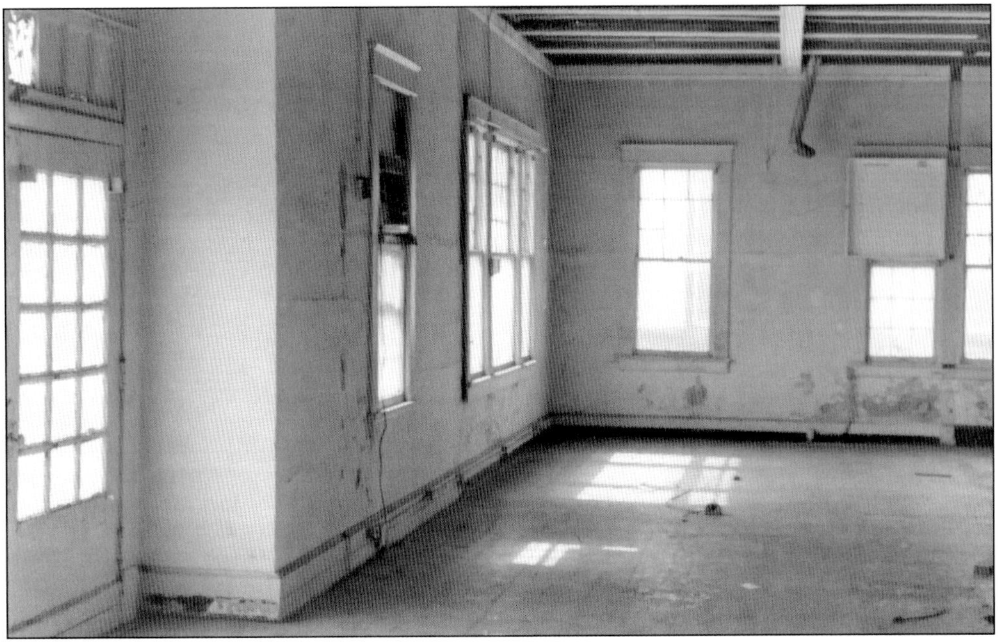

Pictured above is a view of the north end of the depot interior prior to the commencement of restoration efforts. A view of the museum interior from the south side of the interior is shown below, providing a glimpse of the current exhibits on display, including the diorama of the Ennis roundhouse and machine shops. The diorama and model, as well as the model of the old depot on display in another case to the right, were built by the Exhibit Group around 1992. Upon entering the museum, visitors are greeted at the depot ticket window, similar to the ticket window of a century ago. (Above, courtesy of City of Ennis; below, courtesy of Ben Tucker.)

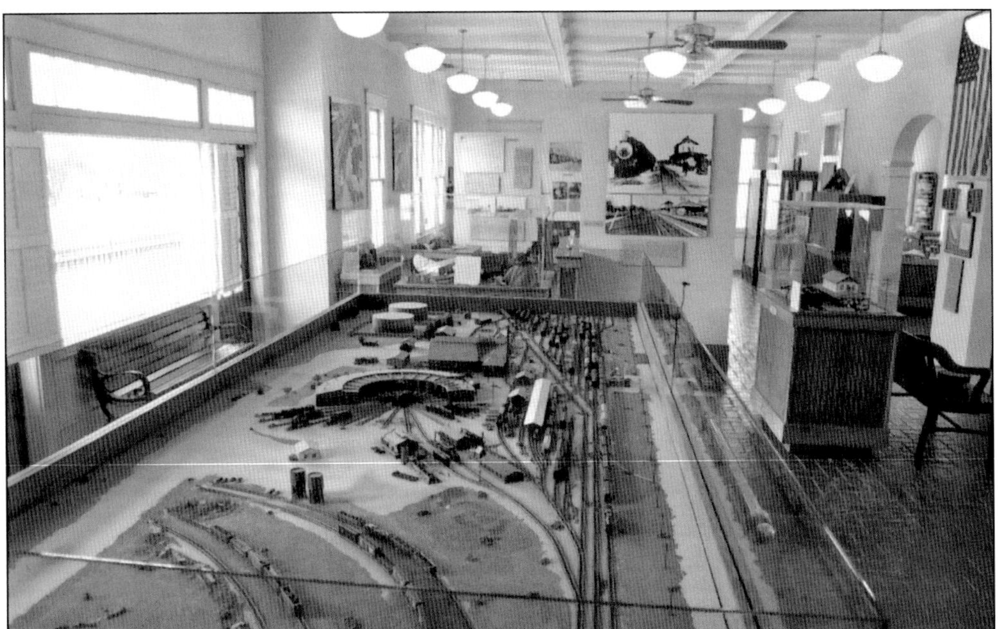

The Houston and Texas Central Railroad pot-bellied stove, found in the dispatch room, is a treasured piece of railroad history at the museum. (Courtesy of Ben Tucker.)

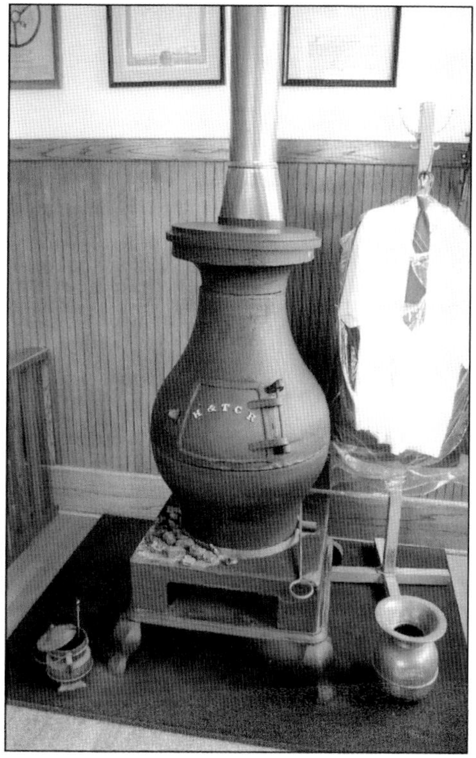

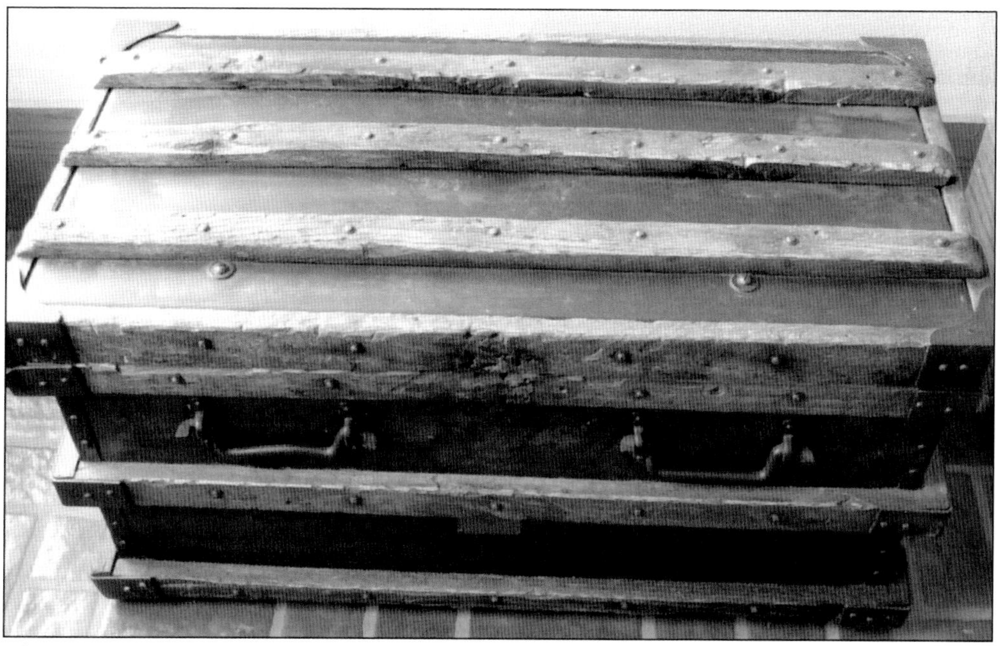

The Vanderman Strong Box, such as the one pictured above, was made specifically for use on railroad cars, stagecoaches, and wagons for the safe transport of valuables such as gold and cash payrolls. These steel chests were made extremely heavy and secure with hardwood slats and iron corners to discourage attempts at theft. The Vanderman Strong Box on display at the museum was manufactured around 1897. (Courtesy of Ben Tucker.)

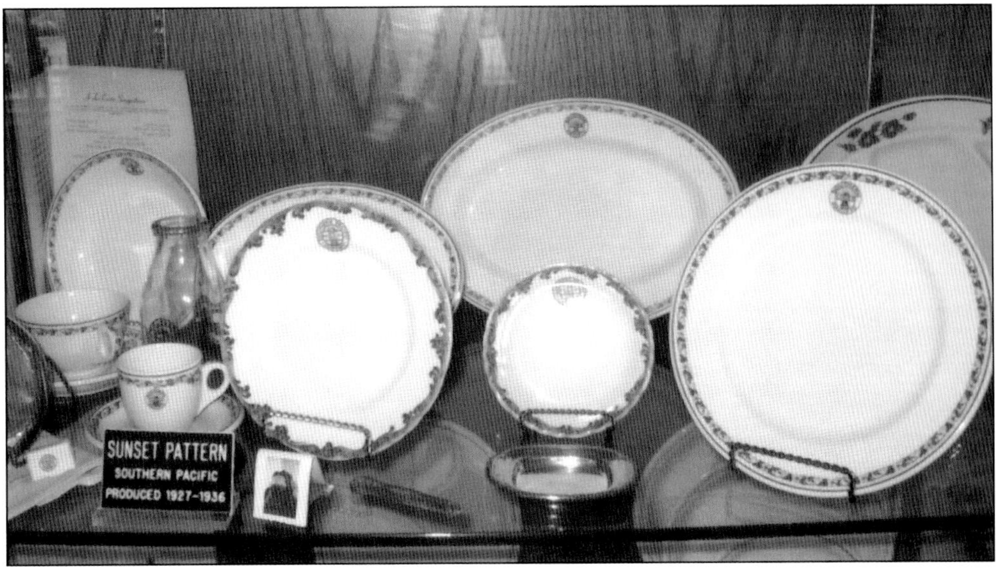

The railroad dining car was a restaurant on wheels. Railroad companies considered it a major factor in attracting passengers from competing lines. Though railroad china was often commercial-grade dishware, necessary to stand up to daily use on a constantly moving dining car, railroad companies served first-class meals on them. The Ennis Railroad and Cultural Heritage Museum has a large collection of railroad china, two of which are pictured. The Sunset dishware pattern, shown above, was manufactured by the Syracuse China Company and was used for a short period of time by the Southern Pacific Railroad, from the late 1920s to the early 1930s. The Prairie Mountain Wildflower pattern was manufactured by the Onondaga Pottery Company for the Southern Pacific Railroad. This pattern, pictured below, was used from 1931 to the late 1950s. (Both, courtesy of Ben Tucker.)

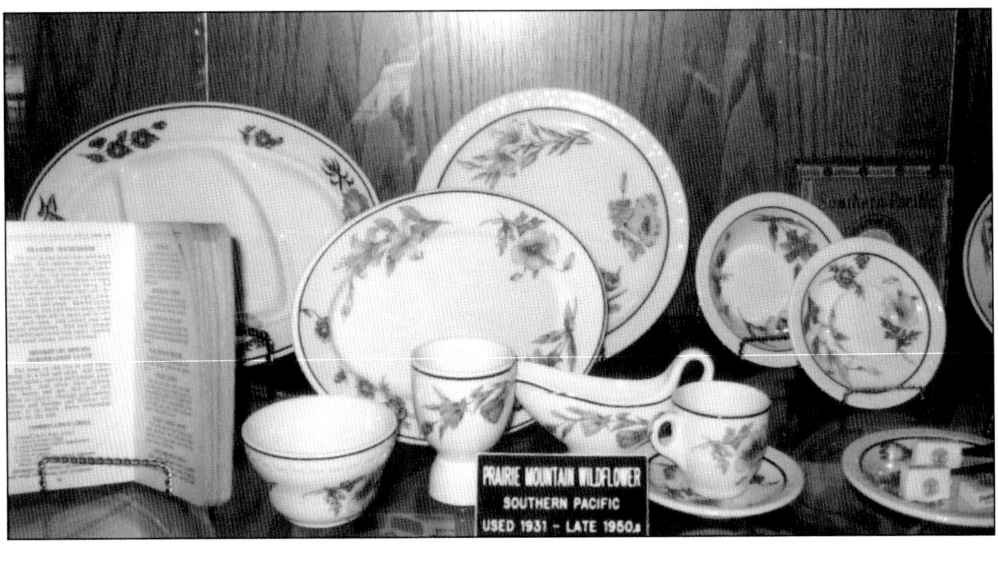

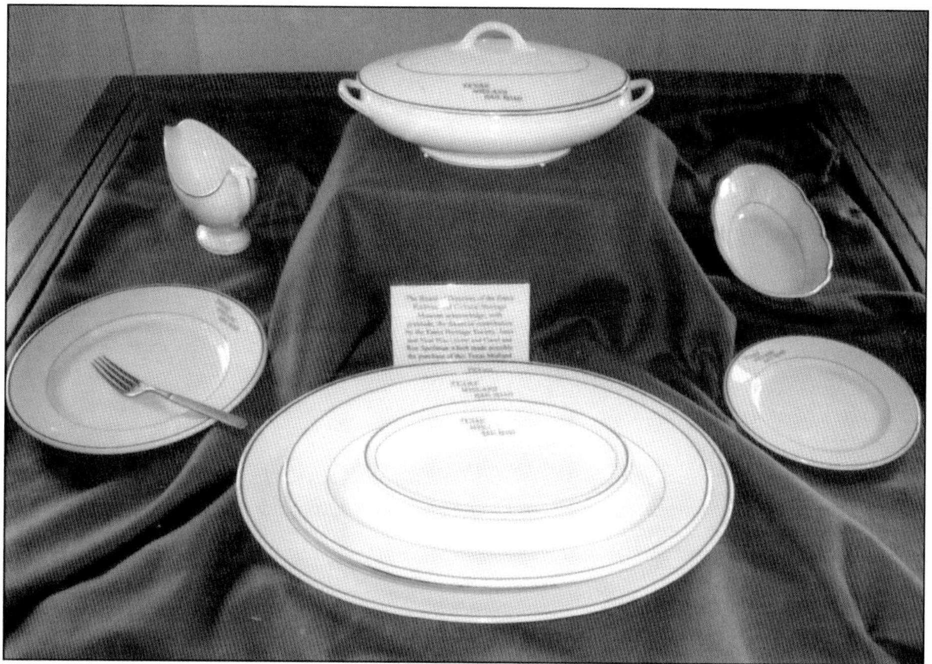

The Texas Midland Railroad reached Ennis in 1894 and connected the community eastward to Paris, Texas. Pictured above in a display case at the Ennis Railroad and Cultural Heritage Museum are some of the few remaining dishes used on the Texas Midland prior to its purchase by the Houston and Texas Central Railroad in 1928. Pictured below is one of the many display cases in the museum that highlight important aspects of railroading. Various watches are displayed, emphasizing the importance of time on the rail. In November 1883, it was the railroad that created the uniform system of four time zones across the United States. (Both, courtesy of Ben Tucker.)

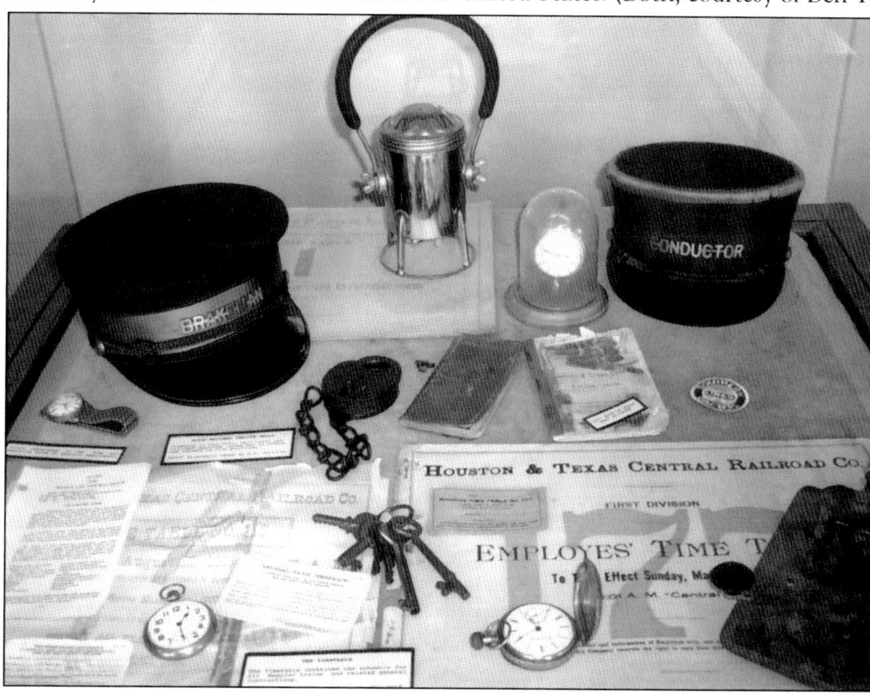

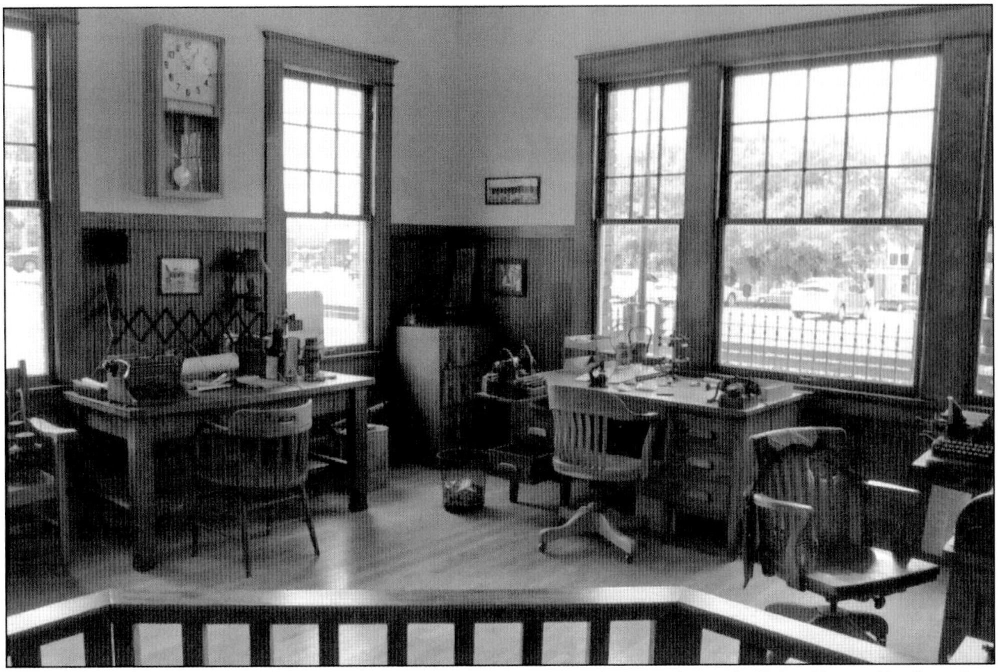

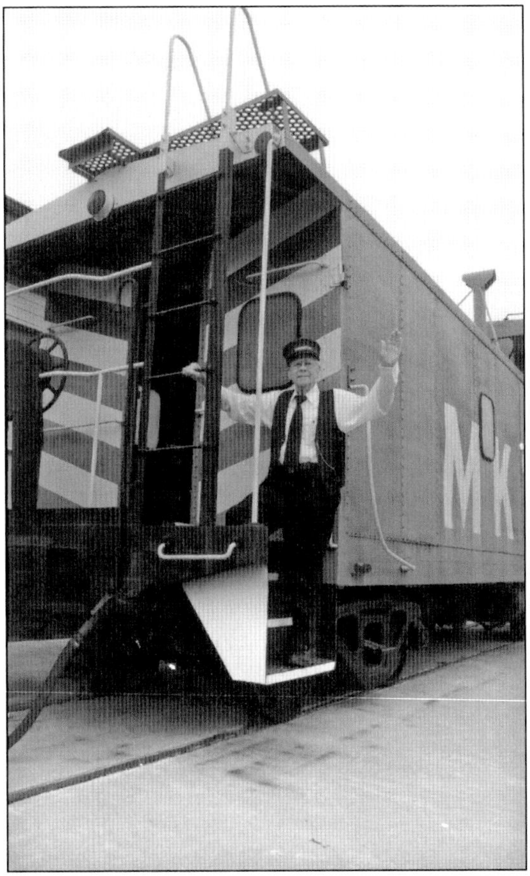

At the north end of the Ennis Railroad and Cultural Heritage Museum, visitors will find a railroad dispatch office, as pictured above, that will take them back almost 100 years in time. (Courtesy of Ben Tucker.)

The Ennis Railroad and Cultural Museum is proud to have in its collection a retired Missouri, Kansas, and Texas Railroad car, pictured at left with longtime museum staff member "conductor" Bill Martz waving the train on. After its arrival in Ennis, numerous volunteers dedicated their time and effort to the restoration of the interior and exterior of the car. (Courtesy of City of Ennis.)

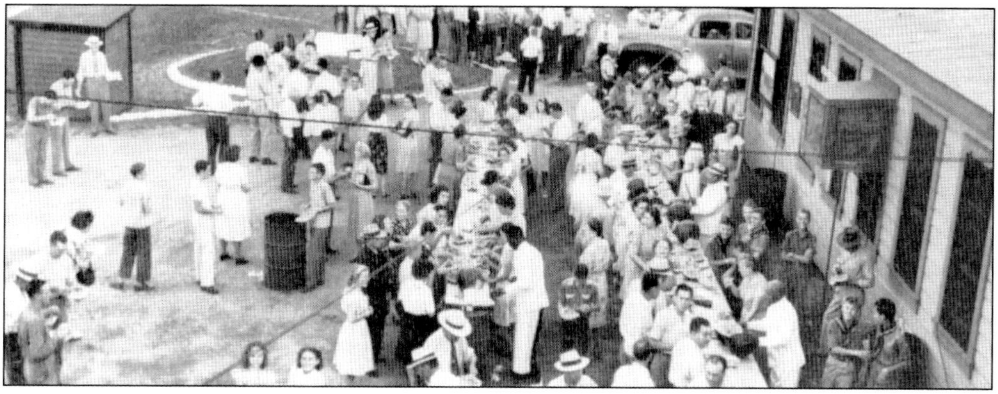

On July 26, 1947, Southern Pacific employees in Ennis celebrated the 75th anniversary of the arrival of the Houston and Texas Central Railroad. Pictured above is the celebration at the division shops, which included tours of the shops. The event also included fund-raisers by the Southern Pacific Service Club, such as the beard-growing contest. Some of the competitors are pictured below. From left to right are (first row) A. M. Grant, file clerk (first place winner); L. McDonald, shop employee (second place winner); "Judge" C. W. Freeland, engineer (third place winner); and H. M. Pruitt, dispatcher; (second row) T. D. Ray, roundhouse laborer; Joe Schramek, drop pit foreman; J. C. Rooker, engineer; Lloyd Johnson, machinist apprentice; J. B. Miller, fireman; Cecil Sledge, rodman; F. M. Cox, sheetmetal worker; and Joseph Odlozil, boilermaker. (Both, courtesy of Joe V. Pool.)

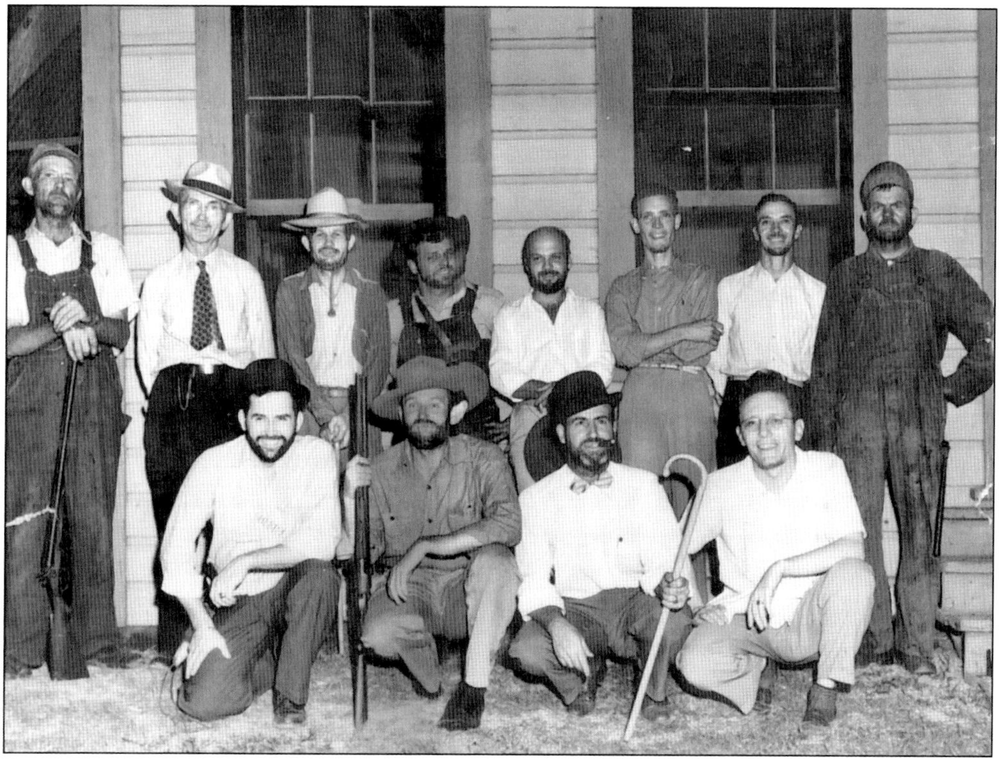

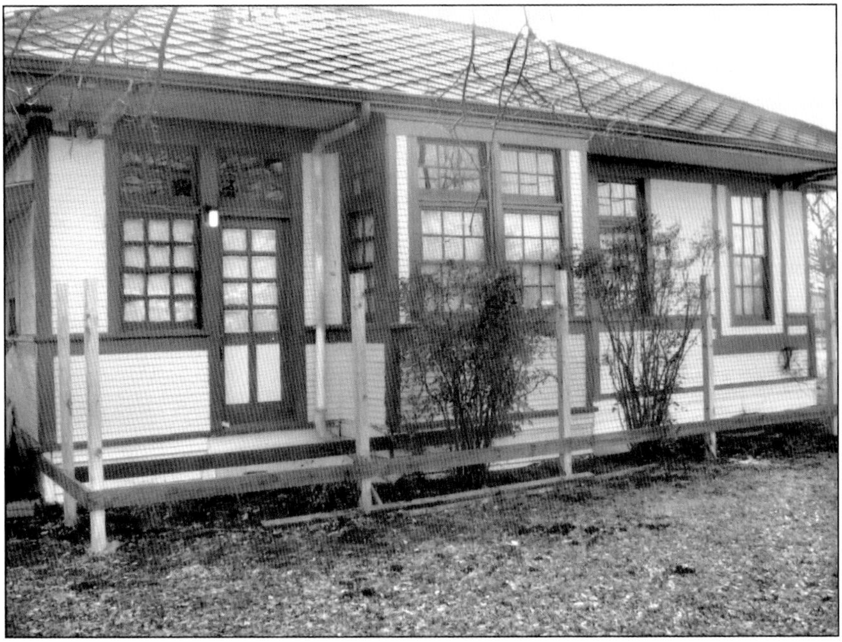

The Forreston depot, pictured here, was built as a prefab structure in Parsons, Kansas, at the main shops of the MK&T Railroad around 1889 and was operational in the spring of 1890. Originally located at Main Street and U.S. Highway 77, it served as a combination depot with four rooms, including two waiting areas, a freight room, and the train master's office. The depot was the only place to use a telephone until the 1930s, and it is rumored that Clyde Barrow was a frequent visitor to its telegraph office. The depot closed in 1947 and was relocated to its current location on Pecan Street in Forreston in 1953. Currently, it is being restored to its original state by the Thompsons. Many of the 286 windowpanes are original, and bullet holes can be seen throughout. (Both, courtesy of Barry and Anita Thompson.)

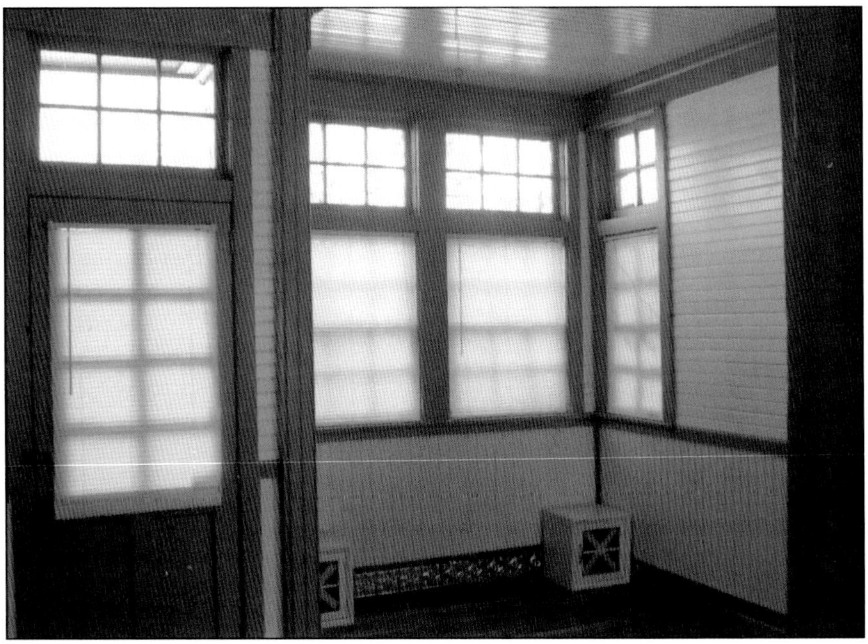

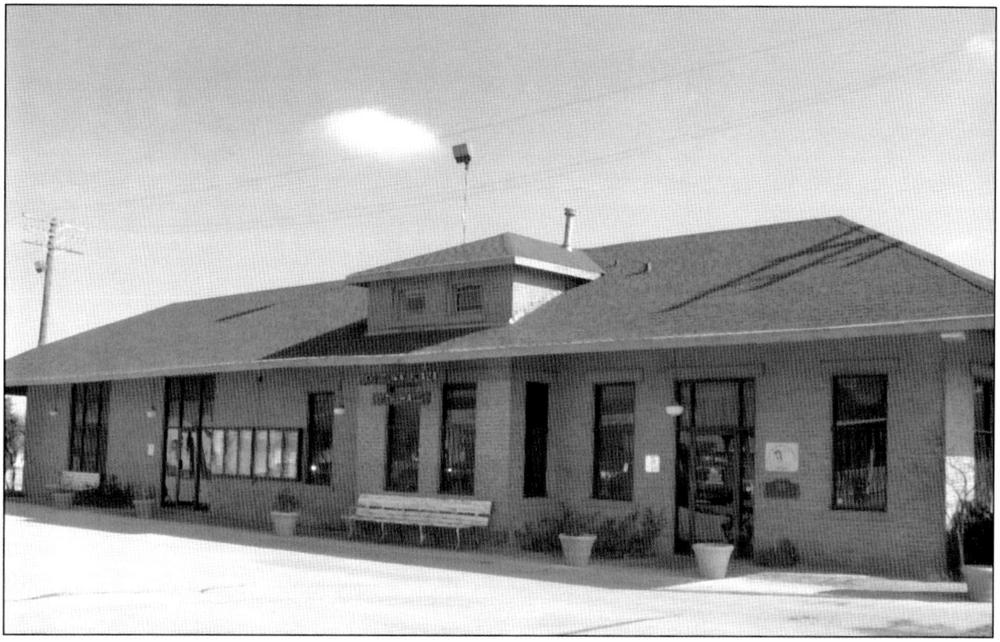

In 1912, the City of Ferris requested that the railroad build a new depot to replace the older wood structure. After resolving a dispute over where to locate the new brick depot, Houston and Texas Central division superintendant W. L. Bisbee approved the plans. The new depot was completed in January 1913. Pictured above, the depot has been restored and has been the location of Ferris City Hall since the early 1980s. (Courtesy of Michael Wilson.)

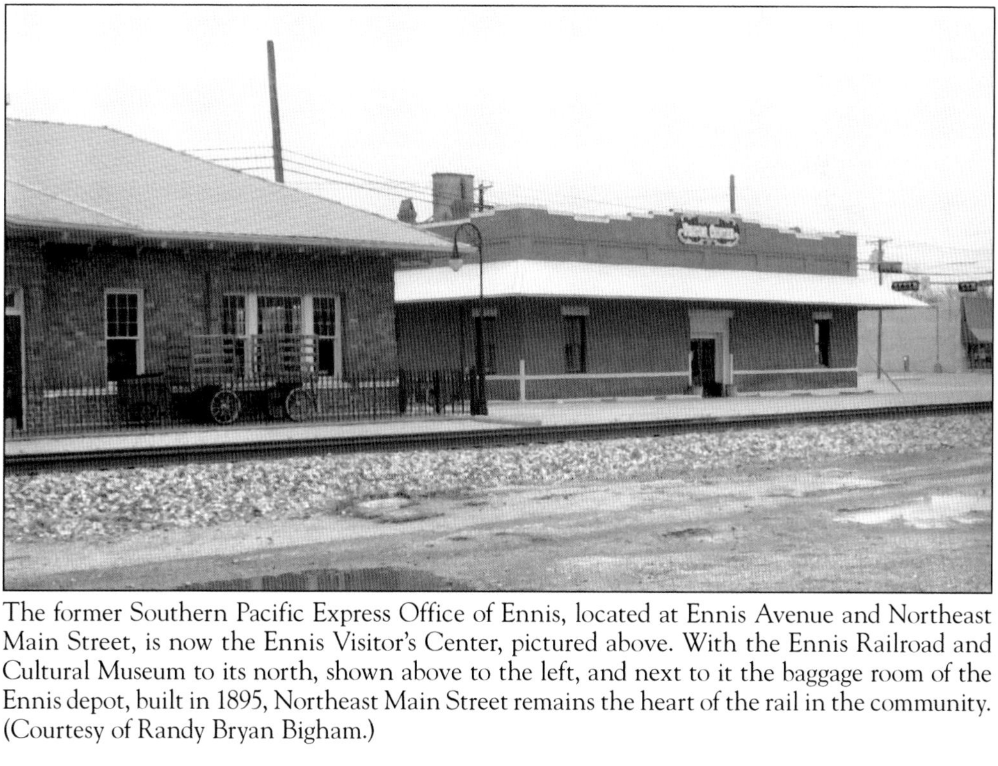

The former Southern Pacific Express Office of Ennis, located at Ennis Avenue and Northeast Main Street, is now the Ennis Visitor's Center, pictured above. With the Ennis Railroad and Cultural Museum to its north, shown above to the left, and next to it the baggage room of the Ennis depot, built in 1895, Northeast Main Street remains the heart of the rail in the community. (Courtesy of Randy Bryan Bigham.)

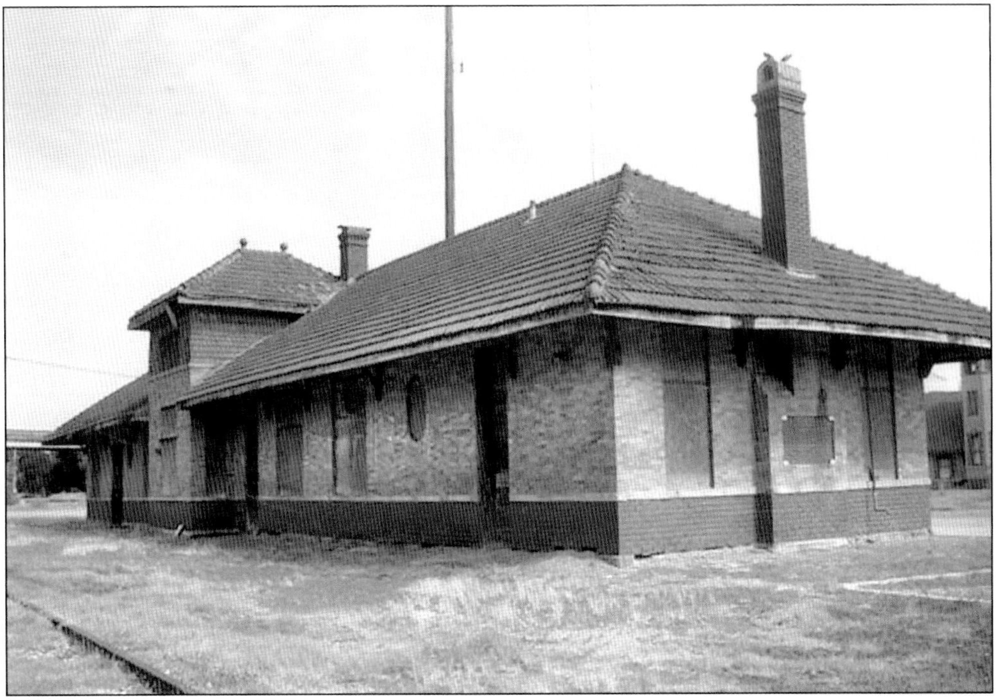

The City of Waxahachie purchased the Missouri-Kansas-Texas Railroad Depot, pictured above, in 2008. Plans for restoration include maintaining the historical integrity of the exterior of the structure as much as possible. Part of this effort includes putting the original roof tiles back in place after reinforcement of the roof is completed. Pictured below, observing the condition of the interior of the depot prior to restoration, are Debra Wakeland (left) and Hilda Chapman, both members of Waxahachie Partnership, Inc. (Both, courtesy of City of Waxahachie.)

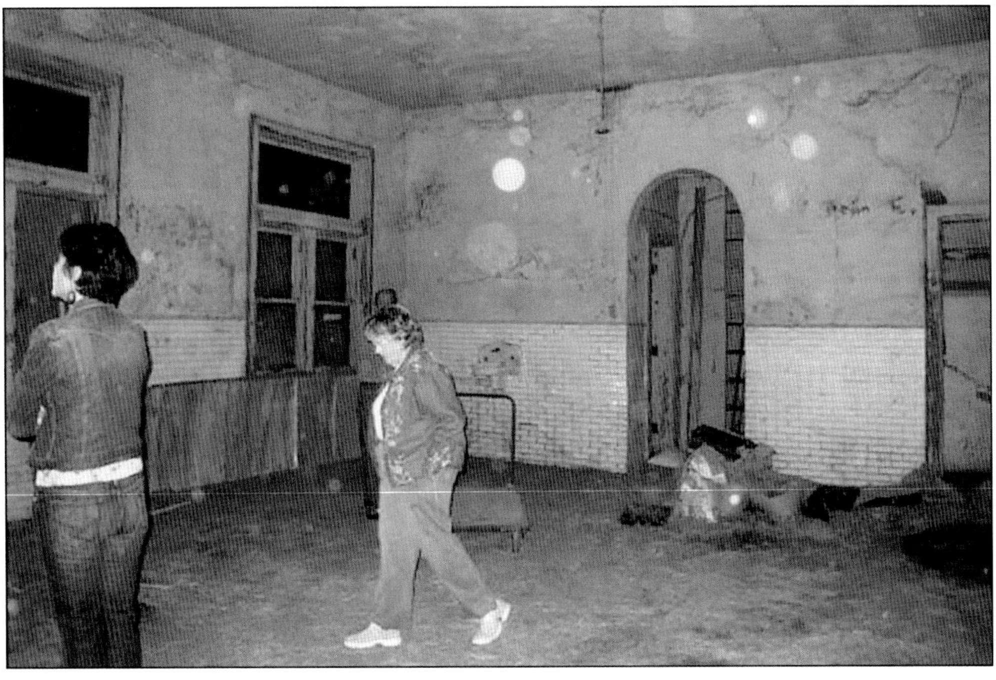

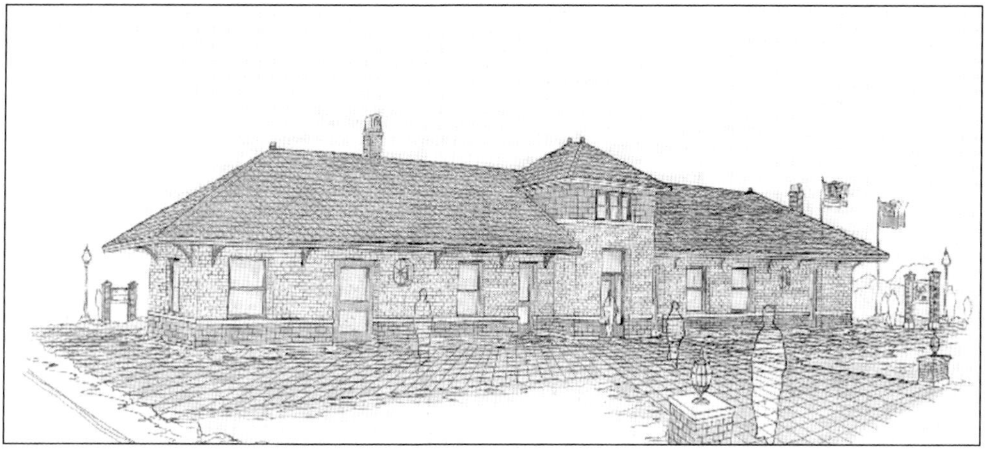

The restoration of the former Missouri-Kansas-Texas Railroad Depot is expected to be completed by early 2011. Pictured above is a rendering of the restored depot, which was prepared by Anthony Mottla, a local architect and Waxahachie resident. The rendering provides a view of the south side of the building. (Courtesy of City of Waxahachie.)

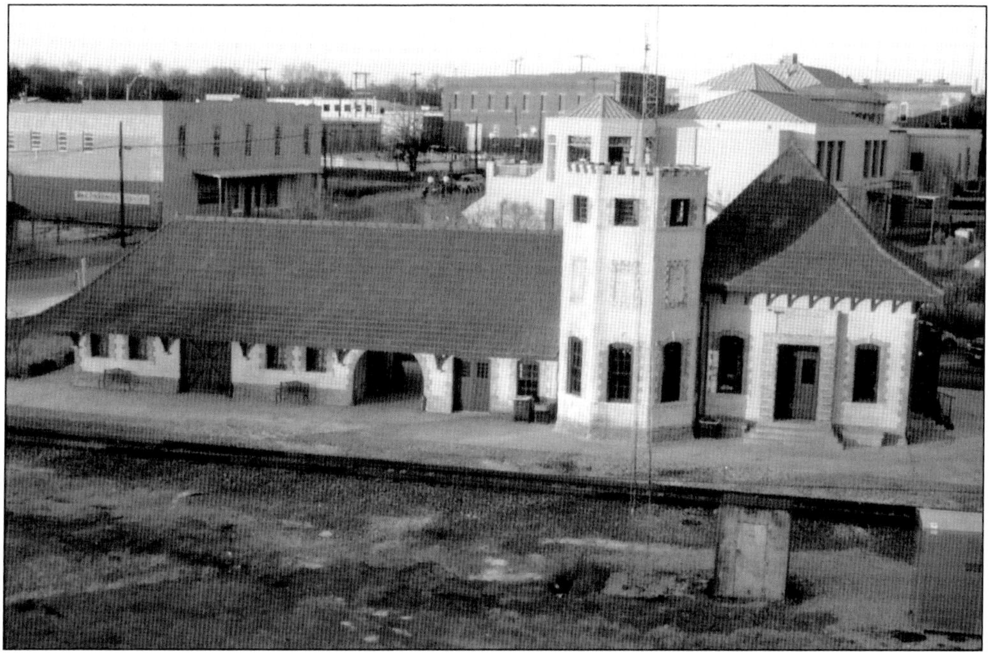

Since 1963, the Nay Company of Waxahachie has been located in the old Trinity and Brazos Valley Railroad Depot. The company purchased the building in 1998 from the Burlington Northern–Santa Fe Railroad Company. Authentically restored, the company has retained much of the original structure, including doors, windows, and wainscoting. The Nay family has taken every effort in the preservation of this historic structure. (Courtesy of the Nay Company.)

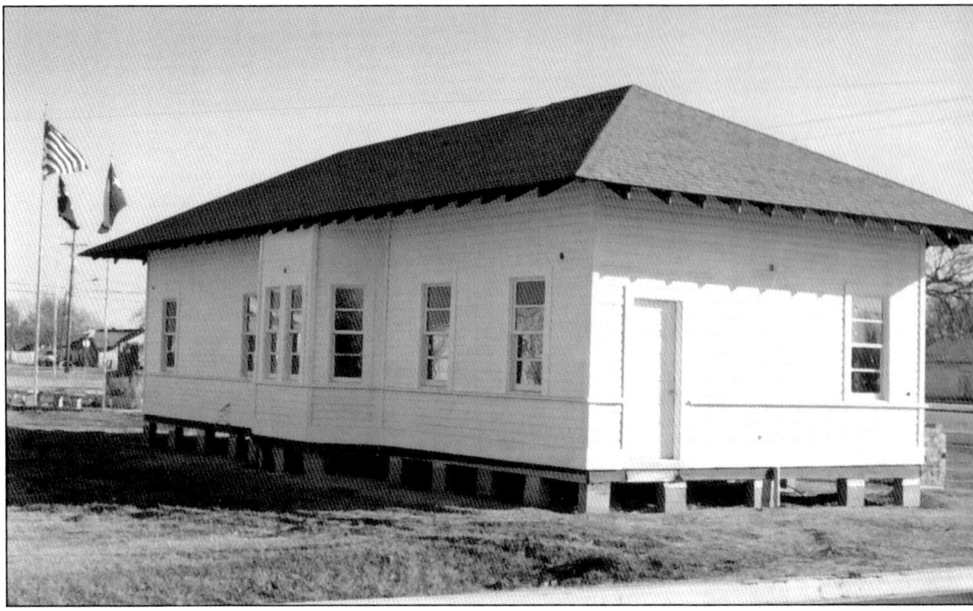

The railroad depot pictured above is being restored by the Maypearl Chamber of Commerce under the direction of the Cowboy Bank. It has been relocated within yards of its original location. It was purchased by the Wilemon Gin in the 1960s and used as a cotton gin office. It has been gifted to the City of Maypearl by the Wilemon family for use as a museum and public gatherings. (Courtesy of Kathryn E. Eriksen.)

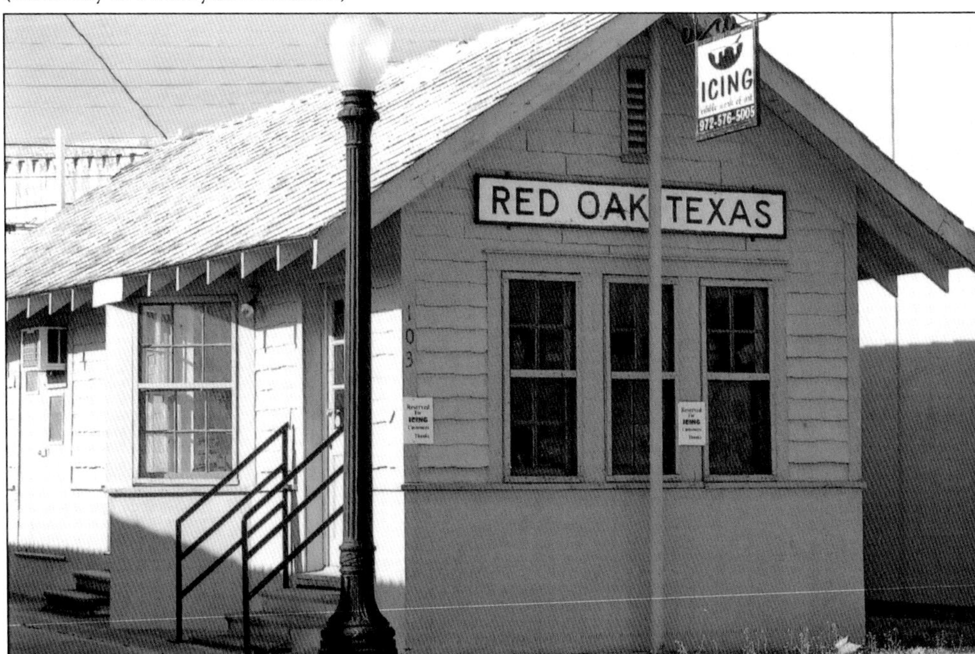

Now located on South Main Street, the Red Oak depot (pictured above) has served many purposes over the years, including as the chamber of commerce office and the *Weekly Herald Newspaper* office. In 1911, the Missouri-Kansas-Texas Railroad enlarged the existing depot of that time by adding 50 additional feet to double its capacity. (Courtesy of Kathryn E. Eriksen/WJ.)

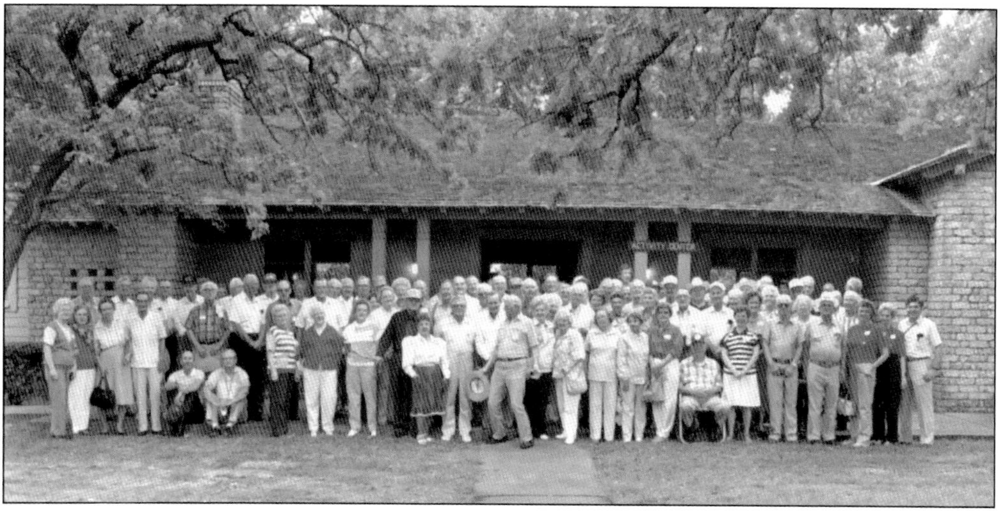

In 1991, members of the Southern Pacific Railroad Retired Employees gathered for a reunion, pictured above, at Fort Parker in Groesbeck, Texas. Two years later, on January 11, 1993, retired railroaders and their families gathered at the Golden Corral Restaurant in Ennis. They were welcomed by Ralph Essary and led in an invocation by Eddie Luksa. This led to the organization of the Southern Pacific Sunbeam Club of Ennis, which still meets the first Tuesday of each month to remember life on the railroad. Pictured below are members of the group at their yearly reunion in 2002. (Above, courtesy of George Graves; below, courtesy of Darlene Denbow.)

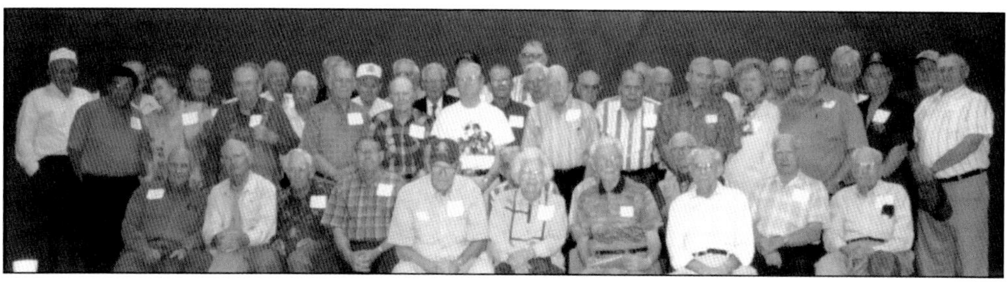

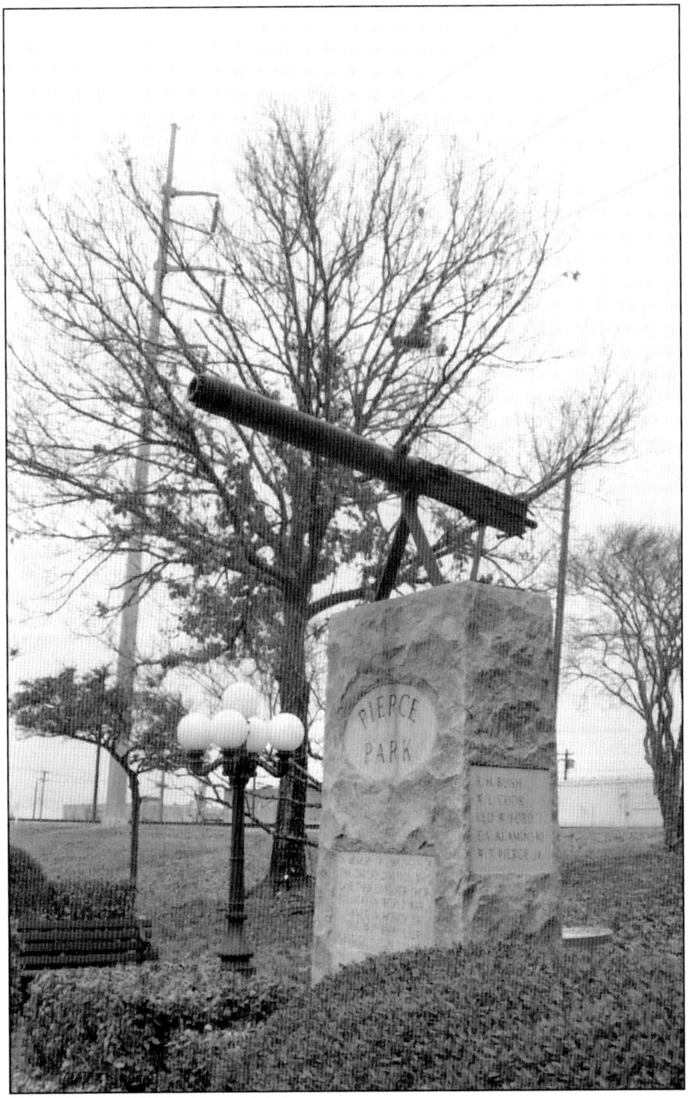

The Pierce Park Memorial was named in honor of William Thomas Pierce Jr., the first Southern Pacific Railroad Dallas division employee to die in combat. Also honored on this monument are E. V. Alaminski, R. M. Bush, W. L. Cook, Leo Ford, Glynn Massey, Fred Reyther, R. F. Rikard, and Guy Youngblood. Stuart Townsend's 1922 portrait commemorating the 50th anniversary of the rail's arrival in Ennis portrays a northward view of Main Street. The depot, built in 1872, is prominent along the tracks. Pictured below in 1947 at the 75th anniversary celebration with Southern Pacific Railroad employees standing in front of the portrait are, from left to right, Willie Love, Richard Vinson, A. J. Hill, and R. L. Smallwood. The portrait, a treasured piece of Ennis history, is now located at Ennis City Hall. (Left, courtesy of Randy Bryan Bigham; below, courtesy of Joe Pool.)

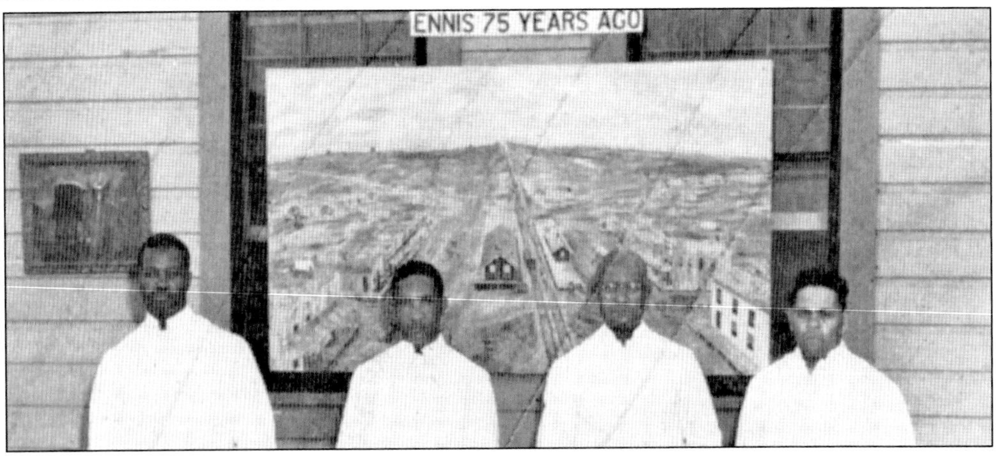

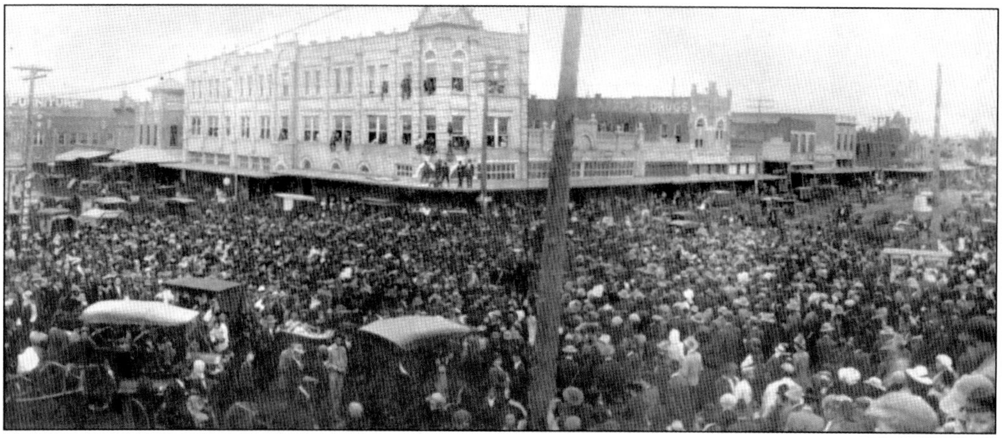

The arrival of the rail to Ellis County brought tremendous growth and prosperity to the entire area. The degree to which commerce, an essential to every community, was impacted is pictured above, where on November 24, 1913, Trade Day crowds packed the streets of Ennis as the city's cotton was bought and sold. Today, almost 100 years later, commerce and its importance to a community continues to be a vital issue. Pictured below is the Ennis Industrial Park. Begun in 1995, the Sterilite Corporation soon became the first to call Ennis home in 1998 with several other companies soon to follow. The park, with the Union Pacific Railroad Dallas Houston main line bordering its east side, running parallel to U.S. Highway 75, demonstrates the continuing importance of the rail to the area. (Above, courtesy of Charlie and Betty Honza; below, courtesy of City of Ennis.)

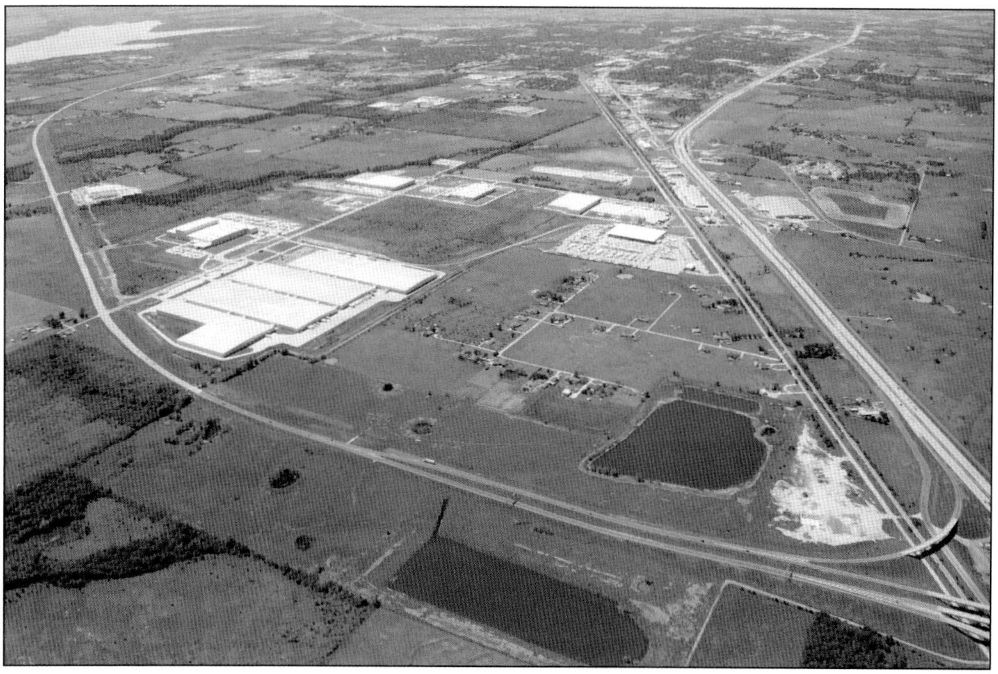